PEARLS OF POWER

IMPLICIT KEYS TO LEADERSHIP

DR. CHARLES A. LEWIS

Psy Press
Est. 1978

Psy Press™

Carrabelle, Florida

2022

Edition: 1.03

PsyPress email.com

ISBN: 978-1984011503

Table of Contents

Introduction ~ First Impressions 1

Chapter 1: Our Choices 4

Chapter 2: Candidate Selection 12

Chapter 3: Gender Roles 21

Chapter 4: Dominance..31

    Testosterone 33

    Pseudo-crises...47

    Toxoplasmosis gondii 48

Chapter 5: Stature..50

    Women's Stature and Leadership 58

    Body Mass 59

Chapter 6: The Appearance of Intelligence 61

    Intelligence (or is it just getting enough sleep)...............................67

Chapter 7: Competence 70

    Competence and Attractiveness 74

    Age of Competence and Facial Maturity 74

Chapter 8: Attractiveness...81

    Smiles 84

Chapter 9: Trustworthiness.. 87

    Who are you going to trust? Me or your lying eyes?...................... 88

Chapter 10: More than Appearance 91

Chapter 11: Beauty Sleep 95

    The Need for Sleep 96

    Sleep Deprivation...97

    Energy Balance.. 98

Chapter 12: Skin Tone and Character 103

Chapter 13: Scleral Health and Attractiveness 108

    Reddened Eyes 111

Chapter 14: Fitness and Exercise 118

Chapter 15: Eyelashes and Eye Makeup 120

    Eye Cosmetics 120

Chapter 16: Other Cosmetics..123

    Contrast 124

    Eyeliner and Mascara 126

    Eye shadow..127

    Foundation and Blush..128

    Lipstick 129

Chapter 17: Faux Pas 133

What Not To Do 133
Body Piercings..133
Halitosis..133
Pearly Whites 134
Tattoos...136
Wrinkly Clothes 137
Messy Hair...137
Hair Parts 139
Other Hair 142
Chapter 18: Dress for Authority 145
Style 148
Chapter 19: Jewelry and Accessories 150
Necklaces: 151
Chapter 20: Contemporary Appearance 155
Chapter 21: Stature and Posture 157
Devices and Support 161
High Heels 163
Exercises 165
Clothing and Perception of Stature 167
Chapter 22: Finger Nails 172
Chapter 23: Sexual Attraction 175
Seeing Red 178
Chapter 24: Voice...183
Find Your Radio Voice 185
Prosody...186
Using a Microphone 189
Vocal Fry..191
Upspeak (Valley Girl)...192
Chapter 25: Mug Shots 194
News Flash 195
TV and Video 202
Final TV Check List 207
Chapter 26: How We Choose..210
Partisans...212
Chapter 27: Where Power Lies 216
Perspective 216
Chapter 28: Executive Presence...219
Charisma...220
Chapter 29: Getting It Done 222
References 229

Introduction ~ First Impressions

The first time I saw Susana, more than 30 years ago, she was sitting on a bench under a tree in front of her house. My very first thought was "Is this going to be my wife?" What made this young woman stand out so much that called for such an extraordinary first impression? She was skinny, making her eyes look huge. She had big frizzy hair. Her posture was erect like that of a dancer, making her appear poised, fit and self-assured. She was engaged in conversation, appearing to be actively listening. And she had (and continues to have) a lovely, pleasant, bright face that, to me, showed exceptional emotional stability. Fortunately, I guessed right.

First impressions have a tremendous impact on how we relate to those around us. We all make implicit multifaceted evaluations of people we meet, or see photos of, in a fraction of a second. This automatic function of the human brain occurs without our consent; we cannot help ourselves from doing it. This does not mean that we cannot override our implicit evaluations, or that we are stuck with biases and prejudices. However, unless we get to know people, we usually stick with our first impression. Even when we get to know a person, our initial implicit perception wears a path that usually self-reinforces, rather than dissipates, that first impression.

While I am not advocating that we trust our first implicit and instinctual reactions, I am warning that we humans do it all the time. We can't help ourselves, and these automatic assessments have a great impact on our selection of political candidates, the hiring of employees, and our choice of intimate partnerships.

After screening job candidates by reviewing their resumes to assess competence, most hiring decisions are made within the first seconds of the interview, often before the interviewee has time to take a seat. Much of the rest of the interview is used to make it look as if the decision was not made on the first impression. It also gives a chance for the person doing the hiring to develop a relationship with the person and to make sure that they have not made an awful mistake. Thus, when you walk into an interview, the first two seconds are the most important. If you get chosen for the job in those seconds, the rest of the interview is about not muffing up enough to lose the opportunity.

Most of the time, our political leaders are chosen in the same way. People generally follow their first impression and then, selectively gather evidence to reinforce their conviction.

People can hardly help but believe what they see, even when they don't realize what they are seeing. If you look confident, people generally assume you are, and if you look vulnerable and weak, they'll see this too. *"Unreflective trait inference,"* the tendency to infer attributes to people based on their face and countenance is a powerful influence on voting choice for candidates and for hiring people into positions of responsibility and leadership. Unreflective trait inferences, a.k.a. implicit perceptions, have an enormous impact on how we are perceived and how we perceive others.

Some common heuristic inferences include the assumption that taller individuals are more competent and intelligent, and that people with more mature faces are more powerful, dominant, and have higher social competence. We make inferences on trustworthiness, aggressiveness, and hostility based on people's faces in a fraction of a second. These inferences shape how we approach people and how they perceive us.

In this book, we will explore what it is that we see and hear that guides our perceptions of people, and how women in particular, can curate their appearance to gain access to leadership positions. While public service leadership (elected office) is a principal focus of this book, the same influences that work in politics work for private and public sector leadership roles.

Looking the part is essential to getting a role, but obviously, looking the part is not enough. If someone gets a leadership position but is not competent, honest, and dedicated to the organization, their tenure can be a disaster. This book is not a guide to feigning competence, but rather for polishing it. Incompetence is dangerous. We need incompetent leaders like we need actors dressed as doctors doing brain surgery. Unfortunately, competent and dedicated persons who seek leadership positions or want a voice in civil society may be stymied by not looking the part. Understanding what it takes to fit the part can help competent, dedicated individuals be competitive in their pursuit of leadership roles.

Most elections are won and lost by a few percentage points. The final choice between qualified job candidates is commonly decided by subtle impacts of unreflective trait inference rather than by large differences in merit. Thus, the focus of this book is narrow; it examines a small but important component of ingress to leadership. By examining the implicit biases and heuristic shortcuts we all use in daily life, we can sidestep some of the biases that prevent new voices from being heard and hinder wider access to leadership.

We all use implicit perceptions to streamline our assessment of others. By being mindful and understanding the factors that influence these inferences we can decide when we wish to override these automated choices that influence how we judge and perhaps misjudge people; not just in our choice of candidates and employees, but as well in how we assess and treat our students, neighbors, and coworkers and choose our friends.

We can learn to think and make rational choices in selecting friends and foe, and in deciding who the best candidate is. We can teach our children critical thinking, how to assess decisions more mindfully, and to be alert to attempts at manipulation of our choices. Nevertheless, even if we are conscious of our perceptions, when we walk out the door, in most of the interactions we have with new people, we will be implicitly judged.

You can lead a horse to water, but you can't make it think. It is hard enough to change ourselves and to maintain mindfulness; changing others and their unreflective biases is nearly impossible. Although we cannot change how others make their perceptions, we can influence their instantaneous implicit perception. We can change how others perceive us.

Understanding how people form these implicit decisions and knowledge of the factors that influence them can help us change how we are perceived and help us create a public persona that empowers our goals. My hope is for this information to help women, minorities, and the marginalized gain equity in earnings and influence in our society. Better governance will come from more inclusive and more collaborative leadership.

The chapters ahead discuss the perceptive factors that affect how implicit judgments of leadership are made, and how to wield this knowledge to project an image of competence and leadership. The information herein can help provide access to those with talent and industry, and provides insight on how our automatic biases can diminish us and those around us.

Chapter 1: Our Choices

Who selects our leaders? In a democracy, we do. We are the sexist, racist, and prejudiced people that limit each other's potential. We are also busy limiting ourselves, as most of us don't perceive ourselves as leaders, nor as sexist or racists.

Don't blame yourself – it is part of being human. Mostly, we don't intend to be prejudicial. We make most of our decisions without conscious thought; thinking is slow and subject to recurrent revision after revision. So we use shortcuts hundreds of times a day so that we can function effectively. We expect a pencil to be where we left it so that we don't need to do a systematic search every time we want one. We expect that we can sit on an object that looks like a chair. We assume that we can trust the food in our refrigerator to be edible, that our loved ones are not a danger to us, and that strangers may not be so friendly; especially if they don't look like people from our tribe.

We use heuristics and pattern recognition. Pattern recognition allows us to identify objects, sequences, music, places, and people. Each time we recognize an object, we don't consciously go through a set of descriptive criteria to analyze its size, shape, and colors to decide what it is – we just recognize it as a cup, a house, or a cat. We immediately recognize people we know, distinguishing them from millions of others, and know when someone is a stranger.

A heuristic is a simplified decision-making criterion, using rule-of-thumb estimates, intuition, learned biases, and other shortcuts. These usually work well enough for most of our day-to-day choices. Heuristics are especially well suited for decisions between two possible choices. They allow us to rapidly select between options without deep reflection or analysis. This reduces the cognitive workload on our brains and lets us focus on tasks that require more insight. It saves time and mental energy that would be needed to deliberate and second guess the hundreds of choices we make each day. So we simplify it. This is useful and works well most of the time.

In well less than a quarter of a second, we make numerous appraisals about people we meet. We quickly assess their gender, approximate age, whether they are familiar or not, and if they are our tribe. We judge them for mating potential, their health, and whether they appear to be risks for transmitting infectious disease – all in the blink of an eye. We also assess how dominant a person is, their likability, and trustworthiness. The flash assessments that form our first impressions have considerable depth and detail. These first impressions of people stick. These are all instinctive, intrinsic reactions that people have made since we have been human and likely long before.

> The human brain slowly and continuously increased in size over the last couple of million years, but had not changed much in the last 100,000 years. That is, until about 3,000 years ago when something remarkable occurred. Over the last three millennium, the average adult human brain has gotten notably smaller.[1] Until very recent times, most people lived in small villages. Hunter-gatherer and swaddle agriculture societies, even in the first half of the 20th century, typically lived in villages of about 150 people. The population for an entire tribe averaged about 1200 individuals.[2] Over human history, most people only met a small number of people outside of their tribal group over their entire lifetime.
>
> Nowadays, we may see more than 1200 people in a single visit to a shopping mall or on the drive to work; the number of people we interact with on a personal basis has not gotten larger. The average American has about 500 acquaintances, that is, people whose name they know and would at least briefly speak with if they ran into them while shopping or during other leisure time activity. Still however, few people maintain social networks larger than 150 persons and on average, we trust to varying degrees only around 17 people.[3] [4] We are still "engineered" for living in small villages.

We judge people on their appearances, especially when we have little else to go on. And they judge us in the same way. But how likely is our first impression to be correct? Aren't these just prejudices?

I had a wooded lot that I planned to build a home on. It had good sized oaks but had many large pine trees, and pine beetles had moved into the area that would destroy these trees within a few years. I contacted a logging company, and they came out and offered me a couple thousand dollars for the pine trees that I wanted removed. However, when I met the logger, his truck was filled with empty cola cups, hamburger wrappers, and other trash. Perhaps it should have, but it didn't bother me that his clothing was sloppy, his teeth were yellow, and his hair was a mess; he was a logger after all. But the trash in his truck was too much of a sign that he didn't care about order in his personal space. I thought, "If he doesn't care about his own space, how much will he care about mine?" I turned his offer down and I met with another company. The other logger was neat and although dressed for his trade, was clean and well groomed. I sold him my trees for $1800, and his crew came and did a great job. I could hardly tell where the pines had been, and the large oaks looked great. They left all the pine branches in a small, compacted pile. My lot looked like a four-acre wooded park.

A few weeks later, perhaps after seeing how my lot came out, a neighbor up the road used the first logger to remove her pine trees. He trashed the land. The ground was left deeply rutted, and most of her oak trees were broken and severely damaged. There were stumps visible and large branches covering most of her land. It looked like it had been hit by a tornado and remained so for many years.

People are actually pretty good at using their personal filters to determine certain personality traits quickly, but this does not mean that they are necessarily right. We can judge, with some accuracy, how intelligent a man is by looking at a photo of his face. However, this does not work so well for women's faces.[5] People that are judged from a photograph to be more trustworthy are not only more likely to have money lent to them; they are less likely to default on the loan.[6]

Countenance and bearing tell us about a person's confidence and station, and we use this to judge competence, social status, and health. We also judge a person's character based on heuristics. We rely heavily on implicit clues we see in people's faces to assess them, and these characteristics are among the most potent influences on people's choices for leaders. Implicit evaluations not only determine who is successful in elections but also which persons rise up in corporate leadership.

So returning to who's in charge, we tend to select taller, healthier, stronger appearing people as leaders. In times of crisis, people give power over to more dominant figures. During turbulent times, people are willing to give up some autonomy in exchange for a sense of security. This handing over power to a "strong-man" during a crisis is not a prejudice limited to men, as women also do this. In more settled times, we look for more likable and trustworthy leaders that are more likely to collaborate and are less likely to be self-serving.

Female personnel officers commonly offer to pay men more for the same job than they offer women. Most women favor men over women as leaders. Why would women participate in such unfair practices that prejudice other women? It is not misogyny. It is subliminal instinctual cues that we are born with, that the persons most fit to lead are those that best can protect the family and tribe from danger. Cultures rewarded the best hunters for being able and willing to reliably provide meat in slim times. In primal societies, the taller, stronger, faster, and more competent appearing men were chosen as leaders and rewarded with privilege. Meanwhile, in primitive cultures a woman's desirability was largely based on the appearance of health and fertility. Health, in both men and women, serves as a proxy for competence; the ability to thrive, especially in difficult circumstances. In a primitive society, even after reproductive age, a healthy appearing woman might be assumed to know how to find and gather resources and have a wider skill base than less healthy appearing women of the same age.

We no longer live in hunter-gatherer societies. Competence as a leader takes other skills than physical strength and stature. Nevertheless, we continue to assess our leaders largely from traits adapted to survival advantages useful in primitive times.

The selection of leaders, at least in politics, is largely an implicit (subconscious) decision. This does not imply that it is a baseless decision. Rather, these implicit judgments are more like the fuzzy logic used in big data to target advertising or to seek out terrorists. This heuristic method allows fast processing of subtle data by the brain quickly and with minimal effort.

Unfortunately, fuzzy logic does not always get it right. When computers use fuzzy logic to target advertising to your Facebook page, it causes little harm if it shows you products that you are not interested in; targeted advertising still benefits advertisers by increasing the hit rate over indiscriminately targeted ads. Even though the targeting is not entirely accurate, it still cuts the advertising costs to sales ratio. The risk is low for both parties.

Targeting individuals as terrorists using fuzzy logic will increase the number of persons tagged as terrorists. Here the risk is high and can be deadly to those falsely targeted.

When our brains use implicit heuristics to assess a situation and get it wrong, it causes problems. It is dangerous and criminal when implicit racial bias causes police to target and use undue force against individuals they heuristically assess to be a miscreant.

Although we depend on reading the emotional content of facial expression, we are far less accurate when assessing people of races we are not in close social relationships with. It is dangerous that medical professionals, from every area of the globe that has been studied, have been found to underestimate the level of pain that persons of other races and cultures are experiencing.[7] It is dangerous when psychopaths evade our implicit detection of dangerousness. Medical professionals and police need to be trained and remain vigilant to the innate propensity to act according to these biases.[8]

We, as humans, are prone to making snap "implicit," "emotional," "gut-level" decisions. This is how we make most of our choices; whether is which dessert we want, which person we are attracted to or avoid, or which team to root for. These are typically heuristic decisions based on pattern recognition, usually made with the right hemisphere of the brain with little conscious thought or internal dialog or deliberation. The inner dialog, which is mostly a left brain activity, actually comes after we have made our choice. Then, the brain acts as a lawyer, defending the choice rather than prosecuting it. The time between the actual heuristic decision and the dialog happens so quickly that we think the choice was made entirely from the "rational" inner-dialog adjudication.

This process was unmasked for me one morning when I hopped out of bed. I started running towards the bathroom at top speed because I was excited to get the day going. At least, that is what my brain was saying. Actually, I had stood up too fast and was busy passing out; my central vision had gone black, and my feet were moving in progressively smaller and faster steps as I careened forward into the nightstand and fell hard on the floor. As I lay on the floor recovering my wits, I couldn't figure out why I had decided to run at top speed all of 12 feet to the bathroom – it made no sense at all. The reality was that I had not been in a hurry at all; the left half of my impaired brain was aware of the fancy reflexive footwork as quickly stumbling forward, and it created a back-story to explain it. If it had not defied logic and had not been such an unusual set of circumstances, I might have just accepted that I had been in a rush. What my brain told me was the result of a heuristic evaluation of limited data (rapid forward movement and quick steps), followed by a barely plausible reasoning that I had made an a priori decision to run because of some special enthusiasm for that day. In reality, the explanation for my behavior was made after the fact. This is how we come to most conclusions in life, heuristic evaluations followed by rationalization; yet, we are almost never aware of the process.

While we can learn to use the left half of the brain as a prosecuting attorney, picking apart our decisions, we rarely do. Mostly we just reinforce our heuristic choices with clever defenses and then give ourselves a little squirt of dopamine as a reward for being so cunning. It's hard to avoid and much less work than actually weighing data and making a truly logical choice. As a physician for over 30 years, I use heuristics to make diagnoses as well as to sniff out cases that don't fit patterns closely enough, and thus, cause me concern. Next, I use objective data to confirm or rule out the diagnosis. It is not the heuristic pattern recognition that gets us into trouble, but rather the failure to backcheck and validate our decisions. It is fine to use heuristics, but we also need to monitor our reasoning.

Most of us do not do a great job of monitoring our intuitive reasoning. Please take a moment to answer these questions and jot down your answers before reading on.

1. It takes 6 seamstresses 6 hours to sew 6 dresses. How many hours would it take for 60 seamstresses to sew 60 dresses?

2. You go to a restaurant for lunch, and the meal and a cup of coffee cost a total of $11. The meal cost $10 more than the coffee. How much did the coffee cost?

3. A forest fire breaks out in the mountains of Montana and spreads quickly, doubling in size every hour. After 48 hours, it has burned 10,000 acres. How long did it take to burn 5,000 acres?

Got your answers?

The first three questions were adapted from those used in a study by MIT professor Shane Frederick to test Cognitive Reflection. When tested, Harvard students, on average, missed half of these simple questions; one in five students got all three wrong. When students from Michigan State University were tested, half of the students missed all three.[9] These questions have semantic clues that prompt intuitive answers. Even when asked simple, numeric questions, our brains make intuitive conclusions that feel right, but that may not be correct. Perhaps because they appear to make semantic sense, we have a hard time suppressing our feeling that we have the correct answer, and that no further thought is required. Top level students overcome their intuitive responses and back-check their answers, and thus, make fewer mistakes. The correct answers are six hours, fifty cents, and forty-seven hours. Imagine how inaccurate we are when we are not even aware that we are being tested.

When investors buy stocks, most often it is an implicit choice. It is a sum judgment rather than a logical decision. In the rational market theory, the stock of any company should quickly rise or fall to its fair value – it is sold at the consensus value the informed traders are willing to pay for it. When information, positive or negative, is available, the price should reflect that. Although there are certain "inefficiencies" in the market that perhaps can be exploited to beat the market, once these are made public, they too tend to be factored into the price and disappear. Very few professional traders beat the market over long periods of time, indicating that when traders do beat the market; it is more often by chance and luck than ability. Thus, although it appears to be a rational choice, most stock market purchases, despite the hours dedicated to researching a company' SEC filings and news feeds, are in fact implicit, emotional choices. In fact, adding more information usually does not help, but rather only adds to the burden and confusion of decision making, without improving the choices. If there is a talent to investing, it is in knowing when to take a profit or cut losses, rather than insight into which companies stock to purchase.

Perhaps the reality is that the most important decisions in our lives are too critical and too complex to leave to rational thought. These are the choices that alter the trajectory of our lives. In truth, we have far too little knowledge of the future to make these critical decisions. If we make a career choice or choose among universities to attend, we try to be rational and weigh the probability of success, the difficulties, and potential benefits of those options. It can be a sensible choice to attend a particular college or to move to a different city or country, but there is no way of knowing how a choice of which city or university would turn out in comparison to other choices. For such complex decisions, especially when overloaded with information, we make implicit decisions and then stick with them.

After our heuristic or emotional choice, after the fact left-brained justification, and dopamine reward, we feel better. This is essential to happiness. When we try to make rational decisions based on limited evidence, we are continually second-guessing, and looking for more evidence. But the additional data often does not help in making a decision, but rather adds to confusion and prolongs indecision, and thus causes unhappiness and lost opportunity. Thus, making heuristic decisions makes us feel good; while truly rational decisions can be second-guessed later, making us miserable.

> ***Pearl:*** If you are having difficulty in making a rational decision between two choices, it is likely because there is scant evidence that one choice is superior to the other. When there is a clear difference in cost, risks and benefit between choices, decisions are easy. Thus two close options are likely to be just as good and just as bad as each other. For most difficult decisions, one can relax and just select one. In the circumstance of a selection of two apparently equal benefiting choices, one can base the decision on a value appropriate for the decision; values may be ethical, economic, aesthetic, or based on other criteria. Make the choice, be happy and don't look back.

> One of the decisions that has the most significant impact on our lives is our choice of life-partner. Wouldn't a rational choice make more sense? Yet, the selection of potential partners is implicit, emotional and often driven by chance encounters.
>
> We make an implicit decision to engage in a relationship, and then we either X-them-off our potential candidate list or commit to the choice. Like with stocks, the engagement is an emotional, implicit choice; the disengagement more often explicit. If we find out that our choice of potential life-partner candidate cannot be trusted, that their values do not align with ours, or that they are unwilling or unable to provide our needs in the relationship, we will likely seek to end it. And sometimes there is just a failure to bond, and we simply fall out of love.

NOTICE AND APOLOGY: Many of the recommendations for physical presentation, style, and dress outlined in this book may seem stodgy, out-of-date, and even biased. They are, and this is intentional, even though they often do not reflect the style or personal preferences of the author. The styles recommendations are socially conservative as these are ones that are most accepted as a professional norm and that are least likely to hinder ones acceptance into leadership positions in work and society. If you seek to change the world, it may make it easier if you don't make it obvious to those you plan to overthrow.

Chapter 2: Candidate Selection

The viability of representational democracy would seem to rely upon voters making rational choices to elect candidates that best represent their personal, family's, and country's best interests. In democratic societies, one would expect that citizens consciously deliberate their choice of candidate. This, however, is not how we make most of our decisions; instead, most voters make implicit judgments. Our brains use the same implicit processes for job candidates. At least for job candidates, there is a pre-screening with a resume to try to assure that they have sufficient knowledge and experience to perform the job. Not so for political candidates. Here is how elections actually work:

In a study published in 2009, participants were asked to watch ten-second clips of U.S. gubernatorial debates from around the country. The clips were of politicians that the study participants were not familiar with, and the participants did not know the political party of the candidates. The videos were silenced so the participants could not tell what was being said or even hear the voice of the candidates. The clips showed the candidates one at a time, from the waist up, to avoid height comparisons. The study participants chose which candidate they predicted would win the election based solely on the silent video clip comparing two unknown candidates.

In these two-party gubernatorial elections, the study participants, who knew nothing of the race other than what they had seen in the clips from the debates, were able to choose the actual winner of the real elections 58 percent of the time, a highly statistically significant outcome. Random guesses would have given a 47 – 53 percent range. Furthermore, the predictions were well correlated with the actual percentage vote in these elections. It was estimated that twenty percent of the variation of the election could be accounted for by the implicit choice made from viewing clips in which nothing was known about the two political candidates or their party affiliation.

The heuristic clues, such as seen in these silent clips, influence voters enough to swing most competitive elections. In the elections in this study, incumbency was found to provide only a seven percent advantage compared to the 20 percent implicit advantage.

The participants in this study were not adept at guessing the political party of the candidate; doing no better than random guessing, and their rating of candidate likeability and physical attractiveness had little predictive value on the election outcome. The participants perceived their predicted winners to be more confident, in spite of contemporary polling data at the time of the debate, in which many of these confident appearing candidates were behind in the polls.[10] Something about these candidates, the way they looked and moved, gave them a sizable boost in support.

In a different study using still photos of unfamiliar gubernatorial candidates, participants were asked to pick the winner after only seeing the still photos flashed on a screen for one-tenth of a second. One-tenth of a second is enough time for people to judge a variety of personality traits; allowing additional time serves to increase the person's confidence in their judgment.

In this still photo study, each participant judged 89 gubernatorial race pairs and decided which of the two candidates was more *competent*. Results were not included in the analysis if any candidate in any pair was recognized by the subject. The study participants correctly chose the winners an average of 57 percent of the time. Compared to those who viewed the paired choice for 100 milliseconds (1/10th second), there was no significant additional advantage for participants viewing for 250 milliseconds or for unlimited time. When the participants were scored on how much more competent one candidate appeared to be than the other, on a -3 to +3 scale, the results correctly predicted the winner even more strongly. The pooled the results of the participants viewing the photos for 250 ms, accurately predicted the actual winner of the election 68 percent of the time.

In races in which there was no incumbent, the candidate that appeared more competent in their photo won 59 percent of the time. Incumbents have a considerable advantage. They are assumed to be competent. Furthermore, they are from the party that the district or state voted for in the previous election; thus they may be in a less competitive race. In cases in which the incumbents lost, the challenger candidate was perceived to have had a more competent face 86 percent of the time.[11] The incumbent advantage is at least in part because the incumbent likely had a competent face in order to have won the previous election.

In another study of facial perception, 681 children aged 5 to 13, were invited to play a computer game in which they chose the best captain to sail a boat. Unknown to the children, they were presented pairs of photos of 57 sets of runoff candidates for the French parliament and asked which person in the pair would make a better captain. The children chose the winning candidate 71 percent of the time! When adults were asked to rank the candidates on perceived competence, the results were substantially identical to those of the children.[12]

In another study of voting choices, the faces of actual political candidates that were not recognized by the subjects were rated in forced-choice selection, examining different pairs of faces of the two candidates on a screen. Thus, given images of two people, they were asked which of the two was more competent. They were also asked to rate faces on trustworthiness, attractiveness, and whether the candidate had a "baby face." The subjects then rated the candidates on these attributes on a scale from -7 to +7. Later, subjects were asked to vote on which candidate from various pairs they would vote for. There was no political content for these choices; they were made solely on the appearance of the photo of the candidate.

By far, the most critical criterion for voting for the unknown candidates was the perceived level of competence. These "voters" preferred candidates that were rated from the photographs as being more competent, by a 40 percent margin. This preference was even greater among younger voters. In contrast, having a baby face decreased the chance of being voted for, likely because baby-faceness is inversely associated with the perception of competence. Surprisingly, after adjusting for competence, having a trustworthy face did not give a statistically significant advantage in being elected in this study. Being very attractive increased the percent of vote received by 4.5 percent among young voters and about two percent among older voters.[13]

Perception of competency has less influence among strongly partisan voters in partisan elections. Nevertheless, less committed voters may stay home on Election Day if they feel their party's candidate appears less competent than the opposing candidate.

Even for well-informed, rational voters, decisions are influenced by facial characteristics. Early support within the party likely goes to the candidate that most closely fits the part. After coming to an implicit, heuristic decision to support a candidate, the early adherents create the buzz and generate rationalizations of why their favored candidate is superior. They then sing praise for his or her qualifications, ideas, and experience. Later, other party members, including those seeking a judicious selection of the candidates that are most closely aligned to their viewpoint, receive what is billed as impartial information on the candidates' attributes. Nevertheless, these are already biased, filtered facts based on rationalized, post-heuristic implicit choices. Moving forward, social proofs guide later supporters who assume that the earlier advocates are well informed, and thus, follow their lead. When voting within parties, such as during primaries, the choices made are just as likely to be implicit among adherents as they are for non-committed swing voters.

Implicit judgments of facial images predict the outcome of elections in studies from the United States, Canada, Australia, Ireland, Britain, Italy, France, Japan, Bulgaria and other countries. There have been several studies that have tried to sort out which implicit influences have the most substantial effects on voting behavior. These influences vary according to the situation. These studies have been done in Asian, European, Australia, and North and South American countries. I have not found any studies on implicit facial value voting from Africa, and have seen no American studies that mentioned Black American politicians, other than President Obama. While I cannot cite evidence for implicit influences on the selection of black candidates, it is likely the same implicit factors guide candidate selection of them.

When Americans and Japanese rated photos of Japanese and American politicians on power (dominance and facial maturity), and warmth (trustworthiness and likeability), they came up with very similar assessments of the politicians. Nonetheless, when selecting which candidate from a pair would win an election, the Japanese assessment of American candidates did not pan out, nor did the American's choices of Japanese politicians. The score the Japanese gave the American politicians on power predicted the American election results, and the American's score for the warmth of the Japanese candidates, predicted victory for the Japanese candidates.[14] Thus, in Japan having a trustworthy and likable face is essential to winning elections, and in the U.S.A., facial maturity and dominance were foremost. In another cross-cultural study, comparing Caucasian Americans and Korean politicians in predicting election outcomes, competence was equally important in both cultures. However, the Koreans chose not to vote for faces with attributes associated with threat or corruption but were more likely to select faces they rated as open minded. These last three traits, however, had no significant influence in the outcomes of the American elections.[15] When Americans rated the faces of Bulgarian candidates, competence ratings most strongly predicted actual outcomes, with attractiveness having a small additional effect.[16]

A cross-cultural study of ten different nations found that photos of American political candidates, corporate leaders, and university presidents showed bigger, toothier smiles than those of other countries, reflecting a state of excitement, while in France, Germany, and the UK, calm smiles were most common among leaders, and smiles of either type were less common in China. The level of arousal shown by politicians and leaders was found to reflect the "ideal affect" of the country. The "ideal affect" was not what the populace was actually feeling, but if instead indicates the desired emotional valence of the constituents.[17]

In 2016 Bernie Sanders reflected the frustration of young people trying to start their careers, while Trump reflected the dissatisfaction of less well-educated, white Americans at their perceived erosion of social status. Especially for Trump, it gave his supporters a vicarious sense of legitimacy in voicing previously socially unacceptable xenophobia and anger.

Pearl: A candidate's emotional valence should reflect the desired mood of those selecting the candidate. In the U.S., this is generally one of happy arousal and confidence.

In a study of candidates for the Finnish parliament for non-incumbent seats, being more attractive, (by one standard deviation) was associated with an increase in the votes received by women by 24 percent and by men by 20 percent, even when the "beauty rating" came from raters in other countries. In some studies, beauty has been found to be more helpful for male than for female candidates. Meanwhile, beauty only garnered about four percent more votes in Germany and just 0.7 to 1.8 percentage points in Australia.[18]

Although implicit face reading is very similar across cultures, what we look for in our politicians is not cross-cultural. American history has been blessed with less, or at least less apparent, political corruption and has avoided dictatorial rulers; thus we have been less sensitive to potential risks from candidates that have less trustworthy or more dominant faces.

In countries with very strong party-voting, the appearance of the candidate has less impact than those countries where partisan loyalty and issues are less compelling. Additionally, we have different expectations for different positions, and these expectations can change with time and culture. The implicit choices of candidate we choose for school board, sheriff, judge, congressman, governor, or president are different. When voting for a member of the U.S. House of Representatives, we understand that the 435 members need to work together to get work done and that they will be subordinate to the President. When choosing the CEO of an organization, we select using different implicit valuations.

Pearl: When curating a look for a position, make sure that it matches the expectations for that post.

For example, trustworthy faces are preferred in a simulated voter choice in a time of peace, while more attractive faces are favored in times of war.[19] Trustworthy faces are seen as more pro-social,[20] and likely to move forward domestic policies in areas such as healthcare and education. Democrats tend to prefer more trustworthy faces and are less swayed by attractive candidates. The ideal face may vary by the constituency; the ideal heuristic for a Republican district may be different than for a balanced or predominantly Democratic one.

More attractive faces are perceived to be healthier and fitter. This may explain why voters that lean Republican, who tend to be more hawkish and care less about domestic policy, prefer more attractive candidates than do voters that lean Democrat. Thus, an attractive democratic candidate would likely gain more swing voters than one that was less attractive but had a more trustworthy face. A Republican candidate that has a trustworthy face might gain more swing voters than a more attractive one.

These first impressions can easily make the difference between who is elected or chosen for a position of trust and authority or not. These choices affect our income and our chances to shape the world.

Implicit choice largely determines what occurs in the voting booth, and it also impacts decisions made in hiring, the boardroom, in police lineups, and in the courtroom.

Pearl: In the United States, in competitive races, the more competent appearing candidate for the U.S. House of Representatives wins about 70% of the time, thus providing a 20%

edge. Competence is the most important facial characteristic for most elected offices, and for mid- to upper-level management positions in the United States.

We make subliminal and emotional choices that have substantial influences on the outcome of elections, and make similar decisions in our daily life about nearly every person we meet. We make these assessments in less than a quarter of a second. These assessments have an enormous impact on decisions of who gets which job and who gets voted for, particularly when there is little or insufficient data to make an informed decision.

Let me ask. Did having a long nose make me a bad doctor? I admit, my nose was deviant from the norm, but I wasn't. Early in my career, things were not progressing. I was involved in research but was having difficulty finding full-time work in research or clinical medicine. I took a few months off and volunteered at a third-world Caribbean hospital and then later had a nose job so that my hood ornament would actually properly function as an air exchange device. When I returned to the States, I was able to breathe easier, but things also became so much easier professionally. I was no longer treated as some suspicious deviant. I found work and was treated with respect. My patients seemed more comfortable with me and would laugh at my jokes. From the inside, I do not feel that I changed at all; same brain, the same sense of humor, and same personality, however, people treated me as if I were someone else. This is how we select and winnow-out our potential employees and politicians.

If you want to win elections or are a candidate for a competitive position, you can sway the vote and increase your chances of being selected for a position by swaying people's implicit perceptions. I am not advocating the pursuit of positions that potential candidates are not qualified for or competent to do. Competence and integrity come first. But how can a person with those abilities serve if they are unable to attain a position of influence because they do not fit people's idealized heuristic mental image of what a leader looks like?

Thus, attaining leadership position may require management of one's persona.

1. Some of the counsel included in this book may seem dated or sexist. It is not for lack of sensitivity or that it reflects the writer's personal preferences or biases. It is included because the goal of a candidate is to appeal to a broad population of people from

various communities, and in particular, those who make heuristic choices on candidates with little other information. In fact, this book is in a sense, a manual on how to ethically circumvent people's implicit biases that prejudice our chances of success and opportunity to contribute to our community. These biases also impede many qualified persons from getting hired into positions of responsibility. As you read, remember that an important goal is to avoid alienating people who have different perspectives and that may have less contemporary viewpoints.

2. For most elective offices, other than in a small town, most voters will never meet or get to know their elective candidates. Your name and physical attributes will determine a large portion of their decision. Even campaign volunteers adhere to their candidate based mainly on implicit choice.

3. Whiten your teeth, buy the clothes, and do the other steps outlined so that you look the part you wish to play. Need braces? Get them. Most of the important tweaks to appearance, as outlined in the coming chapters, however, are more subtle and less extreme. Creating and maintaining a professional image does require attention and discipline.

4. Is it disingenuous to manage or create a persona? The word persona came from the Greek word for mask. We all create our persona, intentionally or unintentionally. Adolescence is a time of creating one's identity. Teens often distinguish themselves with hairstyles and dress to show individuality, nonconformity, and to identify with a group they want to be part of. Young adults adapt their personas as they move into the job market. I am not advocating for conformity of persona nor of psyche. I recommend however, being intentional in creating a persona that facilitates personal and professional goals. If you are asking for a position of responsibility and influence, looking the part will facilitate getting it. You are not selling out by changing the details of your appearance – you are buying into what works.

5. In a general election, unless you totally screw up and alienate people, your committed party base will vote for you, and thus, you do not have to preach to the choir. The job of a candidate is to get the snap-judging, less-informed, less-committed people who lean in their political direction to show up and vote for them, and to get marginally committed swing voting individuals that lean away, to question whether the other candidate is worth taking the effort to vote for.

6. After people have made an implicit choice and defended it, they are unlikely to change their decision. We are usually quite unhappy when reality conspires against us to do so. When it turns out that our "gut" instantaneous reactions were fallacious, we feel betrayed and wonder how we got it wrong. It often takes a long time to reverse these erroneous decisions – much longer than there is time for during an election. The more publicly a voter has shown themselves to support a candidate, the less likely they will change their view, and the more likely they will disbelieve or justify any negatives about their candidate.

7. You can assume that as a candidate, you will not change the mind of anyone dedicated to or even leaning towards the opposition. You don't want to make enemies that will motivate those leaning to the other side to turn out to vote, but don't waste limited resources and energy trying to change the minds of those on the other side. Your goal should be to get as many as possible of those leaning in your direction to turn out to vote for you, maybe pick up some in the middle, and to avoid seeming so alarming that those leaning away from your side show up in great numbers to vote against you. The less committed a voter is, the more likely that implicit judgment will determine their vote.

8. Swing voters decide most elections. Candidates need to campaign to win votes from the people from the center. The goal is to appeal to the middle, where most swing voters are. A clean, conservative, professional appearance alienates no-one.

9. Once people have made their implicit choice to follow you, they will listen to your ideas, and likely support those ideas. It is backward from what it ought to be. The first step is to get people to make the implicit choice to support you. It is afterwards that they adopt your ideas.

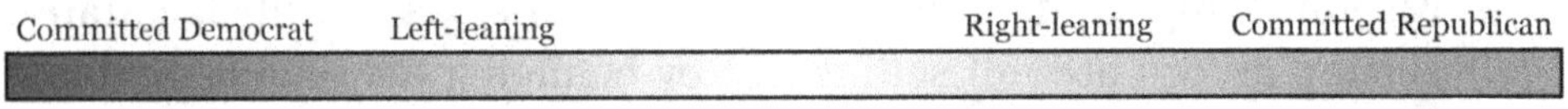

| Committed Democrat | Left-leaning | | Right-leaning | Committed Republican |

Figure 2-1: A representation of the main political spectrum in the U.S.

> Less than half of Millennials turned out to vote in 2016. Millennials that don't vote let old white boomers and geezers decide their future.

"What the human being is best at doing, is interpreting all new information so that their prior conclusions remain intact."

Warren Buffet

Chapter 3: Gender Roles

There is a glaring gender gap in American politics and business leadership. At the time of this writing, only six of fifty governors are women, and three of these women ascended to the governor's position after their male governor resigned their office midterm. Just 37 women have been elected as state governors in U.S. history, and no woman has been president. During the Twentieth Century, only 27 out of the nearly 2000 leaders of 199 different nations were women. In the year 2000, just two U.S. Fortune 500 companies had women CEOs.[21]

In 2017, 21 percent of US Senate seats were held by women, and 19.3 percent of the seats in the U.S. House of Representatives were. This finally brought up the percentage of female representation in the U.S. Congress to that of the Bangladeshi parliament. The gender gap is even more significant within the Republican Party, where only 5 percent of the Republican senators are women, and 22 of the 240 (nine percent) of the Republican members of the House were women. This suggests that women have a far greater disadvantage in partisan politics in conservative districts and states.

Most societies have distinct gender roles. Traditionally, men are seen as stronger and more assertive, if not outright dominant, and a woman's role is traditionally nurturing and cooperative. In the United States, Republican candidates often espouse the premise that government should be run like a corporation, with a focus on lowering taxes, getting out of the way of market capitalism, beefing up the military and not acting as a "nanny state." These encompass a very masculine role for government.

The corporate metaphor is a dangerous one. The fundamental purpose and responsibility of a corporation is to profit its investors. Corporations by their nature are psychopathic; they focus on the short-term gain of wealth and are not guided by altruism or empathy. Dollars are fungible; life, liberty, and happiness are not.

A saner model for democracy is to pattern its governance and roles more like an extended family in which there are multiple stakeholders and needs. These needs are not limited to income and security, but also include housing, education, a safe environment, healthcare, economic justice, cultural development, promotion of social responsibility, quality of life, and sustainability for future development. These more traditionally "maternal" responsibilities are somewhat more closely aligned with the Democratic Party, and thus, may explain why more women are elected from that party.

There are various gender and racial differences among different demographic groupings. American men, and especially white men without a college degree, are more likely than women to be right-leaning and vote Republican. Sixty-five percent of white men without a college degree lean Republican. Since these men have conservative viewpoints, they are less likely to favor candidates that promote a social agenda. Fewer women run on a conservative/ testosterone platform, thus, disadvantaging female candidates; even if no gender-based voting-bias is present, there is a policy bias.

The voting bloc that is most likely to include Republicans and independents that lean Republican are white, non-Hispanic, Protestants and Mormons that do not have college degrees. Hispanics, African Americans, Jews, and Asians are more likely to lean Democrat in voting. Overall, women lean Democrat, but white women in the United States are about equally divided in their vote between the two parties. Conservative women, however, are reported to have a separate bias against female candidates.

Table: 3-1: Voting groups (Data from Pew Research, 2016)[22]

	Registered voters without college degrees Lean Republican	Registered voters with college degrees Lean Republican
White Men	65%	54%
White Females	51%	41%

In a 2017 study of voting patterns in Chile, a country that at the time of this writing has a female president first elected in 2006, found that women were slightly less likely to vote for female candidates than men were. Women living in districts where traditional gender roles are more prevalent showed a preference for male candidates. This included educated women in higher income areas, where women were less likely to be part of the workforce.[23] These women may feel their identity and self-esteem threatened by female leaders. They apparently felt that their role as homemakers and mothers was diminished when compared to women that serve as political leaders, making their life-roles seem less valuable.

The richest man, and really the only wealthy person, in my Peace Corps village, was Sergio Gomez. He had a small wooden house on the edge of the canyon with a zinc roof and the only flush toilet in town. He was the only one in town with a personal vehicle, a very old ex-military jeep. He was the big man in town in physical stature, wealth, political, and firepower. He was the only guy to wear a gun, and since his brother was a provincial judge, he had gotten away with using it after picking fights in bars. No one crossed him. He had vast land holdings and by far the most cattle. When I knew him, he was about 70, and he offered to sell me his house, ranch, and 180 cattle for the equivalent of $10,000. Most of the men in town were probably earning about $30 a month, so for them, it was a fortune. Alas, as a Peace Corps volunteer, it was out of reach for me too. Here, having $10,000 does not make one rich.

Wealth is relative. People judge their own success by looking to see how others are doing. When people look at others showing their vacation photos and special events on Facebook, they feel worse about themselves. They feel diminished, even though nothing has changed in their wealth or social status. I wonder if seeing minorities move out of the historical poverty and marginalization they have suffered causes Caucasians to feel somehow diminished and if this does not explain the resentment many whites have for them.

We all have error detection alarms that warn us when things are out of place or don't fit our expectations. This is a normal and handy feature of our brains. It means, however, that we have to do something with the alarm – we have to determine if there is real danger or not and either respond to the danger or if we determine that it was a false alarm, make a mental note of it, so the alarm stops bugging us. Until we do, it can cause anxiety and discomfort. The whole process creates a cognitive burden. We are most comfortable when things are normal and when people match our expectations. That way we don't have to think or react to "not-as-expected" alarms.

People are more comfortable with the normal and known than with the unknown or ambiguous. In general, both men and women are more comfortable with masculine men and feminine women than with androgynous men or women. Men and women prefer male voices that are lower and more masculine over men's voices that are high pitched, and women's voices that are distinctly feminine over those that are less feminine.

In an experimental study, 170 young women were asked to wait in a man's office for an interview and allowed to sit in one of three offices. One room was decorated with items indicating that the man likely had a daughter and supported women's issues, the second office was decorated with items that clearly indicated sexual chauvinism, and the third office was ambiguous. After a few minutes, the attendant let the woman know that the man was not going to be available and the subject was given a brief cognitive test. Women that were placed in the chauvinist office scored equally well as did those who had waited in the office decorated as a progressive man. The women, however, scored significantly lower on the cognitive test after being in the office that was ambiguously decorated. It was more unnerving for women to wait to interview with someone that was an unknown. This indicates that these women had a lower cognitive workload from preparing to be interviewed by a man who was clearly sexist, than from one that was more ambiguous and difficult to peg.[24]

Gender identity is an integral part of our self-image. Especially for older and more conservative people, when others are non-conforming to traditional gender roles it sets off a cognitive "error detection alarm" that produces a cognitive burden and discomfort. Seeing people outside of our range of our "acceptable range of gender role" causes an error detection alarm. When women have higher power than men, it can cause men to feel less powerful in their gender role, and this is discomforting.

An example of a challenge to gender roles was observed in a study done in New Jersey prior to the 2016 presidential election. In the study, the participants were randomized to the order of the polling questions. They were either asked about their household income distribution between the voter and their spouse, prior to, or after being asked which political candidate they supported. The income question was designed to remind the participants of societal changes in gender roles from the traditional roles of a man as a breadwinner and woman as homemaker. If income distribution was asked before asking which candidate was preferred, it prompted the participant to consider gender roles, before stating their choice of candidate.

When male participants were first asked about political preference between Trump and Clinton, the men voiced a preference of Hilary Clinton over Trump 49 to 33 percent. However, when male participants were first primed with the income distribution question, they preferred Trump over Clinton 50 to 42 percent; *the reminder of gender roles shifted male voter preference by 24 percent!* When the same questions were asked of men, but the choice was between Trump and Bernie Sanders, there was a one percent shift in preference towards Sanders.

Among female participants, asking the income distribution question before candidate preference raised the preference for both Clinton and Sanders over Trump. Thus, the reason for the shift is unlikely to have been caused by increased concern for lost income, but rather a result of discomfort men felt after a reminder of changes in traditional roles.[25] Like the homemakers in Chile, these men felt their status and self-esteem was diminished when the income comparison was made, and it affected their voting behavior. A 2014 study found that 59 percent of college-educated American women aged 35 to 50 earn at least as much as their husbands do.[26]

Clinton's repeatedly reminding voters during the campaign that she was breaking the glass ceiling was a tactical error that likely cost her the election. In the face of a reminder of the perceived loss of gender-differential empowerment, one in four men shifted their support from a highly capable female candidate to an almost cartoonish, stereotypically masculine candidate for president.

The author of the New Jersey study pointed out that sociological research has shown that "in the face of personal or societal threats to their masculine identity, some men become more likely to endorse anti-gay stances, pro-gun policies, or anti-abortion views"... "Men who feel that their gender role is threatened by a wife who earns more money than they do may become more likely to embrace religious justifications for male superiority, or play up their role as the protector of the household."[27]

Male and female voters also look for slightly different virtues in male and female leaders. Men are perceived to be more effective leaders in situations where there is top-down leadership, such as in the military or directing traffic. Women are perceived to be better leadership roles that require interpersonal skills and collaboration.

In a study, voters were asked to rate photos of faces of male and female candidates for the U.S. House of Representatives on a one-to-seven scale for competence, dominance, attractiveness, and approachability. They were then shown pairs of candidates and asked which candidate they would vote for in a presidential election, having no other information about the candidates.

As in other studies, the voter's perception of competence was the single most influential determinant in deciding their vote. However other factors do have an influence. Men prefer female candidates that are more attractive, and women prefer male candidates that look approachable. In the mock elections for president, dominance (an appearance of power) was not a significant factor in candidate selection. In the actual election of these candidates in 2006 however, only male voter's perception of male candidate competence was statistically correlated with the election outcome. Dominance was not a significant feature in the mock or real elections in this study. [28]

Table 3-2: Influences Impacting Voting Behavior, Male vs. Female [29]

	Male Candidate (Explained variance)	Female Candidate (Explained variance)
Male Voter	Competence: R = 0.53 (R^2 = 41.7%)	Competence: R = 0.71 Attractiveness: R = 0.78 (R^2 = 70.8%)
Female Voter	Competence: R = 0.57 Approachability: R = 0.56 (R^2 = 49.3%)	Competence: R = 0.74 Attractiveness: R= 0.66 (R^2 = 63.6%)

Univariate R values, R^2 = correlation for multivariate adjusted model.

The lack of significant correlation to actual election outcome likely occurred from the use of university students as study participants. University students are younger, more educated and liberal than most voters, and are less prone to gender bias, while the majority of voting districts in the U.S. are non-competitive and conservative. Nevertheless, this study strongly suggests that male and female voters look for different qualities in male and female candidates.

Pearl: The perception of competence is the most critical face-value quality, with attractiveness important for female candidates and approachability for men. Other studies suggest that for Republican-leaning voters, attractiveness is an asset for men.

Approachability is likely a combination of openness and lack of hostility. Openness is likely appearing alert, friendly (smiling) and having a less, rather than a more, masculinized face.

In times of conflict or threat, more physically formidable leaders are preferred. In a study conducted in Texas in 2009, approximately 300 subjects who had been called for jury duty, all registered voters, were asked to complete a short survey while they waited to see if they would be selected to serve on the jury. They were asked how they would likely vote under different scenarios where the presidential candidate had either male or female first names. When the economy was good, there was no significant bias for a male candidate, but when the economy was in trouble, there was. The researchers also found a strong preference among both men and women to have male CEOs of companies they would be interested in working for, and this preference was even stronger if the company was under economic threat. The study also found that men were preferred as candidates even more strongly if the voting scenario was in a time of war.[30]

Entrepreneur Daymond John is quoted as saying *"Pioneers get slaughtered, and the settlers prosper."* The concept comes from a 1993 paper demonstrating that the first company to bring a disruptive, innovative product to market fails about half the time, while companies that follow have much higher success rates. Part of the advantage of following is the creation of a market and acceptance of the product while avoiding errors. The first company to sell personal computers was not Apple, IBM, or even Commodore, but rather the nearly forgotten company, MITS.[31]

Similarly, the first people to break gender-traditional work roles also have a hard time, whether it is men as nurses and librarians or women as coal miners and loggers. These people get little assistance and much resentment from their traditional gender co-workers, and they are often sabotaged.[32] In August 2017 a male software engineer at Google made the news (and got fired) for issuing a detailed, ten-page letter that argued that Google was wasting resources on promoting the hiring of female engineers, as he contended that women are not as adept as software engineers because of inherent physiological differences, and that women are not as productive as they are less competitive and less self-reliant.[33]

> It is for inherent differences that the owner of an engineering firm I know prefers to hire female programmers. He feels that women are better software engineers as they are more patient, detail oriented, make fewer programming errors, create fewer bugs and that women communicate more effectively, and thus are more likely to deliver a product that meets the product's requirements.
>
> Women did most of the computer program coding in the early days of the computer industry but were squeezed out of the industry as it developed into a well-paid career. According to NASA, prior to John Glen's historic space flight in 1962, he did not trust the computer's trajectory calculations for where the capsule would splash down and

asked the head engineers to ask a Black female mathematician working for NASA to check the numbers. He said "If she says the numbers are good... I'm ready to go."

Women moving into more traditionally male roles and careers can threaten gender identity of both men and women. Women pioneering into leadership positions and into non-traditional roles for women also experience difficulty. Women seeking leadership roles are often treated badly. It is not uncommon for men in the U.S. Senate to treat female members dismissively, especially if the woman has the temerity to speak out and do her job. As a senator, Kamala Harris was not uncommonly cut off and silenced by her male counterparts. Pioneers do have a hard time, but as more women and minorities gain leadership positions, they will have easier inroads to power and influence to represent American democracy.

Gender bias in leadership is common even in female-dominated professions. About 76 percent of the 3.6 million full-time school teachers in the United States are women. In primary schools, men make up less than 20 percent of the teaching staff, but hold 40% of principal positions. Only 28.5 percent of secondary school principals are women, although 59 percent of high school teachers are female. [34] [35] Of 13,728 school district superintendents, just 14.5 percent (1,984) are women.[36]

Women may be better adapted as teachers of children than men. Women, on average, are more patient, less impulsive, and have better communication skills; traits that help in managing and teaching easily distracted and unruly children. Men tend to be more aggressive and explosive, while women exhibit more restraint and inhibitory control, and are more likely to diffuse anger.[37] [38]

One reason that fewer men teach may not be gender bias, but rather an attrition of men from positions that don't offer advancement, inducing men to leave the teaching profession. In the many years that I served on school advisory councils, I saw many male teachers crave the principal position and move from one district or state to another to pursue a job as a principal, but don't recall any women leaving for this reason. I saw high school football coaches try to build their careers off of school athletes, pushing them to victory and lifelong injuries, so they could move to better-paying coaching positions. But why do more men become superintendents?

Table 3-3: Leadership in a female-dominated profession.

	Percent of Female Teachers	Percent of Female Principals or Superintendent	Male to Female Leadership Ratio
Primary Schools	78.5	60	1.34
Secondary Schools	60.5	28.5	2.1
School Superintendents	76	14.5	5.24

For CEO positions, private, public, or elected, a different heuristic is selected than when choosing for more collaborative positions. As of June 2017, 32 (6.4%) of the 500 CEO positions of the S&P 500 were held by women.[39] [40] As noted there are only six women governors, and three of these were elevated to the position when their governor left office during his term. In comparison, about 20 percent of the members of the U.S. House of Representatives, and 22 of 100 US Senators are women at the time of this writing.

One reason that more women are not in positions of power is that they do not seek these positions. A study performed by the Center for Talent Innovation in 2014, found that only eight percent of Caucasian American women professionals aspired to a position of power with a prestigious title. Interestingly, 22 percent of African-American professional women interviewed did.[41] Caucasian women do not start their careers uninterested in advancing to leadership status. Women do as well in college and have similar or slightly higher career aspirations than do men when starting out. However, after a couple of years, the reality of their prospects and lack of support becomes apparent; women then lower their expectations to fit their perceived reality. They become less enamored with their career, and it becomes a job rather than an aspiration.[42]

The best way to gain leadership skills is through experience, and this only comes with a dive into the action, taking risks, and seeking positions one is not yet qualified to do. Men are less timid about taking risks than women are, and thus are more likely to seek leadership roles. Additionally, women are less likely to ignore their lack of competence and abilities than are men, while men tend to overestimate their capabilities. Women tend to have a more negative perception of their abilities than do men, even when there is no significant difference in their performance or abilities.[43]

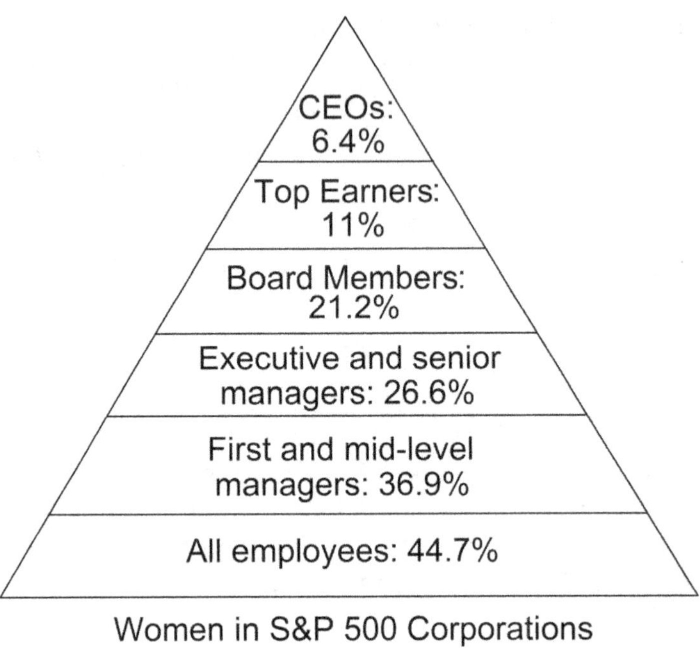

Figure 3-1: Proportion of females in various levels of corporate hierarchy. Thus, women make up only 11% of top earners and 6.4% of all CEOs.

People should choose their own paths; not everyone needs to aspire to leadership or high power professional careers. While men tend to overestimate their skills and experience, women often impede their career ascendency by a misperception that positions are not open to them, by misplaced sense of inadequacy, and laundry list of anxieties of what might possibly go wrong in seeking promotions or leadership roles. These self-limiting factors can be just as tough as external barriers. Other than for CEO positions, where there truly is a glass ceiling, women hold themselves and each other back just as much, and probably more than men do. Women should realize that they are not alone; there is an invisible ceiling that likely affects 90% of men who also do not fit the implicit model for top leadership. A substantial difference for men is that most men are unaware that the glass ceiling applies to them.

Women who aspire to collaborative leadership roles should assume that these positions are open to them as much as they are to their male counterparts. For top leadership roles, there remains a large gap; however, it is narrowing. I fully expect that by the time the young women, now in college, reach the azimuth of their careers, the gender gap will have closed. Thus, young women should presume that top leadership roles are equally open to them. We will have a better society and a more successful business economy as a result.

Chapter 4: Dominance

Imagine then, a fleet or a ship in which there is a captain, who is taller and stronger than any of the crew, but he is a little deaf and has a similar infirmity in sight, and his knowledge of navigation is not much better. The sailors are quarreling with one another about the steering --everyone is of the opinion that he has a right to steer, though he has never learned the art of navigation..., and will further assert that it cannot be taught, and they are ready to cut in pieces anyone who says the contrary.

Plato's Republic

(Plato argues that philosophers, the educated and trained, should lead, rather than the most dominant man.)

There are two distinct leadership roles. One is the singular, supreme commander role. This is the role of a CEO, president, governor, and superintendent. There is only one person in this role in the organization, and it is the top seat. Most other leadership roles are collaborative or subservient to the supreme commander in charge. Collaborative positions include congressmen and senators, members of parliament, commissioners, board members, other representatives, and partners.

People appear to make different implicit judgments as to who is fit for these two types of positions. People tend to choose more dominant individuals for the supreme leader roles but look for less imperious, more cooperative individuals for the collaborative roles. This makes sense, as a congress or board would not get much done if everyone on the committee was trying to boss the others around. This may be why there is far less, and perhaps minimal bias against women in gaining access to collaborative leadership positions.[44] Women are seen as being good at collaboration. However, it is more difficult for women to attain the supreme leader in charge position.

In competitive environments, facial dominance in the leader may be associated with a company's economic prosperity. The facial characteristics of managing partners (MPs) of America's top 100 law firms were assessed. Unlike corporate leaders or elected officials, MPs of law firms advance based on performance. Ratings of facial appearance for *competence, dominance, and facial maturity,* were associated with the firm's profit margin and profits distribution to partners. Likability and trustworthiness were not associated with profitability.[45] Competent and aggressive lawyers are more likely to win cases. When Law school yearbook photos were assessed an average of 33 years after graduation, facial power (dominance) predicted profitability and career achievement as managing partners, while warmth (likability and trustworthiness) was inversely related to profitability.[46]

Dominant, masculine faces are more likely to succeed in military organizations and sports. West Point Military Academy graduates from 1950 who had more dominant faces in their graduating class photos, while not providing a distinct advantage in their early or mid-careers, was related to promotions 20 or more years after the pictures were taken.[47] There may be an advantage for a dominant face for the top CEO (gubernatorial or presidential) positions in very competitive or wartime environments; however, this is not the case in times of peace or for other leadership roles in management and government, where cooperation and deference to top leadership are expected.

Companies with lower cognitive complexity are financially more successful with a CEO with a dominant face. This may be because of increased dominance and willingness to exploit others, including cost-cutting by getting rid of employees, selling off less productive units, or making moves that raise short-term profitability at risk of long-term decline.

Although facial appearance plays a role in the selection of CEOs to the largest American corporations, these facial characteristics do not appear to help in the company's actual success.[48] When the faces of CEOs from non-profit organizations were rated for dominance, those with higher dominance ratings were less successful in multiple measures of the charities success.[49]

In a study of facial characteristics in men within corporate hierarchies, the characteristics of dominance, attractiveness, and trustworthiness were considered. Moving up the hierarchy is central to moving towards leadership, and gives a higher number of positions to compare. Of these three traits, only perceived trustworthiness was correlated with position in the corporate hierarchy. Facial width, which is associated with domineering behavior and untrustworthiness, was unrelated to rank within the organizational hierarchy.[50] Clearly dominance has a role, but it is limited as to where it works.

What about female CEOs? Ratings of photos of 20 female Fortune 1000 CEOs by undergraduate students ranked the perceived competence and leadership of the photos, and these ranks correlated with the profitability of the company, however the ranked dominance was correlated with the individual's compensation.[51]

The selection of leaders and of who gets influential employment positions depends mainly on the perception of leadership potential. It has been mostly men that have held top leadership roles in political and business environments. When women and men work together in teams, it is generally a man taking on the supervisory role. When men lead, there is a tendency for a more autocratic style,[52] and when women take on an authoritarian command style, there are more complaints.

As recently as the year 2000, hypothetical female bosses were perceived to be as competent as hypothetical male bosses, in a study using the same resume, but different first names, but the boss with a hypothetical female first name was seen as self-serving and difficult to work for. It may be that female bosses were resented more if they led with an authoritarian style that would have been accepted by a male boss. The biases against female leaders in the workplace are weakening, and women are now seen favorably as bosses.[53]

Testosterone

In competitive environments, higher testosterone provides both physical and emotional advantages. Since these traits show up in the face, people will often choose leaders with more masculine faces during times of conflict or uncertainty.

A higher level of testosterone during adolescence promotes a taller physical stature and is associated with greater physical strength. Testosterone effects are associated with more aggressive and risk-taking behaviors that may imbue hunting and survival skills in a primitive society. We apparently have an innate propensity to choose taller leaders and choose more dominant leaders in times of crisis and insecurity.

Testosterone itself is associated with increased muscle mass and strength. Men who are more masculinized by testosterone are physically stronger, have broader shoulders, and are more dominant. Furthermore, higher levels of testosterone are associated with specific behavioral traits: increased dominance, competitiveness, aggression, sexuality, and risk-taking behaviors and high self-esteem. It is also associated with being more self-serving, less-cooperative, and having a higher willingness to exploit others.[54]

One characteristic associated with aggressive masculine faces is a high facial width to height ratio (fWHR). This ratio is formed from the width of the face at the zygomatic arches divided by the height of the upper face. The faces of these masculinized men are wider faces at eye level, with more separation between the eyebrows; the nose and mouth are broader, and the lips are thinner. More masculinized faces have a broader, rounder lower face and more prominent jawline than men who are less heavily masculinized.[55] [56] These facial traits are implicitly recognized.[57]

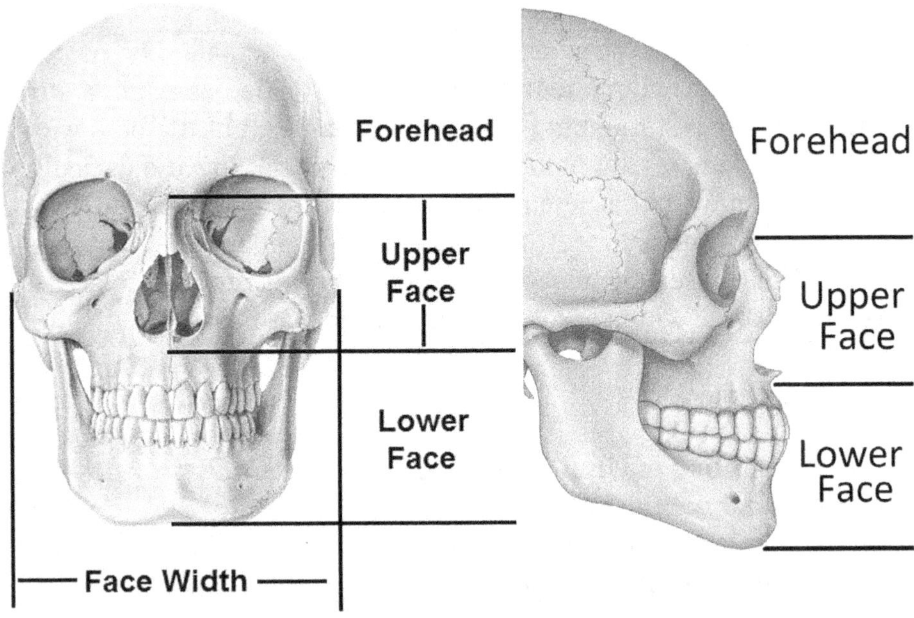

Figure 4-1: Skull showing anatomical face-width and height areas. The upper face goes from the top of the nasal bone to the base of the nasal spine. The fWHR is the ratio of the face width to the upper face height.

In a study of mixed-martial arts fighters, a group that self-selects men that are both very physical and competitive, those with a higher facial width to height ratio were not only perceived to be more aggressive competitors but were also found to be more successful fighters. Those of higher body mass were perceived as, and also found to be better fighters.[58] [59] In Figures 5-2 below, notice the downturned curve of the lips at the corners of the mouth, the decreased space between the eyes and brows, and the broader nose in the more aggressive face. These are all testosterone-mediated effects on facial structure.

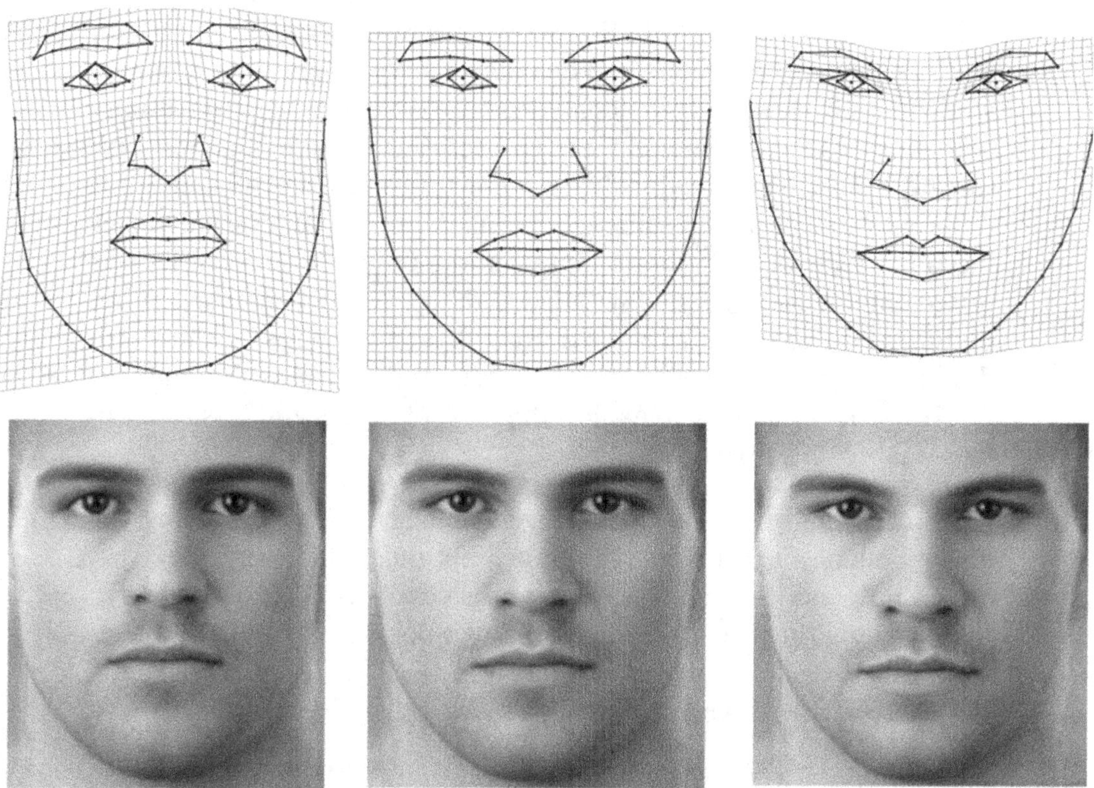

Figure 4-2: The central image is a morphed composite image of mixed-martial-art athletes. The left and right spline-deformed images portray the averaged faces of those perceived to be less aggressive fighters on the left and the more aggressive fighter on the right, with spline-deformations magnified 3X to make the differences more visible. Used with permission.[60]

Figures 4-3 and 4-4: A cartoonized, accentuated view of the right-most image above along with a cartoon of an angry bulldog. Artists unknown.

In a study of two groups of hockey players, Canadian professional athletes and undergraduate athletes (already men selected for aggressive and athletic prowess), those with a higher fWHR, were found to commit more penalties and spend more time in the penalty box. As part of the same study male hockey players and female students completed psychological testing and were pitted against one-another in computer games. The computer game was designed to rate aggressive behavior. They were told the other player (in a different room) was the same gender as them. The men with higher facial fWHR were more dominant than the others. When fWHR was tested among men, it was associated with aggressive behavior but not dominance. The fWHR of women was not found to be associated with dominance or aggression.[61] In another study men with a higher fWHR were more likely to exploit the trust of others and less likely to trust male counterparts.[62]

Humans and other animals can show aggression by making the angry bulldog face; raising the upper lip and pulling the eyebrows downward and closer together, in effect increasing the fWHR. In men, angling the face downwards 15 to 30 degrees while maintaining forward gaze, also enhances the appearance of aggression by bringing the eyes closer to the brows, giving a more aggressive appearance.

A statistical review of multiple studies on fWHR found that men have a slightly higher fWHR than do women. Nevertheless, while fWHR is strongly associated with the perception of masculinity in men, it is not in women. fWHR is strongly associated with threat behavior in men, especially among younger men, but again not in women.

"Fearless dominance," a measure of aggressiveness and risk-taking, is associated with cheating behavior. Men, but not women, with large fWHR, cheated more often in game situations where money could be won.[63] In men, fWHR is correlated with physical and verbal aggression and is highly associated with anger (short-fuse) but not with hostility (being ready to fight all the time). Men with higher fWHR have been found more prone to engage in deception and to exploit the trust of others. One study found that in men, a high fWHR was associated with pro-social or self-sacrificing behavior towards in-group members – but against the out-group in competitions; thus these high fWHR men will fight for their in-group. In women, fWHR was correlated with verbal aggression, and cold-heartedness, but these women had lower scores on self-centered impulsiveness.[64] Men with higher fWHR are more likely to endorse racially prejudicial beliefs,[65] a manifestation of in-group against out-group competitive behavior.

In men, a high fWHR was found to be strongly associated with success in business. This may result from the high correlation of the perception of dominance associated in men with a high fWHR. Studies have found that measured dominant behavior is associated with fWHR, but the strength was weaker than was the measure of perceived dominance. There was no significant association between the fWHR in women and perceived dominance. The fWHR is associated with body mass index (obesity), and this may weaken the relationships between perception and behavior, as body mass "inflates" the perception of masculinity, but not the hormonal underpinnings of the high fWHR. Finally, the review found that fWHR was inversely associated with attractiveness. Women perceive men with high fWHR faces to be less attractive.[66]

While fWHR is related to the perception of dominance and leadership ability in some realms, facial adiposity, which correlates to BMI, is judged to be less attractive and individuals with high facial adiposity are perceived to have lower leadership ability.[67] An unhealthy elevated body mass index (BMI higher than about 26) is associated with a lower perception of leadership ability.[68]

Several studies have shown that men with higher fWHR have a higher propensity to aggression and unethical behaviors including deception, cheating, self-interest, and are less likely to trust others. A high fWHR in women, however, is not associated with these traits.

Although demonstrated in multiple studies and used as a proxy for testosterone effect, the fWHR is far from an ideal measure of the impact of testosterone. The first question is whether it is the bone structure of the fWHR, or the soft tissue landmarks that are best correlated with fWHR-associated behaviors. The soft tissue landmarks are affected by obesity which may add error into the fWHR measurement, weakening the association with testosterone. Alternatively, obesity and its effects on growth may be part of the fWHR effect. Also, fWHR tends to increase with aging, as the eyebrows sag and facial adiposity increases.

Anatomically, the upper face is measured from the top of the nasal bone down to the base of the nasal spine/top of the alveolar ridge (the tips of the upper root of the teeth). Most studies use photos and measure the upper face height from the midpoint of the eyebrows down to the margin of the top lip. The anatomical measurement of bone structure, however, appears to more accurately reflect the effect of testosterone but is not convenient to measure as it cannot be accurately measured from photos. The facial width is measured as the distance across the face at the zygomatic arches.

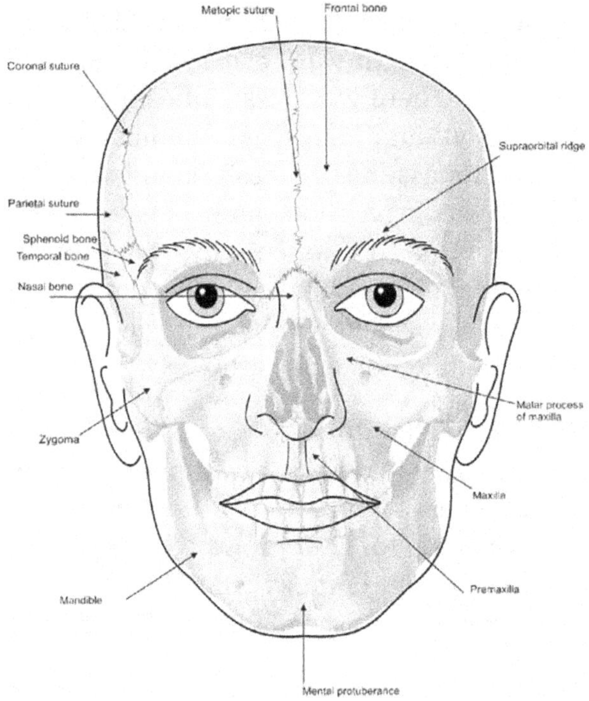

Figure 4-5: Head illustrating soft tissue placement in relationship to bony landmarks

Although fWHR is clearly correlated to aggressive behavior in men, the link is tenuous for females, although fWHR has been found to be associated with verbal aggression and cold-heartedness in women. The average fWHR is only slightly higher in men than women, thus then fWHR does not appear to be impacted by testosterone effect during adolescent development.

It took 25 years to complete the study, but in 2015, data was presented that demonstrated that testosterone during fetal development has a strong influence on facial features of masculinity. Blood from the umbilical cord was collected at birth and frozen at −80°C. After waiting for 21 to 24 years, 97 young men and 86 young women from the study were contacted and had their facial features measured using 3D scanning. A mathematical model including 12 facial measurements was created that accurately discriminated male from female faces. A male to female gender score from zero to one was formed, so that the mean male score was 0.25, and mean female score was 0.75. There was essentially no overlap of male and female scores.

> Faces that have average gender features (i.e., a gender score close to 0.25 for men and 0.75 for women as scored in this study) are considered to be the most attractive to raters. Thus, rather than highly masculine, highly feminine, or androgynous faces, male faces that have average masculinity and female faces with average femininity scores are considered most attractive.

Blood testosterone levels at birth were highly and inversely correlated with facial gender score. The higher the testosterone levels were in the umbilical cord blood, the more masculine the faces were for both males and females at the time of early adulthood. As in other studies, the fWHR did not differentiate male and female faces. In this study, fWHR was only weakly correlated with umbilical cord blood testosterone levels. Thus, fWHR is neither an adequate metric of fetal testosterone nor of fetal masculinization. Contemporary testosterone levels were also analyzed in the young men in this study, and were found to have substantially zero correlation with facial gender score but did have a weak association with the neonatal cord blood testosterone levels. [69]

It is not surprising that a 12-factor measurement from 3D modeling gives a much higher gender discrimination score than does a two-factor estimation from 2D images used to derive fWHR scores. What is surprising is that fetal, rather than adolescent testosterone appears to be the relevant influence on gender-typical facial bone structure.

During adolescence, testosterone level dramatically rises; increasing 20-30 fold in males as compared to females. These levels are reflected in and can be tested in the saliva. These higher levels of testosterone are associated with a broader forehead, chin, jaw, and nose.[70]

Nevertheless, the fWHR and gender scores are only marginally correlated with testosterone levels during adolescence. Furthermore, fWHR remains similar from just before the onset of puberty to young adulthood and is not associated with physical strength or voice pitch. The ratio of the face length to forehead height, however, increases significantly in boys during this time period and is strongly associated with testosterone levels and muscular strength.[71] Thus, and lower face length is associated with adolescent testosterone levels, and these changes are correlated with muscular strength and depth of voice.

It is likely not the masculinization effects from pubertal testosterone that are associated with hostile and aggressive behavior, but rather the prenatal testosterone exposure. The average child with autism spectrum disorder (ASD) has a facial masculinization score that falls in the upper end of the typical distribution for other children of their gender, and their facial gender scores are inversely correlated with their social affect score, showing more social and communication difficulties associated with more masculine features. Facial masculinization, however, is not related to autism-associated repetitive or restricted behaviors that are present in children with ASD.[72] Boys with higher levels of umbilical cord blood testosterone have also been found to have a more limited vocabulary at the age of two,[73] and to have delayed language, fine-motor skill, and personal-social skills at the age of three.[74] The behavior of girls was not significantly affected by higher umbilical cord testosterone levels. Females appear to be protected from testosterone-induced communication and behavioral changes; even females at the lowest end of the distribution have higher facial gender scores (more feminine) that differentiate them from all but the least masculine male facial scores. Behavioral changes associated with prenatal developmental exposure to testosterone may explain the aggressive behaviors related to high fWHR. These changes are likely affected by the timing, duration, and degree of prenatal testosterone effect.

While testosterone during adolescence is associated with face length ratios, vocal tone, muscular strength, the prenatal exposure has much less effect on these areas. Athletes with a higher fWHR while participating in more contact sports and being more aggressive; tend to gravitate to sports that require less endurance.[75]

Baby-faced men have rounder than average male faces, thus giving them a high fWHR. Baby-faced men on average demonstrate higher academic achievement, higher motivation, and are more likely to earn military awards. Their temperament is less inhibited (fearful) as infants. Baby-faced adolescents from lower socioeconomic environments demonstrated more criminal behavior than their less baby-faced peers. As adults, they exhibit assertive and aggressive behavior, in line with other men with high fWHR. Nevertheless, they are misperceived to be naïve, more trustworthy, honest and warm. Baby-faceness likely results from prenatal testosterone effect,[76] perhaps with a muted adolescent effect of testosterone, which thus results in a limited vertical mid- and lower-face elongation[77] and a less pronounced lowering of the voice and muscular development.

Facial clues allow us to distinguish men that were exposed to higher testosterone levels during fetal development and as well during adolescence and early adulthood growth. Those with higher levels during adolescence presumably, continue to have higher testosterone levels during adulthood. Testosterone increases the output of growth hormone which causes bone growth. In adulthood, the long bones do not get longer, so we do not get taller, however, in men, the shoulders get broader into their twenties, and facial characteristics continue to mature.

In acromegaly, a disease caused by excess growth hormone (GH) secreted from a pituitary tumor, there is the growth of the bones in the brow and mandible, a widening of the nose, as well as several other physical changes. These give a hyper-masculine appearance.

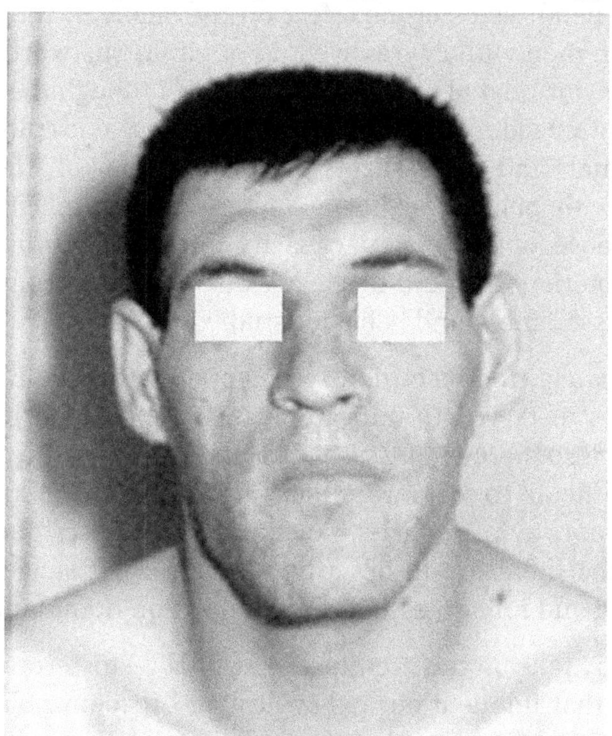

Figure 4-6: A man with acromegaly, a growth hormone tumor that causes over-accentuation of the masculine facial features that develop during adolescence.

The effect of adolescent and early adult testosterone can be recognized; men with higher testosterone levels have a more prominent brow, and jawline, wider nares, and a deeper pitched voice. When there is increased growth hormone present before the end of the pubertal growth phase, higher levels of testosterone also increase height.

During adolescence, testosterone influences growth of body and facial hair, development of the genitalia, the development of acne, a lowering of the voice, an increase of muscle mass, the growth of the bones with increased stature and broadening of the shoulders and rib cage, and also affects the soft tissues in the face. Thus, men's, and to a much lesser extent, women's, faces are shaped by the degree of testosterone activity during the adolescent growth period. A higher testosterone effect gives a more masculine appearance. The "testosterone effect" is not simply controlled by testosterone production and its metabolism, but also by the presence and activity of androgen receptors and their downstream targets.

The adolescent testosterone effect likely gives a more dominant behavior, although not a more aggressive, hostile, or subversive one. It is the prenatal testosterone effect on the shape of the face that is associated in men with aggressive and often untrustworthy and self-serving behavior related to a high fWHR, even though the fWHR may not be an optimized model for determining these masculinized traits. Both prenatal and adolescent masculinization of the face are associated with behaviors that are assessed in implicit judgments including those of leadership capacity and trustworthiness. Thus, these characteristics should be clearly distinguished from each other in implicit assessment and behavior studies.

Unfortunately, the term dominant appears to have been used in some studies of fWHR to indicate aggressiveness and in studies of adolescent testosterone features to indicate assertiveness. This makes it difficult to be sure which attributes are associated with which behaviors across studies. Thus, where the descriptor dominant is used in the literature to describe high fWHR, I suggest the term domineering and for adolescent masculinization dominant.

Here is my take on the literature: The fetal testosterone has effects on the face that imbue a normal-typical and recognizable male face. It also affects behavior and language ability and gives a broader face, although this is an inadequate description of the multiple effects on the shape of the face associated with fetal testosterone. High levels of fetal testosterone are associated with hyper-masculinization and aggressive and hostile behaviors. Adolescent testosterone, in conjunction with growth hormone also affects the face, giving it more distinct masculine features, as well as being associated with other behavioral changes. Some behavioral changes are adaptive; if you end up inside a tall, muscular body, it changes your approach to human interactions compared to being small and weak. Other effects, such as sex drive are likely largely influenced by hormones, but how a person deals with their sex drive is a separate matter.

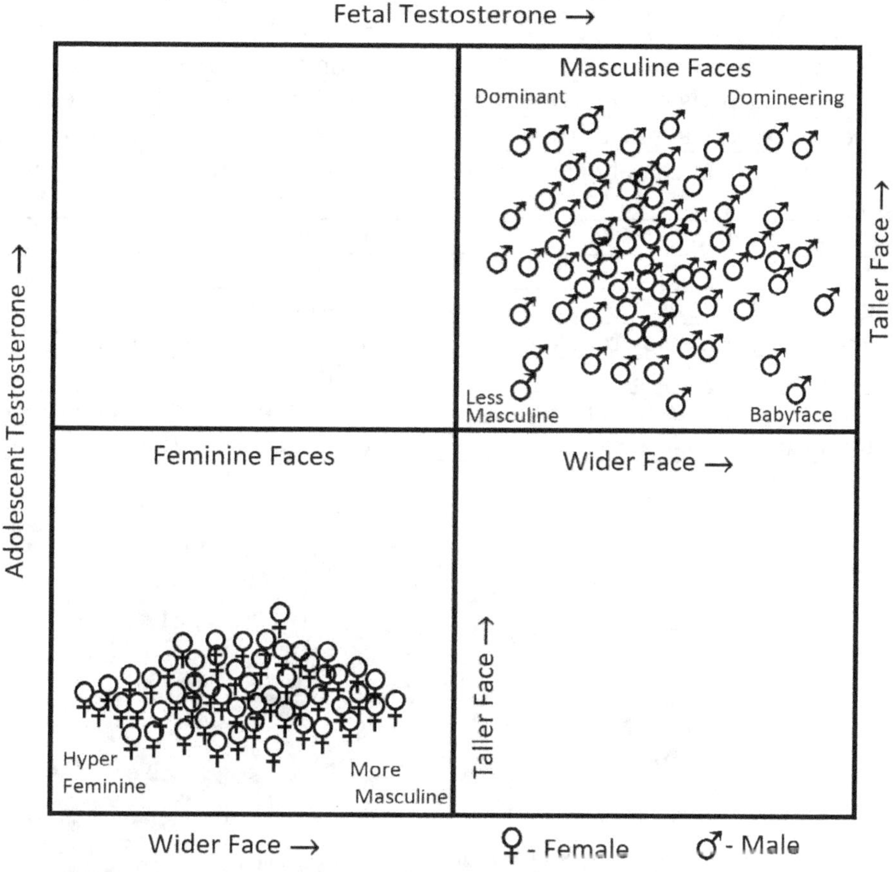

Figure 4-7: An imaginary distribution of the testosterone effect on the faces of men and women. Note that facial width is a poor descriptor for the effect of fetal testosterone on the face and that growth hormone and other factors have important influences on face shape development. The term domineering is used to differentiate the more aggressive and hostile behaviors associated with fetal testosterone influence from that of the adolescent testosterone effect that promotes dominant but not aggressive traits.

The adolescent effect of high testosterone is associated with increased stature, a lower-pitched voice, increased muscular strength, and a longer mid-and lower face, giving an angular jawline. Testosterone is also associated with more melanin production and thus a darker skin color.

Fetal masculinization is associated with a wider face, a higher tip of the nose (shorter nose) and longer columna (increased length of upper lip), down-turning corners of the mouth.

Table 4-1: Effects of testosterone on the face.

Less Testosterone Effect	More Testosterone Effect
Rounded hairline	Square hairline, M-shaped with age
Thinner eyebrows	Thicker eyebrows
Center two-thirds of eyebrows arch up	Center two-thirds of eyebrows flat
More space between eyebrows	Less space between eyebrows
More vertical space between eyebrow and eye	Less vertical space between eyebrow and eye
Narrower mouth	Wider mouth
Longer chin	Longer chin
Higher "Cheekbones:	Lower "cheekbones"
Narrower zygomatic arches	Wider zygomatic arches
Narrower base of nose	Wider base of nose
Higher forehead to face ratio (shorter mid and lower face)	Lower forehead to face ratio (longer mid and lower face)

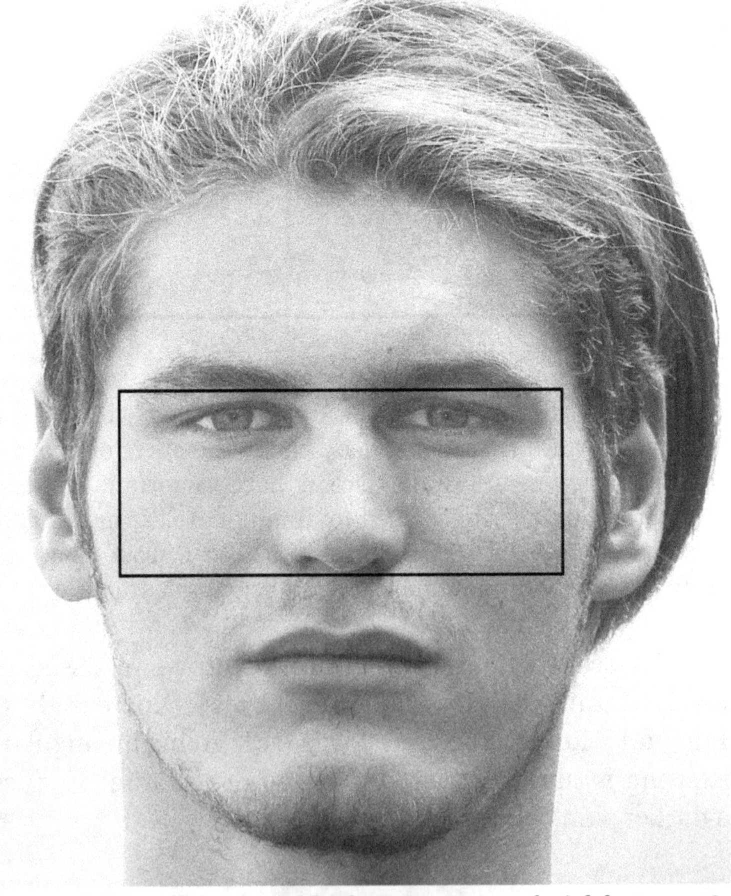

Figure 4-8: Man with several high-testosterone facial features.[78]

In a democratic society, leadership is chosen. Social skills and capacity for cooperation are valued over authoritarianism in most situations. Nevertheless, in times of war, voters prefer candidates with domineering faces that are less trustworthy.[79] In this context, trustworthy likely relates to cooperativeness and the lack of hostility and exploitative behavior.

Perception of *aggressiveness* is inversely associated with upper face height. Thus, a shorter upper face is associated with aggressiveness. Here, the taller the upper face, the less aggressive the face is perceived to be. This effect has also been found in women; however, it was not as potent as it was in men. Thus short and wide faces are associated with the perception of aggressiveness as well as with actual aggressive behavior.

The perception of *trustworthiness* is modulated mostly by the upper face height, with medium to tall upper faces perceived to be more trustworthy. This is true for both men and women. Very tall upper faces do not appear to be as trustworthy as medium tall faces. Faces that are narrower than average are also perceived to be slightly less trustworthy, but the effect is smaller than for face height.

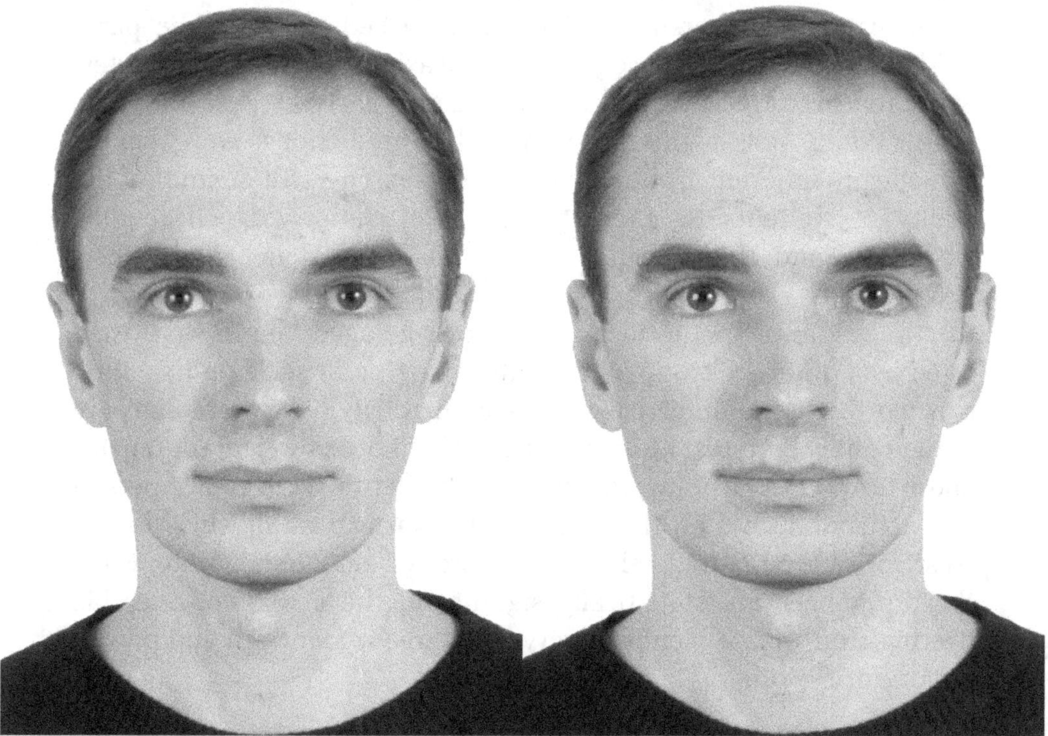

Figure 4-9: The jaw and nose width has been altered in these photos. The wider face on the right appears more dominant, masculine, confident, and trustworthy.[80]

The perception of *femininity* is also judged by bone structure; however, it may be more accurate to call it the absence of hormonal masculinization or lack of virilization. Perception of femininity is linearly associated with face height and inversely associated with face width. The effect size for height is somewhat smaller than it is for aggressiveness but still active.[81]

Faces that are judged more trustworthy and thus more prosocial are preferred by voters in peacetime, but not in the time of war.[82] Faces that have cues for masculinity and height are also preferred as leaders in times of war.[83] In a separate study, trustworthy faces were again preferred in a simulated voter choice during a time of peace, while more attractive faces were favored in times of war. This suggests that health and vitality are considered a sign of the physical fitness of a leader in a time of war.[84] This may explain the preference that conservatives have for more attractive candidates; they perceive that the more attractive candidate will perform better in time of conflict, and are more likely to perceive anytime as a time of hostility, and competition for resources.

In a study specifically designed to determine whether the political party of American political candidates could be differentiated from facial features, university students were asked to guess the party affiliation of 118 unrecognized Caucasian Senate candidates. Students correctly identified the candidate's party 57 percent of the time. While not highly accurate, the predictions were highly statistically different from chance. The researchers then studied the ability of students to guess the party affiliation of college-aged Democrats and Republicans that they had never met. Here, their guesses were even more accurate, guessing correctly 62 percent of the time. Photos of the faces of the college-aged voters were then rated by a different group of students on a 7-point scale on likability, trustworthiness, dominance, and facial maturity, who were unaware of the political interest of the research. The more powerful (dominant and mature) the face was, the more likely that the college-age person was a Republican, and the stronger the warmth rating (likable and trustworthy) the more likely that they were Democrats.[85] Note, while the differences are statistically significant, there was considerable overlap, and we are blends of varying degrees of warmth and power, not one or the other.

This data indicates that not only do people vote for candidates that have faces that reflect their political viewpoints (power vs.

warmth), but more strikingly, people's political views are influenced by their personal approach to the world, and this is reflected in their own face. Do we vote for people that look like us, or do the influences that shape our faces, also shape our approach to the world?

Pearl: Domineering faces prevail in conservative districts as conservative audiences prefer dominant leaders. Liberal voters prefer less dominant, more trustworthy and cooperative faces, and thus these faces do better in more liberal districts.[86] Women, therefore, have a better chance of winning in less conservative districts.

Pseudo-crises

Although men have traditionally been placed in leadership positions, it may be surprising that men with faces that reflect these stronger and more authoritarian traits are not favored in democratic elections in most situations. Highly masculinized faces are preferred in troubled times and times of war. In times of insecurity, people are willing to cede some control to a more aggressive and authoritarian leader in exchange for a greater sense of security. This is not the case in times of peace.[87]

However, the selection of highly masculine, high facial width to height ratio-faced leaders does not only occur in times of crisis but also during times of pseudo-crisis.. More dominant political figures often create a sense of crisis in order to get elected. They warn of decaying military strength; Bush, Romney, and Trump claimed this, although it was, in fact untrue and misrepresented in each case, as America's military remains strong and continually adapts to the geopolitical situation. These men, like Chicken Little, warn of decaying society which is often coded words for fear-mongering and racism. They trumpet warnings of impending economic collapse when they have no way to alter the situation. They use demagoguery and division to gain power. They say that they alone can fix the problems that will otherwise doom the society, and that you are either with them or against society. They create division, creating the illusion of in-group from out-groups. This is one way that dominant figures can rally support, by creating the illusion of troubled times. When people have fallen for a deceptive pseudo-crisis, they have often ended up with Fascist or Nazi dictators, and division.

Toxoplasmosis gondii

There is a bizarre, non-genetic environmental agent that can affect both testosterone influence and modify behavior in humans. Infection with the parasite *Toxoplasmosis gondii* causes changes in brain behavior and increases the output of testosterone in male animals including men. This alteration in testosterone is sufficient that infection with this parasite before adolescence causes men to be taller, more masculine, and more dominant. It also appears to increase the formation and activity of dopamine in the brain, affecting the reward system causing more impulsive behavior and making affected individuals less keen on delayed gratification. It makes male animals more fearless. The infection is associated with a shorter attention span and with lower conscientiousness. Infected men and women are subject to riskier behavior and are more prone to both workplace and driving accidents.

Toxoplasmosis infection may change personality to a more masculinized one with more risky behavior, and one with a higher likelihood of short-term sexual relationships that increase reproductive propensity. These men may have more opportunities for leadership roles based on their stature, risk-taking behavior, and a higher level of extraversion.* However, they have shorter attention spans, tend to be jealous and suspicious, and break social rules more frequently. Thus, they make poor leaders. Incarcerated men were found to be 2.9 times as likely to have antibody evidence of *Toxoplasmosis* infection as did the general population in the city where they were imprisoned. Women infected with this parasite are also more impulsive. They are more likely to be depressed and twice as likely to attempt or commit suicide as are uninfected women. New *Toxoplasmosis* infection during pregnancy can be associated with severe neurological injuries in the child.[88]

This disease affects 30 to 40 percent of the human population worldwide and thus may have a tremendous impact on behavior and culture. In the U.S., it is estimated that 11 percent of the population over 6 years of age has been infected. In other areas of the world, as much as 95 percent of the population has signs of previous infection with this parasite.[89] Mostly, humans are infected by contact with infected cats and their feces.

---

* Herein the spelling of extraversion conforms with its original use.

Since *Toxoplasmosis gondii* increases risky behavior and short-term liaisons, control of the disease might decrease the rates of sexually transmitted diseases and the number of unplanned pregnancies. Infected persons may have lower IQs, or perhaps just lower academic performance as a result of a shorter attention span and decreased ability to delay gratification, which is an essential determinant of academic success. Eliminating this disease would make people happier and less accident prone.

Preventing unintended, out-of-wedlock, and teenage pregnancy, favors planned pregnancies when parents have the resources and maturity to care for their children. This would provides society with a happier and more intelligent and successful populace. Access to birth control and *Toxoplasmosis* prevention could shift society to a more responsible, less aggressive, more cooperative one.

Chapter 5: Stature

Being tall has a tremendous advantage in politics and society. Height is associated with career success, higher income, and being selected for leadership positions in public and private organizations. Both taller men and taller women are more likely to run for leadership positions. Taller men and women tend to be less anxious, and more assertive and dominant and are perceived to be more intelligent.[90] A high IQ is a great asset for a successful leader. Thus, one of the implicit judgments in selecting leaders is facial characteristics that imply height.

U.S. presidents tend to be tall men, and when the presidential race has not had an incumbent, the taller candidate has usually won. Since 1854, when there is no incumbent, the taller candidate has won 16 times and the shorter candidate only seven times. In the last 120 years, there has not been a president that was not taller than the average American man from his generation.

In a study of presidential candidate polls, taller candidates were considered by voters to have greater executive ability and be better leaders during a crisis; be more willing to take risks; be more persuasive; were destined to have better relationships with Congress; have greater vision, and have a more significant historical legacy. Taller candidates are even perceived to be better endowed with luck.[91]

In a study of perception, participants were presented with images of faces and asked to estimate how tall they were on a scale of one to seven, with one being 5' 0" and seven being 6' 8". They were also asked how good a leader the person would be. The images were manipulated images of men and women, adjusting facial ratios, but otherwise the same faces.

Masculinity scores did not correlate to leadership scores or height scores for either men's or women's faces. The perceived height, however, was associated with leadership ability for both men and women. These faces were taller and less baby-faced. Taller male faces were considered to be more attractive, but this effect was minor in women.[92] Men with faces perceived as tall and masculine and older, up to the age of 35, were regarded as more dominant.[93]

Shorter presidential candidates have a harder time. In the 2016 Republican primary debates, Trump (6" 2") derided his five-inch shorter opponent as "little Marco" at 5' 9". Ted Cruz is about 5' 10". Both Rubio and Cruz usually wear boots with heels to add a couple of inches to their stature. Republican presidential candidates Ron Paul and Lindsey Graham (both 5' 7") were never considered likely to win the nomination. Barack Obama (6' 1.5") overshadowed John McCain (5' 9").

In early 2017, Senator Bob Corker, chairman of the Senate Committee on Foreign Relations in the 115th Congress, was apparently on the "short list" for the Secretary of State position under incoming president Trump, but Trump is reported to have discounted Corker (at 5' 7") as being too short for the position.[94]

Taller persons are more likely to emerge as leaders and managers. Height also provides an advantage in professional and educational achievement. Taller men are given higher starting salaries, have higher overall incomes and are more likely to be promoted. Thus tall men have more social dominance than men of shorter stature.

The average height of fortune 500 CEOs is estimated to be 6'2",[95] nearly five inches taller than the average height of 5" 9.5" of American men.

As of this writing, there are currently 32 female CEOs of the Fortune 500 companies. Marissa Mayer (Former CEO of Yahoo) is 5' 8", Sheryl Sanberg (COO of Facebook) is 5' 8", Carli Fiorina (Former CEO of Hewlett-Packard) is 5' 6", Indra Nooyi (CEO of PepsiCo) is 5" 9". Thus the average height of female CEOs is probably about 4.5 inches taller than the average American woman, at 5' 3.5". Thus, having a higher stature is associated with top-level leadership opportunities in women as well. Height gives a substantial advantage for those seeking leadership in CEO positions, but it is less crucial for collaborative leadership positions, such as members of boards and of Congress.

People tend to prefer leaders with a greater physical stature. Nevertheless, this is not just an external bias but also an internal one, resulting from self-selection. Taller men have greater self-esteem and are more likely to seek leadership positions. This self-confidence is likely the product of how the people in their environment respond to them, and reinforce this self-perception. People develop their self-image during adolescence, and when taller than those around them, they are likely to feel more dominant. Men of greater physical stature are more likely to see themselves as qualified for leadership, and as a result of this increased sense of efficacy, are more likely to pursue leadership positions.[96]

Contrary to the obvious expectations that taller, more formidable men would have advantages in physical professions, it is shorter men that are more likely to work as laborers, while taller men are more likely to work in offices and administration, doing sedentary work.[97] Being taller is also worth a considerable amount; thousands of dollars in annual income each year. Men in the U.S. and Great Britain earn about 2 percent more each year for each inch of height over an approximately 6-inch range so that men in the top quartile for height earn on average 13% more than those in the lowest quartile.

In a study aimed at unraveling how height influences income, it was found that when comparing men of equal adult stature, it is men that were taller at the age of 16 that held the economic advantage. This advantage remained even after adjusting for the influence of native intelligence, family resources, and health. Height at ages 7 and 11, did not impact income outcome. While self-esteem during adolescence had a small effect on adult income, it did not explain the impact of adolescent height on income. Height at age 33 did not impact income after adjusting for height at age 16.

The study found that shorter adolescents were less likely to participate in social activities, and thus, may have had fewer opportunities to develop interpersonal (including dating), social, and productive skills. Further analysis of the available prospective data collected and used in this study found that about half of the income disparity associated with height appeared to be explained by participation in extracurricular activities such as athletics, youth groups, student government, newspaper, yearbook, performing arts, and other clubs. For males, participating in athletics during high school was associated with an 11.7 percent increase in income, and in addition to athletics, for each extra-curricular activity, earnings increased by 5.1 percent.[98] Participation in these non-academic activities likely helps develop agency; non-cognitive traits including outgoingness and grit; emotional stability, initiative, independence; and willingness to assume responsibility; characteristics that have been shown to be associated with stature.[99]

When data including women were analyzed, women had a similar two percent increase in income per inch of stature. Women's height at age 16 however, was not significant but the height at age 11 was. The defining difference from boys is that girls start and finish their adolescent growth spurt at an earlier age than do boys.

Height at mid-adolescence is associated with adult earnings may be because of a decrease in earnings among adults who had a growth delay. Nutritional and social deprivation can cause a delay in the adolescent growth spurt and a reduction of final height. Peak adolescent growth velocity for boys occurs on average at age 13, and they gain about 10 centimeters that year.[100] Thus, a delay means they may begin high school four inches shorter, and socially, emotionally, and intellectually disadvantaged. The adolescent growth spurt is accompanied by an intellectual one as well, putting those with delayed growth additionally at an academic disadvantage.

Damn, that explains a lot. I was the smallest boy in a class of 50 kids throughout grade school, except for a few days in the daily lineup, when I put enough cardboard in my shoes, to cover the holes in the soles and nails coming up through the heels, that I could outstretch Danny Galvin in the daily lineup. I was scrawny, sometimes wormy, and was so accustomed to the gnawing sensation in the pit of my stomach that I assumed it was normal. There were eight kids in the house, and times were lean. For months the standard menu was oatmeal for breakfast, two slices of white bread with mayonnaise for lunch, a piercing headache as an afternoon snack, and spaghetti with margarine for supper. Otherwise, the cupboards were bare.

When I started high school with about 2000 others, there was one other kid who was just as short as me – but I never walked up to him to determine who was king of the runts. Eventually, I grew to average height but never caught up with my brothers who on average have four inches on me. They grew up in better times or were better at making friends whose houses they could eat at.

Participation in competitive sports increases success in adult life. There is a pervasive belief that athletics increases leadership skills and teaches teamwork. Not only do I doubt this, but I maintain these are not the reasons participation in sports harnesses success.

Forced to play sports in school, I was always the last-pick for any team. My team-mates kindly reminded me of my status as a liability, before, during and after games. When the weeds got tall enough to hide in, I didn't even bother moving from my seat in the extreme left field during the team's batting inning and my teammates didn't mind. On the swim team, I could barely breathe through my nose when standing on my tiptoes in the four-foot section of the pool at age 12. My same-aged teammate, John Bly, had broad shoulders, was already six feet tall, and won most races at swim meets. I reliably came in last. I was so slow that it sometimes delayed the next race. Other times the gun would fire and someone would dive over me or swim by me in the lane before I had a chance to drag myself out of the pool. I did not mind coming in last. Someone had too — I saw it as my public service to other non-athletic kids, and I was accustomed to it.

I contend that competitive sports are a spectacular venue for public failure. Yes, during sporting events the participant can literally fall on their face, trip up, be pummeled, humiliated and ignobly trounced. It is most effective when the players share the defeat with a team, so that even if they perform adequately, they are still a loser. It's even better when their father is there to see them fail.

Football is a great metaphor for repeated failure. You can get tackled, knocked down and miss the catch, as long as you keep moving the ball forward 10 yards, you get another chance for four more tries.

Sports can be a safe place to fail. It still hurts, but in this arena, there are more games in the season, and more chances to try again, and to lose again. Losing inures one to failure, and allows us a perspective that failure is an acceptable outcome. It teaches that one does not have to be the best, but you have to stay in the game to win. It teaches one to evaluate the losses and try new strategies and build new skills. It teaches that failure is not the end; most players survive and go on to new things. Failure, especially when shared, builds grit.

Stature is largely related to income simply because taller individuals are on average smarter and have better language and mathematical skills as a result. When cognitive tests are included in the analysis of stature and income, much of the height advantage disappears.[101]

Imagine identical twin sisters, but one is born a few ounces lighter and an inch shorter as a result of not getting quite as much placental blood flow. The mother, a teenager, plans to give them up for adoption, and like many mothers in this situation, did not get much prenatal care during pregnancy. The children are adopted by two different families. The larger twin goes to a family of good means which are dedicated to the child and her education and well being, and she quickly catches up on her growth. She is tucked into bed after a bedtime story and has meals with her family each day. She plays T-ball and gets piano lessons in elementary school.

The other girl goes to a loving family that soon falls on hard times, there is unemployment, divorce, and the child is raised in poverty and hardship. Both girls have allergies, but the advantaged one lives in an allergen free house, the other has chronic sinus and ear infections. The disadvantaged girl often skips breakfast, and dinner is a happy meal with a coke and fries. Entertainment is a TV, and she puts herself to bed when she is tired. By the time they get to high school, which of these girls with identical genetic makeup would you guess to do well in terms of academics and social skills? Which one will be more likely to be shorter and overweight, and which of the sisters is expected to be taller and more socially adept?

Is stature actually related to intelligence? Yes, however, indirectly. Height is associated with prenatal, childhood, and adolescent nutrition and health. Intelligence is also related to nutrition during the growth periods. Since affluence is associated with the quality and adequacy of nutrition, medical care, and enriched environment, children raised in prosperity tend to be healthier, taller, better educated, and more intelligent than those raised in deprivation. Individuals that are genetically shorter are not genetically less intelligent. It is deprivation that limits intelligence, not stature.

A tall stature is a sign of health and fitness. Obviously, healthy, well-nourished children grow taller than undernourished or sick children or those with intrauterine deprivation. With better nutrition and the treatment or elimination of many childhood diseases, people have gotten taller over the last hundred years. Japan has almost no immigration to affect changes in population genetics, so it is an excellent place to see this secular change. The average man born in Japan in 1870 had an adult height of 156 cm (5 feet, 1.4 inches). The average adult stature for Japanese men born in 1980 is 172 cm (5 feet 7.7 inches). Following World War II, between 1950 and 1980 the average height of 20-year-old Japanese men increased just over one inch each ensuing decade.

The average height of Caucasian men serving in the U.S. armed forces was about 5' 8" from 1790 through 1890, slowly gaining an average of about half an inch over 100 years. Then the average height of Americans began to decline slowly over the next 60 years. This was likely the effect of urbanization, crowding, and poorer nutrition, especially among recent immigrants as compared to those living on farms or rural areas. The average male height fell to 5' 6½" in 1950, representing men that grew up during the great depression. Since then, the average height has steadily risen, now with an average height of 5' 9.8" for younger American Caucasian men.[102]

While the population as a whole is getting taller, the height gain is actually occurring among the historically less privileged population, as their nutrition and health care catches up with the more affluent population. The average IQ in the United States has increased about 30 points over the last century, so much so that IQ tests need to be realigned about once a decade so that the average IQ can remain set to 100. This is largely the effect of better health, nutrition, and enriched environment, and control of disease, such as intestinal parasites. It is not the descendants of people like Jefferson (6' 2" and an IQ of over 145)[103] that have grown two inches taller and become 30 IQ points smarter; it is the underprivileged that are catching up, creating a healthier, smarter, and more productive society.

Men, on average, are about 5 inches taller than women. The average adult American man in 2014 was 5' 9" and the average American woman 5' 3.5 inches, a 5½" difference. Younger adults aged 20 to 29 are about half inch taller than those over 30 and stature continues to increase as a secular trend.[104]

But are taller persons really inherently better at leadership, vision, and luck? Consider the men who were not hired, but instead, founded several of the most successful companies of our time. These entrepreneurs are no taller than average. Steve Jobs, founder of Apple, was 6' 2", and Elon Musk, founder of PayPal, Space X, and Tesla, is also 6' 2". Warren Buffet and Bill Gates are both 5'10. The two founders of Google, Larry Page and Sergey Brin are 5' 11" and 5' 8". Jeff Bezos, the founder of Amazon, is 5' 8", the same height as Michael Bloomberg. Mark Zuckerberg, the founder of Facebook, is a towering 5' 7". The point is that while height gives the illusion of leadership ability, which is helpful, but it is perception only, and not talent, creativity, vision, foresight, cunning, or competence. Height does help with self-confidence, as when people look up to you, you can start to believe you are a leader or at least believe you have access to leadership roles. Keep in mind that many U.S. senators including Bob Corker, Ron Paul and Lindsey Graham are short. Former Senator Jeff Sessions, now U.S. Attorney General, is 5"4". Retired Senator Barbara Boxer is 4' 11" and stood on a box to speak. Stature is mainly an issue for CEO positions.

Being tall and looking the part clearly helps in getting CEO and other top-level positions. But do these leaders lead better? Do these extraverted, tall, white knights with glinting smiles and degrees from top universities have the edge when it comes to running companies? The answer is likely not, and perhaps that they do worse. When these leaders are chosen to come into troubled companies as saviors, they can inspire faith, and rally stock prices, but often fail to effect actual progress or reform, so the company languishes.[105]

Figure 5-1: Nancy Pelosi (highest ranking female member of Congress) appears to be standing on her tiptoes, but is still several inches shorter than Marissa Meyers, former CEO of Yahoo.[106]

The archetypal masculine autocratic leader often fails to listen to, and thus alienates their most talented employees. More effective leaders bring people together, promote collaboration and attract diverse talent. Rather than aplomb and self-assuredness, it is humility and honesty that are associated with successful CEOs. These leaders are more likely to be curious, open-minded and driven by logic. They are more likely to listen and adapt. Collaborative leaders are more trusted by employees who understand that their contributions will be listened to, and thus the employees contribute more and better ideas, and better products are created.[107] So while looking like a leader, having suave self-confidence, and a tall stature create leadership opportunities, they do not determine actual leadership acumen. Don't trap yourself into believing that a lack of stature limits your ability to be an effective leader, nor that fitting the role will make you one.

Taller persons are considered to be more attractive in mate selection. This likely comes from the survival advantage of having a healthier and more robust mate, and the advantages of this trait likely spill over into political and other leadership choices. In a study examining the ideal stature for a mate, on average, men were found to prefer their ideal mate to be 4½ inches shorter than them, and women prefer their idealized mate to be 6 inches taller than them. Men preferred women that are about one inch taller than the average woman and women find men about two inches taller than average to be the ideal height.[108] Thus, very tall men and women, those taller than the ideal, may be judged to be less attractive as mates, and again, this may spill over to choice in leadership.

There may be little leadership advantage to a person being taller than about four inches taller than the average man or woman. The leadership advantage for men appears to currently peak around 188 cm, equivalent to 6' 2".[109] According to the National Center for Health Statistics, only about five percent of US men aged 40 to 60 are between 6' 1" and 6' 3", the "ideal" height for leadership.[110] Thus, only five percent of men fall into this ideal height ranges.

Women's Stature and Leadership

Are women disadvantaged in leadership positions because women on average are shorter than men? For women, the relationship between height and perception of leadership qualities is weaker than for men, but still, it appears to be present between taller and shorter women. Taller women earn more, and this is explained by the association of health, intelligence, and timing of the adolescent growth spurt, as discussed above. The psychological advantage of height is also active for taller women, and thus an internal influence that encourages taller women to seek leadership positions. Women that are taller than average are more desirable mates, likely because of the perception of health.

Women, however, do not need to be as tall as a tall man to be on equal footing for most leadership roles. As with other gender dimorphic traits, being within the gender norm is advantageous and falling outside of it carries disadvantages in social selection. Being female does, however, create electoral disadvantages when voters view the situation as a time of conflict or crisis; a time when individuals choose leaders perceived to be more dominant and less risk averse.

A study from the University of Amsterdam, using images of a man and a woman that had been manipulated to make them appear taller or shorter, were compared for perceived leadership attributes. The image of the taller version of the man was perceived to be more adapted to leadership because of perceived physical dominance, intelligence, and health. The study participants however only weakly projected the attributes of physical dominance and health to women as a result of perceived height. The strongest attribution for a taller appearing woman associated with leadership ability was the perception that the taller appearing woman was more intelligent.[111]

Pearl: While a taller stature is helpful for women in achieving leadership positions, it is less significant than it is for men. Women do not need to be as tall as men to compete for leadership positions with them.

Body Mass

The body mass index (BMI) is a measure of weight for a given height per weight and is associated with health. Having a BMI under 18.5 is considered underweight, while one over 25 is considered overweight and a BMI greater than 30 is considered obese. Being obese carries a high risk of adverse health consequences and of harmful prejudices such as stereotypes that these individuals lack self-discipline and are unmotivated, less competent, slovenly, and noncompliant. In a study of voter perceptions, images of candidates with faces indicating obesity were perceived as having less leadership ability. Obese persons are less likely to run for office and receive a smaller share of the votes when they do.[112]

BMI is not an ideal measure of body fat. It cannot differentiate between a highly muscular individual and an overweight one. In middle and older age, however, BMI usually correlates with adiposity. A better measure of health for women is the waist to hip ratio. This is the ratio of the waist circumference to the hip circumference. The ideal waist to hip ratio (WHR) is 0.7 for women as this ratio is associated with fertility and health and generally considered most attractive. A WHR greater than 0.8 in women is associated with lower fertility and is considered to be overweight. A waist to hip ratio of over 0.9 in men is defined as overweight. The ideal fat mass in men is 12 percent, which is considered to be most attractive and associated with optimal immune function. Men are healthiest with a waist circumference less than 35 inches and women less than 32.5 inches. A waist of more than 35 inches for a woman or more than 40 inches for a man is associated with an increased risk of heart disease and diabetes,[113] and thus, they are indicative of health risks, and therefore such large waists are detrimental to the perception of leadership.

Very thin individuals with low BMI that are underweight are also less likely to be perceived as good leaders. Adults, especially middle-aged and older adults that are thin are likely to be regarded as debilitated and weak. Several diseases can cause wasting, and these include cancer and infectious disease. Thus, being thin individuals may be seen as having disease risk. Voters with poorer health are more likely to vote for more attractive and thereby, more healthy appearing candidates.[114] Tallness is also associated with posture, which gives strong signals of dominance, fearlessness, and robustness.

Thus, taller individuals are judged to be healthier, fitter, more intelligent, and as a result more competent. As with intelligence, a shorter individual can be just as healthy as a taller one, but having a healthy start in life is associated with a taller stature than when life starts out with disease and deprivation. Additionally, healthy, robust people have better musculature. This helps with better posture, which makes a person functionally taller than one that is weak or ill. Height is associated with the Darwinian concept of reproductive and survival fitness. This fitness, rather than height per say, is what we look for in our ideal leaders.

Pearl: It is actually the *perceived height* rather than the actual height that predicts the assessment of leadership ability.[115] Chapter 21 discusses how the perception of height can be influenced.

Pearl: Don't cut your ambitions short as a result of short stature.

Chapter 6: The Appearance of Intelligence

I recall as a young child, hearing my mother comment that a rather attractive man had an intelligent face. On other occasions, I heard her dismissed the behavior of others, noting that one could see that they weren't blessed with an abundance of intelligence. To me, they were all just grown-ups. Some looked scary and mean, others not so mean – but still intimidating.

An important determinant of perceived competence is likely the perception of intelligence. How accurate was my mother, and are the rest of us, at determining intelligence from implicit face value judgments?

A study done in the Czech Republic measured the IQ of 80 university students, half men, and half women, and then had 160 men and women rate the perceived intelligence and attractiveness of each of the 80 students on a score of one to seven. All the students and raters were Caucasian, and the photos were taken in front of a white screen, with the subject having a neutral, non-smiling expression, without facial cosmetics, jewelry or other decorations.

There was good agreement as to which faces were perceived to be intelligent. Both men and women were good judges of intelligence when assessing the facial features of men. The observers however, did not do well when divining the intelligence of women.

The researchers tested general IQ as well as five areas of intelligence. The sub-test areas were verbal, figural, numeric, crystallized and fluid intelligence.

Ψ Crystallized intelligence is the ability to used learned knowledge and experience.
Ψ Verbal intelligence is the ability to solve problems using language-based reasoning.
Ψ Numerical IQ is the ability to work with numbers to solve math problems.
Ψ Fluid intelligence is the ability to solve new problems.
Ψ Figural intelligence is the ability to manipulate two and three-dimensional objects in the mind and is a measure of abstract visual thinking.

Only two sub-areas of general intelligence, however, were statistically associated with the perception of an intelligent male face: figural intelligence and fluid intelligence. These areas are not content driven, but rather are more abstract. Figural and fluid intelligence are useful for adaptation to new circumstances. Thus, these areas of intelligence offer advantage for survival in a changing environment. Figural IQ may assist men in reading social situations.

For women's faces, only verbal intelligence came close to being statistically significant. Otherwise, people were no better at assessing a woman's IQ from a photo than random guesses. Verbal intelligence is at least in part the product of socialization, and more attractive and open appearing women likely have more opportunity to develop these verbal skills. Thus, even the non-significant implicit recognition of verbal IQ may merely be the recognition of an attractive or approachable face, rather than any inherent ability to appraise IQ from looking at a woman's face.

Interestingly, the male faces perceived to be the most highly intelligent were associated with men with an IQ about 135, a quite lovely IQ. Nevertheless, men with even higher IQs were not perceived from their photographs to be quite as intelligent.

The images of the faces used in the study were then digitalized and measured at 72 landmarks for facial features and averaged into three groups for men and women, those perceived to be of lower, average and higher intelligence. No statistical association between face shape and measures of intelligence were found, although figural and fluid IQ came closest. This suggests that this measurement and averaging lost some of the information from the photos. The data lost in this type of the analysis include facial asymmetry, skin tone, and contrast, as well as blemishes such as scars and acne. Nevertheless, there were robust correlations between the observer *perception* of intelligence and the shape of the composite faces.

Characteristics that are perceive to be associated with intelligence in this central European population are the vertical distance between the eyes and mouth (a taller upper face height), the distance between the eyebrows, a slightly longer columella, (the nasal pillar between the nostrils), a longer nose, and a smaller chin; both a narrower jaw and less distance between the lower lip and tip of the chin.

The attributes associated with the perception of lower intelligence were having a shorter distance between the eyes, a shorter nose and upper face, a broader and longer chin.[116] The faces that were perceived to be less intelligent had features associated with a higher fWHR. Meanwhile, the more intelligent faces have a taller upper face.

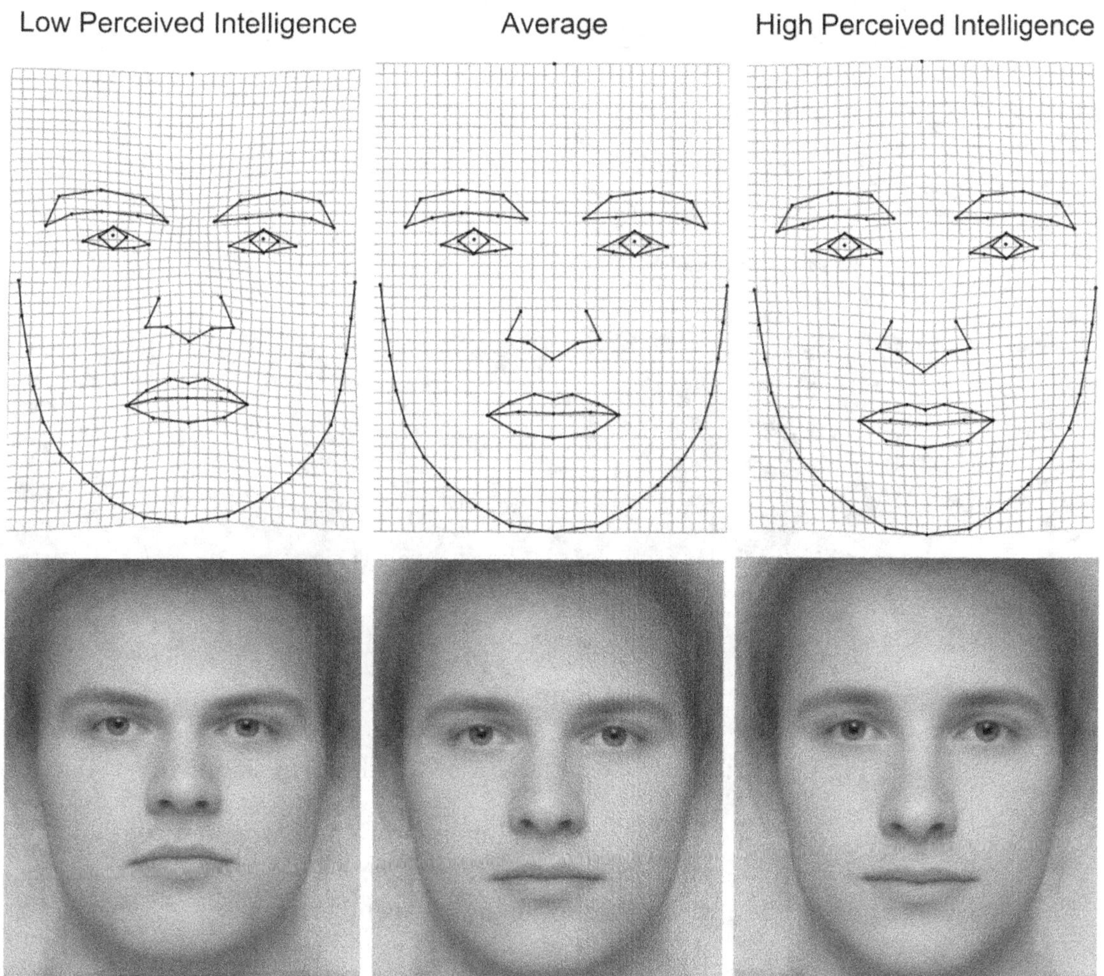

Figure 6-1: Morphed photos. Used with permission. [117]

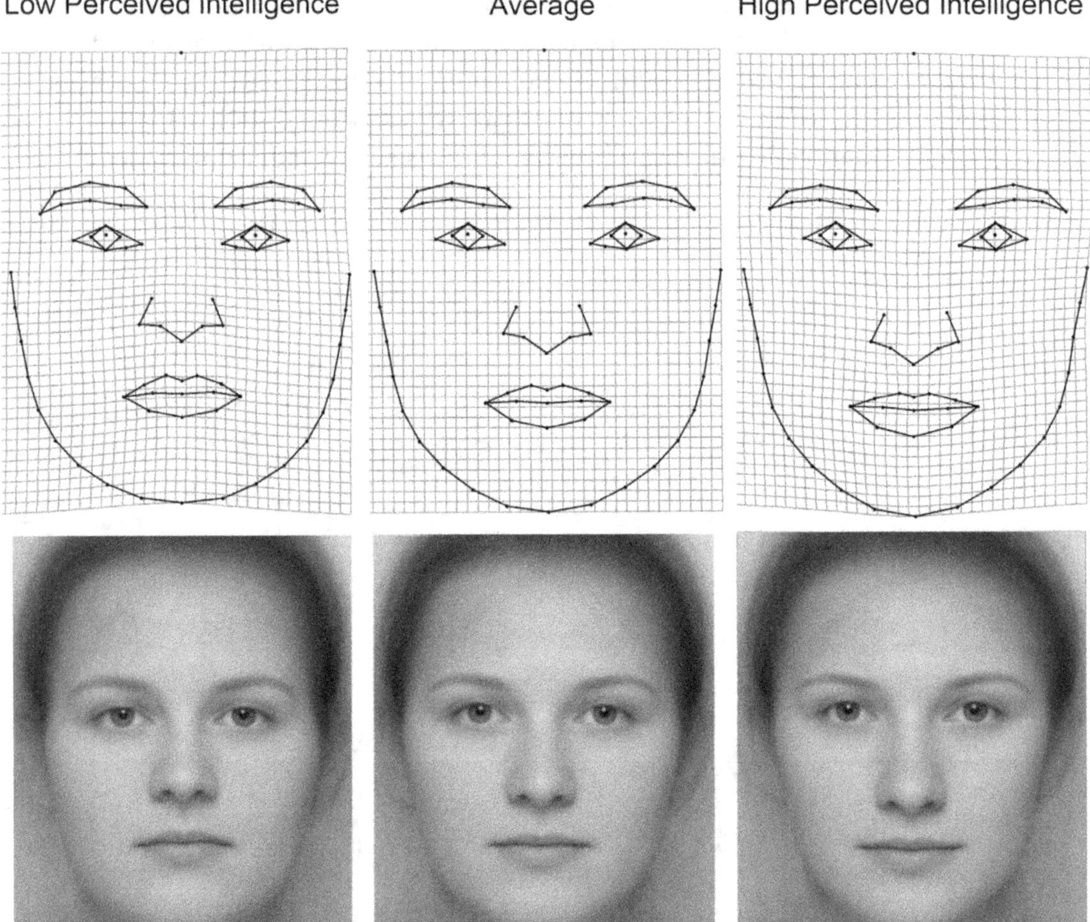

Figure 6-2: Morphed photos. Used with permission.

Thus, faces *perceived* to be less intelligent may be associated with higher fetal testosterone effect, and those *perceived* to be more intelligent associated with more robust adolescent growth.

Another feature of the faces perceived to be more intelligent was that at rest, the corners of the mouth turn slightly up, while those who appear less intelligent have mouths that turn down when the face is at rest. The faces that were perceived to be less intelligent thus tend to have eyebrows that come closer together and downturned corners of the mouth, and a chin with a longer distance from the lower lip to the tip of the chin. These features, when the face is at rest, give a subtle impression of worry, stubbornness, and disengagement. If you look in the mirror and make a pouty or stubborn face, the brows move towards each other, the corners of the mouth fall and the lower lip rises, increasing the length of the chin.

The faces perceived to be more intelligent with wider eyebrows and slightly upturned corners of the mouth appeared to be relaxed, pleasant and interested, thus providing the impression of confidence and accessibility.

It should be noted that because morphed photos do averaging, they remove skin tone, inflammation, scarring, skin blemishes, and asymmetry of the individual faces used to make the composite image. Thus, morphed images give these faces both a more average and attractive appearance than would the individual faces.[118] In these images, a morphed photo was manipulated to fit the measured shape of the average male or female, low, mid or high intelligence group. Thus these images also obscure individual difference in symmetry, skin discoloration, redness, or bags below the eyes that may have been present, and thus leave out some clues that may be used to determine perceived intelligence.

The correlation with actual intelligence with perceived intelligence in women was limited to verbal intelligence. Girls who appear friendly and approachable may become more sociable as a result of a "friendly" face and gain language skills. Boys who appear more interested and open may receive more interaction with adults, and thus develop more opportunities for education during their developmental years. However, there are likely better explanations.

Although intelligence has traditionally been considered to be fixed by early childhood, recent evidence suggests that there can be gains and losses of as much as 20 IQ points during the teenage years, which coincides with the development of grey matter mass.[119] The advancement of area specific in intelligence depends on brain use during these years. Verbal intelligence, for example, increases with increased and more complex reading among younger teenagers.[120]

In the study of Czech university students, when looking at photos of women's faces, people could only discern verbal intelligence, and even this was of marginal statistical significance. I think it likely that while we are not adept at judging woman's intelligence from her face, it is not because it is not possible, but rather that the heuristic is not an instinctual priority. Instead, our implicit trait inference of women is set to determine their receptiveness versus hostility, health, and fertility. These traits are largely determined by facial expression, which was intentionally minimized in this study, and soft tissue traits, such as skin tone, adiposity, and facial symmetry. In women, these traits are not closely tied to the adolescent growth spurt, as they are in men. We can likely learn to recognize intelligence in a woman's face but it would be an intentionally learned skill.

Another factor that may affect the correlation of face shape and features with intelligence may be the timing of puberty. Adolescence is a time of brain development and specialization that depends upon training in those areas of intelligence. Girls reach puberty earlier than do boys. It may be that the aspects of intelligence that we can perceive in a man's face are developing over the age span typical of male puberty, but later than that of female puberty and thus, they may not be evident in the facial bone structure of most women. Perhaps it might, if that skill set development was timed to the stage of puberty.

Teachers invest more attention in children that they perceived to be intelligent. We also know that more attractive children get more positive attention from their teachers and that they judge taller, more attractive, and healthier children to be more intelligent. Thus more open, approachable, and intelligent *appearing* children may receive more favorable feedback and encouragement from teachers and other adults, and this promotes learning and likely the development of a higher IQ. These teens may be encouraged to participate in more activities that develop agency, responsibilities and social skills. How many adults want to interact with annoyed, disengaged-appearing teenagers? A friendlier appearing face likely has more opportunities for social engagement and the development of agency. Thus, the face may shape the intelligence quotient and emotional quotient.

Largely, people settle into a lifetime assessment of who they are during their adolescence, and this often holds us back. Late bloomers may never consider themselves attractive, despite evidence to the contrary, because they did not have fashionable clothes or consider themselves as being highly attractive during their high school years when their self image formed. Young people who attend traditional university (four years on campus socializing with peers) have an extended period of ego development as a result of extra years of social development prior to entering the workforce. During this time they may grow their self-esteem and agency. Adults' lives provide much less social support for ego development, and people tend to stay in the same level of social hierarchy that they had during these periods of ego development.

This is why it is important to curate your face. It is not just during childhood and adolescence; our interactions with other alter the way we perceive ourselves, and how we interact with the world.

Intelligence (or is it just getting enough sleep)

Teachers assume that more attractive students are more intelligent than less attractive ones. However, perceived intelligence is poorly correlated with academic performance. The perception of conscientiousness, however, has a much better correlation to academic performance.

Eyelid openness and an upward mouth curl were associated with the perception of intelligence of young adults and school-aged children.[121] These features give the appearance of attention and engagement. Sleep deprivation causes the opposite effects in the face, presenting with thicker, lower hanging eyelids, and drooping corners of the mouth, as well as paler skin, more lines in the face, and dark circles under the eyes.[122] Thus sleep deprivation causes one to appear to lack attention and engagement. It is no surprise that sleep deprivation does not bode well for academic or professional performance, and in addition it makes us look dull-witted.

Adequate sleep is essential for health in growing children. Growth hormone is released during sleep. Children that have insufficient, disrupted, or poor quality sleep have poorer growth, and sleep deprivation in school children is associated with shorter stature. Ten- and eleven-year-old children who sleep more than 10 hours at night grow taller than those sleeping less than nine hours.[123] Inadequate sleep in children is also associated with obesity.[124] Even during infancy, at three months of age, babies that sleep less than 12 hours per day have poorer linear growth and tend to be heavier.[125] In an American study, preschool children with typical bedtimes before 8 PM were less than half as likely to become obese by adolescence as those with a bedtime after 9 PM.[126]

Pearl: Getting children to sleep at a time that promotes health and growth does not happen naturally in modern life with electric lights, television, and other evening activities. Children want to be engaged with their family in the evening. A regular bedtime schedule and routine, including a bath, lowered light intensity, having television and other screens off, and a bedtime story with a parent helps calm the child and helps them get to sleep. Just as adults need to relax before bed, children also need to slow down before drifting off to sleep.

Pearl: Making sure your child is well slept, will help them with academic achievement and in enjoying school. Helping them be well groomed and having clean, well fitting clothing will also help them in school.

How good are teachers at picking academic winners from photos of faces? A study that found a relationship between implicit facial appraisal and academic performance, however, found no direct statistical relationship between perception of intelligence or attractiveness with actual academic performance. A moderate correlation was found between perceived conscientiousness and academic performance, and a secondary association was evident between perceived conscientiousness and attractiveness.[127] It is not surprising that being conscientious helps with academics. It is this trait that teachers likely perceive and appreciate in their students.

So what does the more conscientious face look like? The top and bottom 25 percent of male and female faces rated for conscientiousness were manually delineated for 188 facial landmark points and average coordinates used to warp a morphed image. The conscientious faces had wider open eyes, with more iris visible above the pupil, and slightly upward rather than downward corners of the mouth. Thus, features associated with low conscientiousness are facial features seen in sleep deprivation. High conscientiousness was also associated with a slightly longer face height and with a slightly lower tip of the nose and shorter philtrum. Thus, features of lower conscientiousness may be associated with higher fetal or lower adolescent testosterone effect, or with a lower growth hormone effect. The weaker growth hormone effect may be associated with chronic sleep deprivation.

The upper face growth that occurs during adolescence that is associated with a more intelligent male face, depends on growth hormone, and is thus contingent on adequate sleep during this period of adolescence.

Pearl: Get your beauty sleep so that you look attractive, alert and engaged. Get your kids to bed early if you hope for them to be successful. Make sure the nose works as intended for oxygen intake.

The slightly longer face and nose and shorter philtrum (upper lip) on faces perceived to be more intelligent correlate with a less prenatally masculinized face, thus, these masculinized faces are associated with a perception of lower intelligence. It may not be masculinization, per se, that is associated with lower intelligence, but rather that testosterone influence promotes less compliant behavior and greater distraction during adolescence, with attention directed towards dalliance than academic pursuits. This repurposing of attention may prevent the IQ boost that comes with area-specific training especially during adolescence.

If the facial masculinization is the result of *Toxoplasmosis gondii* infection, it may be associated alterations in the dopamine reward system that get in the way of delayed gratification, a skill essential for academic success.

Judging intelligence from faces has limited reliability after accounting for sleep.

Accuracy in judging intelligence was found to be higher after statistically controlling for attractiveness. Attractiveness has not been found to be correlated to actual intelligence in most studies. When attractiveness has been found to correlate with intelligence, it is only among those in the lower half of the attractiveness range. This suggests that less healthy individuals, with less symmetrical faces, and that are less well-rested are less attractive and that disease and deprivation also take a toll on intelligence. Thus, a lack of health is associated with lower intelligence, while being more attractive than average was not found to be associated with being more intelligent than average. [128]

While there is scant data supporting the association of attractiveness with intelligence, there is strong and convincing data that attractiveness is linked to the implicit perception of intelligence.

We may be able to read conscientiousness in faces, but this too is likely an inverse reading of the impacts of sleep deprivation and poor health.

Chapter 7: Competence

Competence is the facial characteristic that has consistently been found to attract voters, and to influence the selection of leaders. Competence is the ability to accomplish a task successfully or efficiently. Thus, competence should show capability, efficiency, proficiency, expertise, skill, mastery, talent, and ability. Which of these can we see in a face?

We can detect conscientiousness, which correlates with academic competence. We see age, and maturity is associated with competence. We identify trustworthiness, which has features similar to competence. We assess health, which is associated with self-control as an adult. We can see grooming, which is associated with health, self-esteem, and that gives clues to social status, as primates within a group groom each other. We perceive well-groomed individuals to be accepted by their group.

Competence is also what we don't see. It is the absence of social defeat, disease, anxiety, and depression. We can see emotional stability or the lack of it. We can see when someone is lazy about their appearance and assume they are lazy about their responsibilities. We may perceive others as being ineffectual or weak, ignorant, inept, inappropriate, or lazy.

One study of facial photos found that health and four of the big five personality traits (extraversion, agreeableness, openness, and emotional stability, but not conscientiousness) could be inferred with some degree of accuracy from photos of faces of the subjects.[129] Several of these traits are included in the judgment of competence.

By the age of six, children's ability to discern trustworthiness, dominance, and competence is similar to that of adults. When children five years old and older rated faces on perceived trustworthiness, dominance, and competence, they gave very similar ratings as did adults. The terms used for children, however, were nice versus mean, strong vs. not strong and smart vs. not smart.[130] Thus smart and competent are similar.

There is not one heuristic for the appearance of competence. The gestalt that helps get one ahead in the military or on the football field is not the same as that for academia. The physical attributes needed to wield a 25-pound chainsaw are different from those required for a computer programmer.

But what is the look of competence for an elected official? It is similar for members of the lower house of congress, parliament, statehouse, and most managerial positions. For most of us, and for most political positions, showing up and getting work done on time, taking responsibility, getting along, cooperation, team buildings, and playing nicely with others, are essential to getting things done. Stubbornness, aloofness, self-centeredness and rigidity are anathema to competence.

There are several features that make up the heuristic of competence, including maturity (increasing age at least up to the age og 60). Trustworthiness and attractiveness have been found to be highly correlated with the perception of competence, while baby-faceness was inversely related to it.[131]

Some facial features that are associated with the enhanced perception of competence are eyes closer to eyebrows, which is also a sign of facial maturity and aging, as gravity plays its tricks on us. Other signs of competence are higher cheekbones, and a more angular jaw, rather than a rounded U-shape jawline. When obesity is avoided, fWHR decreases with age, making older faces appear less aggressive and physically powerful but friendlier.[132]

Academic competence was found to be associated with the perception of conscientiousness, which turns out to be associated with wider open eyes and upturned lips, which are associated with getting sufficient sleep at night. Competence is associated with looking alert and engaged, and not looking dull-witted and slow.

Competence for a congressional seat requires looking healthy and displaying both physical and emotional resilience. Thus, frowns, anger, worried, fearful expression, shifty eyes, and embarrassment impede the look of competence. (Break out the Botox; see Chapter 9.)

Good posture is essential as it gives the charisma of health, resilience, and confidence without appearing domineering or threatening. An erect posture avoids the head forward position, which tilts the face back slightly, causing the mouth to appear to curl downwards. Head forward posture also lengthens the anterior neck and gives the shoulders a sloped appearance. Sloped shoulders are associated with social defeat in primates, as discussed in Chapter 21.

Being smart is highly correlated with intelligence, and thus, upturned corners of the mouth, alert and engaged open eyes, and a longer upper face show intelligence. Essentially the same features as academic competence. Thus again, better sleep habits, better health during growth and adolescence, and a less hostile face are associated with the look of competence.

A German study was performed to see how well strangers are at evaluating personality traits from watching people read a brief standard message in a video.[133] The researchers recruited 50 pairs of adults living together, mostly engaged or married couples. Each of these people was evaluated with standard tests for personality measures and intelligence, and they were rated on personality scores by their partner. They were also videotaped; they were instructed to walk into a room, walk around a table to a chair, sit down and look into the camera and read a weather report, and get up and walk back out of the room. The videos lasted about 90 seconds for each subject. The 100 videos were then rated by strangers either on 48 observable attributes or on 21 personality traits. Some raters watch the video with sound and others without.

The positive measures of *extraversion* detected in the videos were a friendly expression, smiling, self-assuredness, relaxed sitting, a powerful voice, frequent head movements, use of makeup, and stylish hair. Negative factors for extraversion were an indifferent expression, walking stiffly, soft-or unpleasant voice, unrefined appearance, unfashionable dress, and avoiding looking into the camera.

On measures of *agreeableness*, the positive traits included having a friendly expression, smiling, relaxed sitting, frequent head movements, and the duration of reading. Attributes inversely correlated with agreeableness were hard facial lines, indifferent expression, unpleasant voice, hectic speaking, and avoiding the camera.

Interestingly, the judges rating the subjects in the silent videos and those rating the videos with sound were in significant agreement with the subject's self-rating of having a powerful voice or an unpleasant voice. Thus, we can accurately infer an unpleasant voice from a silent video of someone reading.

Perception of conscientiousness, emotional stability, and intelligence are traits that likely correlate with the perception of competence, although the perception of agreeableness and even extraversion may contribute to it.

In a bicultural study of Asians and Caucasians, competence was found to be correlated to open-mindedness and to be inversely correlated to the perception of threat and corruption.[134] Thus, a face that appears threatening (down curved lips, eyebrows closer to eyes, heavier and more narrowly spaced eyebrows) appears less competent. Open-mindedness likely includes open eyes, more space between the eyes and eyebrows, up-curved lips and a longer chin that lacks a look of stubbornness. The perception of corruption likely correlates with lack of trustworthiness and a more masculine, high fWHR face. Trustworthiness is discussed in Chapter 9.

The traits to which raters attributed *conscientiousness* included a refined appearance, a well-proportioned body and a graceful gait that combines lifting feet while walking and swinging arms while walking. Other factors judged to show lack of conscientiousness included informal or showy dress, relaxed sitting and frequent head movement. Also, wearing glasses was correlated with a higher rating of conscientiousness, but this may just be a correlate of age and the need to wear reading glasses.

Emotional stability is another correlate of competence. The perception of *emotional stability* was most strongly related to friendliness, (having a friendly and relaxed expression and smiling), and having a pleasant voice. A graceful walk also correlated with the perception of emotional stability. Avoiding the camera and less eye contact with the camera was inversely rated with emotional stability, as was going back and correcting reading mistakes.

Culture and openness were correlated with attractiveness and having a feminine appearance, as well as having a friendly expression and pleasant voice and being easy to understand.

Finally, raters judged the subject's *intelligence* from the films. Heavier individuals and those with unrefined appearance were judged to be less intelligent, while more attractive individuals were rated as more intelligent. An indifferent expression was rated as having lower intelligence, and those with a self-assured expression were rated as being of higher intelligence. Powerful, unpleasant and hectic voices were associated with ratings rated of lower intelligence. Notably, *none of these traits were actually correlated with measured intelligence*. Traits that were related to tested intelligence included reading more fluently; making fewer reading errors, making fewer corrections, and reading the passage more quickly.[135]

Since most of the photos of actual politicians used in voter correlation with heuristic competence studies are smiling in their photos, the up-turned lips while the face has a neutral expression can thus be discounted as a deciding factor in the judgment of competence.

Pearl: One can appear more competent when smiling, relaxed, well-rested, confident, attentive, and having good eye-contact with the camera.

Competence and Attractiveness

As might be expected, the attractiveness of faces decreases with age. Since attractiveness is correlated with the perception of competence, the implicit evaluation of competence also declines slightly with aging. Nevertheless, the perception of competence increases with age for middle-aged and older adults who are and remain attractive.[136] This reinforces the importance of health, vigor, and grooming in the assessment of competence.

Pearl: Immune competence, the ability to fight infection, is integral to physical attractiveness, and likely the assessment of competence.[137]

Age of Competence and Facial Maturity

In a study of facial preferences of voters, over 250 participants aged 11 to 57 were asked to view six sets of photographs of same-gender pairs of members of the US House of Representatives and select the person from each pair that they would vote for on appearance alone. The participants were also asked to rate, on a one-to-six scale, the importance of a leader being dedicated to social issues or to international strength, measures of more liberal or conservative perspectives.

Unknown to the participants, some of the photos of the congressmen and congresswomen had been modified to increase or decrease the size of the mouth and eyes. Larger eyes and mouth give a baby-faced appearance, and smaller eyes and mouth give a more mature look. Babies have proportionately larger eyes, a smaller chin, chubbier lips, a higher forehead, thinner eyebrows that are more arched, and a smaller nose than adults. Thus, this study tested to see if voters preferred younger or more mature faces.

Women were chosen as the preferred candidate only slightly less often than were men, and the difference was not statistically significant. There was a significant increase favoring the selection of men whose faces had been matured, and a decrease in the selection of "baby-faced" men.

When candidates were paired by gender, so that the choice was always between two men or two women, men preferred male representatives with more mature faces and female representatives with less mature faces. Women showed no preferences for female facial maturity but preferred more mature male faces. Men in this study favored international strength over social issues.[138]

The ages at which adults are perceived to be of maximum competence is middle age, between 40 and 60. This is the age range that gives the greatest advantage to being elected to the U.S. Congress for a first term.[139] In 2017, the mean age for being sworn into Congress for a first term was 50.8 years. Women are perceived to be most competent in their 40's and men are in their 50's. No woman has ever won a first-term seat in the House of Representatives after the age of 70. Women have the advantage of being able to begin political careers at an earlier age than do men, and they benefit from starting younger.

Hair color

Photos of women were presented to Polish men aged 18 to 46, and the men were asked to rate the attractiveness of the women. The same women were presented to different men but with a different hair color in the pictures, blonde, brown, or brunette. Blonde-haired women were only considered more attractive when the woman was 30 years old, but not for women aged 20 or 40. Blonde haired women were estimated by men to be younger.[140] A British study also found that brunettes were rated as more attractive than blondes. Hair length was found to only have a weak effect on attractiveness ratings by men and women.[141] Women with dark hair may be considered to be more attractive as dark hair adds contrast to the face, giving the impression of increase femininity.[142]

In another British study, when men rated a photo of a young woman as a blond, brunette or redhead, they rated the brunette as more attractive, competent, approachable, and intelligent, but also as more arrogant, while considering the blonde version of the women as needy.[143] Blonde hair is likely perceived as a juvenile trait, as it is common for Caucasians to be blonde as children (towheaded) but to have their hair turn dark usually before the age of ten as they approach puberty. Nevertheless, when women change their hair color, they more often lighten than darken their hair.[144] This may make them appear younger, but it may also impede their career advancement.

In researching, I could not find any studies on the perception of competence for graying or grey hair. Many male members of Congress have gray hair. Anderson Cooper has commented that his prematurely gray hair was helpful to his early career, giving him an air of authority and credibility at a young age. Nevertheless, both men and women are generally perceived to be most powerful during their 40's and 50's, an age when most people only begin to show scattered grey hairs.

No female U.S. Senator and only one female in the US House of Representatives sports grey or white hair. That one Congresswoman is Virginia Foxx of North Carolina. It can be assumed that most others color their hair. In a search of photos of the 32 women who are CEOs of S&P 500 companies, I could not find any shown with grey or white hair, although many male CEOs of these large corporations have grey hair.

Pearl: When running for a political office or when seeking a higher job status, women with more than scattered gray hair almost certainly benefit from coloring their hair, as it provides the perception of vigor and adds to the perception of competence.

Pearl: Coloring the hair to be a somewhat lighter than natural color than one had in youth will blend graying hair and look more natural than black or very dark hair on older persons.

Pearl: A hairstyle with bangs or without a part may help hide roots between treatments.

Who's old? I like to think that I look fit and healthy (for my age.) Somehow that seems like telling someone they look great for an 80-year-old.

A few years ago, my then teenage son would complain that I was mean to him, and that I was always angry with him, disapproving, and that I was undermining his self-confidence by what he perceived to be negative feedback of his musical performances and other activities. I was mystified by it. I was proud of him and his accomplishments and enjoyed doing things with him. Then I read that teenagers have a hard time reading the faces of adults, and told him this. Well, telling him this just added to his perception that I considered him incompetent in yet another area.

If only I knew then what I know now. Teenagers are actually great at reading faces; they are just slower at ignoring what they see.

It's not like I have saggy jowls, but much of my well-spent youth was done out of doors. During the summers, I hardly came indoors, often sleeping under the stars, and I biked everywhere. I worked as a landscaper and carpenter. I joined the Peace Corps and lived in the tropics, working mostly out of doors for several years. I didn't know sunscreen existed before a dermatologist was whittling off precancerous lesions from my face in my late 20's, and back then, the strongest one available was SPF-10 that sweated or washed off after an hour. Thus, there has been a wee bit of photo-aging along the way, not to mention the slow grind of gravity.

When my face is in neutral, as it is when I am focusing on something or just relaxed, my lips bend down like a handlebar mustache. As we age, our eyebrows sag down, closer to our eyes, giving the face a more stern, dominant appearance. My years have earned me that too.

My face has a great effect. I can easily appear dominant and grumpy, even though I almost never want to. This is what my son saw, and what drove that wedge. Perhaps this is why teenagers rush to get away from their disapproving parents. Not an entirely bad idea, but really! There must be a better way to get kids to make an independent life for themselves than having age turn our faces into an angry-appearing, scowling masks.

It is the appearance of vitality, strength, and experience, rather than youthfulness that provides the gravitas sought in our leaders. Younger women may do well to use makeup and clothing styles that lend an air of maturity if they want to advance in their careers. For example, pink lipstick gives a younger look and brown lipstick gives an older appearance. Older women do well to color their hair.

Clothing styles can give a more mature appearance to a younger woman, but poor choices in clothing can signal incompetence. The goal in seeking leadership positions for women is not to look like a sexy 26-year-old, but rather appearing as a healthy, mature, confident, and capable woman. Looking healthy and being in your forties is an asset.

Candidates do well to appear to have the maturity that provides emotional stability, wisdom, self-control, and the loss of emotional vulnerability that comes with maturity.

An important component in the assessment of competence is grooming. Hair should be neat, clean, shiny and in place. The hairstyle should be practical, to show that you are, and that you don't spend hours of your day preening. Clothing should be contemporary, but not loud, and mostly solid colors. Clothing needs to fit as if it was made for you. Tight clothing (button stretching) causes one to appear to have gained weight, while loose clothing causes the opposite effect. Wrinkled clothing indicates a lack of care, perhaps a state of homelessness, or of sleeping in the dog house.

Pearl: The heuristic of competence includes the appearance of:

- Intelligence
- Health and vigor
- Maturity (but not old age)
- Being well rested and alert
- Practical and organized
- Well groomed
- Appearing taller than the gender average.

The heuristic of competence includes the assessment of delayed-gratification, self-control, discipline, and confidence.

Confidence can be seen in a relaxed face without signs of worry, anger, evasion, or suspicion. Thus, a relaxed brow with eyebrows that are not narrowed or lowered and eyes that are wide open, rather than narrowing in as they do during anger, shows confidence. The eyes also squint when smiling, but here the lower lids rise up, so it is perceived differently than in anger. Confidence is also seen in an upright posture. The assessment of delayed-gratification, self-control, and discipline likely come across by way of a calm face and grooming, and a healthy appearance.

Pearl: For those with eyebrows that are close to each other, a more relaxed appearance may be created by increasing the space between the brows slightly by plucking. Avoid shaping beyond the ideal for the face shape. Botox may help for those who tend to narrow their eyebrows.

Pearl: Ideal eyebrow width conforms to lines beginning from the outermost aspect of the nostril and extending beyond:

➲ the outer corner of the eye, to give the outer tip of the eyebrow,
➲ over the center of the pupil to give the peak of the arch, and
➲ over the medial corner of the eye gives the medial margin of the brows.

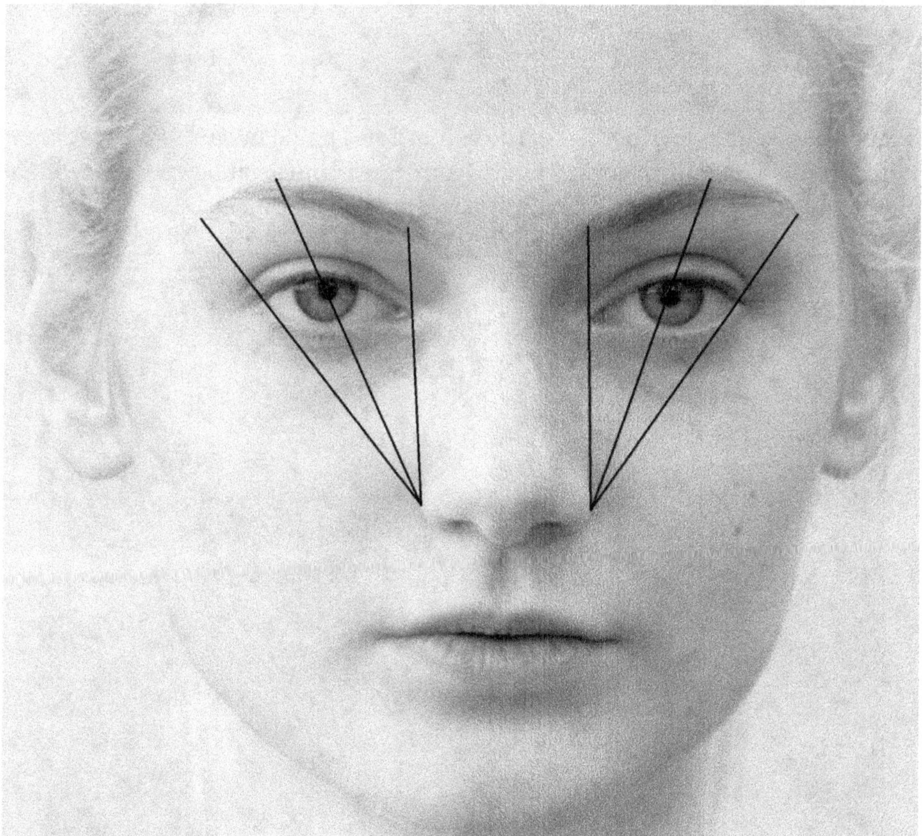

Figure 7-1: In this image, the young woman's eyelids show no iris above the pupils, giving a fatigued appearance, rather than one of competence.

Figure 7-2: With a broader nose, the center lines angle inwards. This woman could remove a millimeter of hairs from the center-right eyebrow, which might give a slightly more relaxed and friendly appearance.

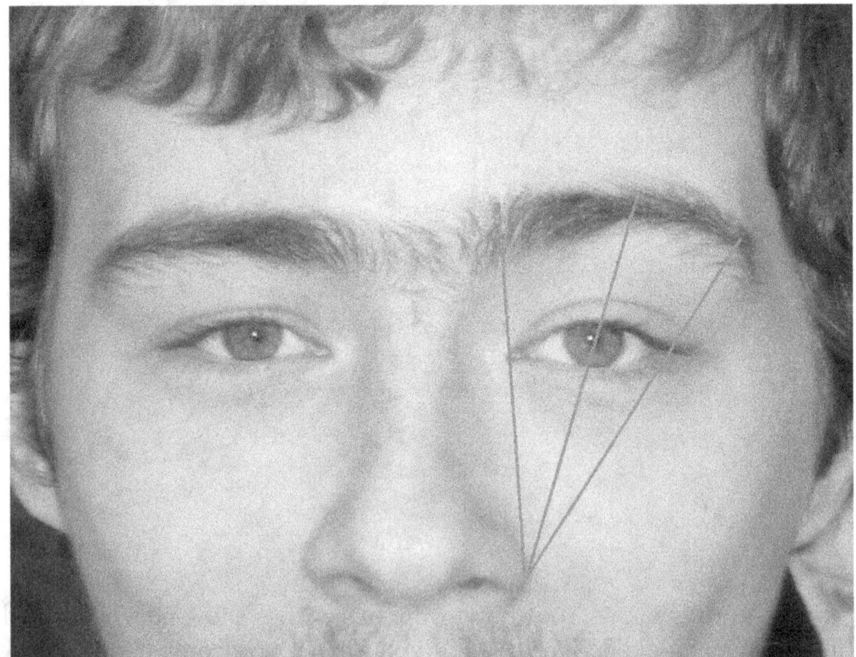

Figure 7-2: The lines mark the typical limits of the eyebrow on a young man with a unibrow.[145] Unibrow (synophrys) is usually an isolated genetic trait but occurs with some rare developmental disorders, giving it a negative association in some cultures. Unibrow is considered attractive in Arabian countries where the trait is common. It generally thickens with puberty and thins in older age, and thus is associated with reproductive health.[146]

Chapter 8: Attractiveness

The most important characteristics by which voters implicitly infer leadership ability are competence and physical attractiveness. As might be expected, in more conservative areas, more gender-typical faces for female candidates are favored. Women who are typically feminine are favored over less feminine female faces among these voters. A bit surprisingly, in non-war times, Republican voters have been found to prefer less-masculine than average male faces. This influence may be limited to Republican women.

When guessing party affiliation of candidates, voters tend to assume that more attractive candidates are members of their own party, a reflection of our natural preference to associate with more attractive individuals. Nevertheless, conservative politicians tend to be more attractive than liberal ones. This suggests that attractiveness is more important in winning primaries for conservative seats than for liberal ones, and perhaps for swing votes in the general election. Attractive candidates, especially attractive female candidates, usually receive more favorable and more frequent media coverage.[147]

First impressions are made automatically and rapidly. There is growing evidence that making the first impression is not only automatic, but our brain makes it a mandatory priority to form impressions of social traits even when they are irrelevant to what we are doing.

Choosing the winning candidate from facial photos in studies works most accurately when the viewing time of the image is just under one second. Many studies have shown that participants form impressions of an individual's personality when an image flashed on a screen for about one-tenth of a second. People, however, rate attractiveness in as little as 13 ms; just over one one-hundredth of a second. This is so little time that viewers can not accurately see the face, and the judgment can be made without conscious awareness of the face.[148]

People are more likely to cooperate with an attractive person. In a study of event-related potentials (ERP; brain-waves) recorded during a trust game, participants had to make a decision whether to cooperate or not with a fictional partner in a game where they had a chance to earn monetary rewards. Choosing a partner presented both the potential for reward and for risk. Participants were more likely to choose a partner if the photo of the partner was attractive. ERP data shows rapid and automatic processing in the discrimination of attractive and unattractive faces.[149] In a similar game-based study where the participant had to accept or reject an unfair offer to share a reward or not, ERP responses were faster when an unfair offer was made by a proposer whose image on a screen was unattractive than when the same offer came from an attractive face. Women, interestingly, showed much less bias against unattractive men than did men.[150]

These studies suggest that attractive people garner more cooperation, an important component in leadership and governance. Women, however, are more willing to cooperate with less attractive people than men are.

Functional MRI (fMRI) studies show areas of increased brain activity. They are useful in determining which parts of the brain are used for different tasks. Both ERP[151] and fMRI studies have shown that attractive faces are identified more quickly and better remembered.

It also goes the other way. In one fMRI study, male faces that were perceived as having a bad personality or to be untrustworthy gave higher activity in the insular and hippocampal areas of the brains of women and these faces were more easily remembered.[152] In contrast, faces that are more attractive are also more easily remembered; however, this is correlated with increased functional MRI activity in the hippocampus and the orbitofrontal regions of the brain.[153] When women wear light makeup, as opposed to heavy makeup or no makeup, it makes them easier to identify and remember.[154] Both attractive and untrustworthy faces make stronger and more lasting impressions.

Once the first impression of attractiveness has been made, it tends to stick. When first shown an attractive photo of a face and then sometime later shown an unattractive photo of the same person, the person rating the unattractive photo rates the second photo as being less unattractive. If shown the unattractive photo first and then shown an attractive photo of the same person later, the rater will rate the second photo as less attractive than if they had not seen the photos of the person before. [155]

Pearl: Make the best first impression you can. People tend to stick with their first impressions.

Our perceptions of attractiveness are instinctual and are largely determined by factors that determine mating quality. Health and fertility are at the top of the list. In our still primitive, post-cave-people society, reproductive strategies are different for males and females. Men have a nearly unlimited reproductive capacity, limited only by opportunity; women are physiologically limited to, on average, a maximum of about a dozen live births. Thus men, while wanting to appeal to the healthiest and largest number of females, are less picky in their mating choices. Women, in contrast, select men with high reproductive fitness for mating.

Men with more average faces are more likely to have genetic diversity of their major histocompatibility complex (MHC), and this is linked to better immunocompetence. Thus men with average faces are considered more attractive mates. Here, the word average refers to having typical and normative features, rather than being of average on a scale of beauty. In contrast, female attractiveness is not associated with MHC genetic diversity.[156] In men, a more masculine face is also associated with stronger immune responses to disease. [157]

Attractiveness is a great asset. Nearly every mother thinks her baby is beautiful, and I agree that most babies are. Nevertheless, more attractive babies get more affectionate care from their mothers than do less attractive ones. Attractive children are assumed to be more intelligent, get more affirmative attention and better grades from their teachers in school. More attractive students are more likely to obtain college degrees. Attractive men are even perceived to have better senses of humor.[158] The advantage continues in the job market where attractive people are more likely to be hired and to be paid more for the same position.[159]

In a series of several studies, five hundred individuals rated images of young people. The images included digital photos of people aged 17-29 years, including photo models and beauty queens, and also photos that were morphed and manipulated to increase or decrease features associated with attractiveness. The more attractive the faces were rated, the higher the faces were judged on perceived success and sociability, and they were assumed to be more accessible, exciting, creative, busy, and content in their lives.[160]

Attractive adults are assumed to be more intelligent than less attractive ones are. There is actually a very good reason for this; people are more attractive when they are healthy and well-rested. And these individuals learn more quickly and are more productive than those who show up to school and work groggy and depleted. This topic will be discussed further in the chapters ahead.

Smiles

Smile. No, really, smile. In a 30-year follow-up study of women, those that smiled in their college yearbook photo had more positive life outcomes in terms of happier marriages, fewer divorces, and better personal well-being, even after controlling for attractiveness.[161] Photos of professional baseball players from 1952 revealed a longer lifespan for those with bigger smiles.[162]

But there are occasions when it is not best to smile. Professional prizefighters that smiled more before going into the ring had less to smile about after. They were likely to get beat by the less intensely smiling adversary.[163] Smiling is associated with being less aggressive and less physically dominance; not the correct message to tell your brain before a fight.

In a study of headshot photos of college football players from the Western Athletic Conference website, the physically larger, more dominant players were less likely to smile than were the medium build athletes, who were also less likely to smile than were the smallest of the college football players. This suggests that the very dominant players neither need to, nor care to play nice. The authors of the study pointed out that high prestige fashion models are instructed not to smile. The high prestige clothing is being marketed to those who want that prestige, and want to be given deference from their perceived subordinates.[164] President Trump rarely smiled in posed photos, as his brand is dominance, rather than as a cooperative manager or leader.

Thus, men and women may demonstrate dominance by avoiding smiling. As a candidate, a smile conveys willingness to cooperate and collaborate with others. A smile indicates friendliness, where the lack of a smile suggests that a person is not open to interaction or negotiation.

Women smile more often than do men,[165] and smiling makes both men's and women's faces appear more feminine.[166] Thus, smiling makes us appear less threatening and less dominant. In a democracy, or when interviewing for a management position, a smile signals willingness to cooperate and be subordinate. This is a plus for working with others and when working as a public servant.

We usually think of smiling as a sign of happiness, but remember that a smile is an act of submission in primates, demonstrating a lack of hostility. Men, more than women, may smile during highly stressful situations. These smiles, however, are considered to be socially inappropriate.[167] Stress situation smiles may reflect social defeat or avoidance. Embarrassment is often expressed with an embarrassed smile.

The perception of smiling faces is also shaped by culture. In India, Japan, South Korea and Iran, smiling faces are perceived to be less intelligent. This may be associated with the perception of submission and of a smiling simpleton in these cultures. In contrast, in Germany, Switzerland, and China, a smiling face is perceived to be more intelligent. When women are photographed smiling, they are perceived to be more intelligent than when photographed with a neutral face, even in countries where a smile is not perceived as showing intelligence in men. Smiling was associated with honesty by observers in almost every country.[168] When viewing images of individuals, women rated smiling faces as being honest more than men did.[169] This may be due to confounding honesty with lack of physical threat; men may feel less vulnerable than women do when meeting a difficult to read neutral face.

Smiling makes faces more attractive, and appear kinder. As the face goes from neutral, to closed smile, to upper smile showing the upper teeth, to broad smile showing both upper and lower teeth, the perception of happiness increases.[170]

Smiling faces were rated not only more attractive and happier but also more optimistic, reliable, sincere, sympathetic and kind, with the broad smile having the strongest rating. A broad smile increased the perception of leadership. A closed smile was associated with the perception of calmness, conciliation, and kindness.[171]

While smiling makes people more attractive, it also makes them appear older.[172] But before you swear-off ever smiling again or decide to Botox away any smile lines, consider that maturity is associated with the perception of competence. Older age only becomes a problem in leadership when it is associated with a decrease in vigor or a perception of obsolescence in health, function, or ideas.

Pearl: Showing your pearly whites, if they are strung in nice even rows, can show health, and vigor. Otherwise, try some whitening strips or visit your dentist.

Pearl: When subjects were asked to assess photos of smiling, expressionless, or frowning faces, they often rated the expressionless ones as frowns; thus, without a smile, you may appear unhappy.[173]

A smile makes your face more distinctive and easier to remember than does a neutral face.[174]

Botox

Many politicians use Botox to look younger. If you are considering this use, I advise rethinking it. Using Botox in the glabella, the area between the eyebrows gives a more relaxed look and keeps one from frowning, and looking worried or angry. In this, Botox can help to provide a more confident and relaxed appearance. It may even help with certain types of headaches.

Many people, however, use Botox to get rid of wrinkles. Often this includes getting rid of the wrinkling of the face that occurs in older folks when they smile or laugh. Yes, big smiles make older adults look even older. I suggest you leave this area alone, or at most, have it treated very lightly. In leadership and politics, maturity is an asset, so long as you look healthy and competent. Lack of smile wrinkles makes the smile look insincere and feigned. People are likely to sense insincerity and may distrust person's whose smiles lack crinkles at the corners of their eyes.

Chapter 9: Trustworthiness

As with intelligence, people make implicit judgments about the trustworthiness of strangers. Using the same faces as used in the intelligence study described in Chapter 6, participants were asked to rate the photos for trustworthiness. Female faces are judged to be more trustworthy than are male faces. Trustworthiness was found to be highly correlated to attractiveness and inversely correlated with the perception of a domineering face. After adjusting for attractiveness, there was no significant inter-rater agreement on trustworthiness when rating women's face shapes.

In men, a high fWHR which is associated with higher developmental testosterone levels was associated with lower perceived trustworthiness, and in other studies has been found to be associated with less cooperative, dishonest and more exploitative behaviors. Nevertheless, other masculine features including a broader and rounder chin and heavier eyebrows were associated with the perception of trustworthiness. This may be associated with the perception of strength and dependability.

Other facial features associated with trustworthiness in men were a broader mouth, the mouth having upturned corners, and having larger eyes. An increased distance between the eyes and the eyebrows was associated with a more trustworthy face.

In contrast to this, faces with a narrower mouth, a mouth with down-pointing corners, smaller eyes and more angular and longer chin were seen as less trustworthy.[175] Of course, when we smile, the face below the zygomatic arch, the cheekbones, becomes wider, the mouth gets wider, the corners of the mouth turn up, and the forehead contracts slightly, lifting the eyebrows, making our eyes more visible. Thus a smile increases the perception of trustworthiness.

Although attractive faces are considered more trustworthy, this only goes so far. It is a face that is average (typical rather than ordinary) that is considered trustworthy.[176]

The condition of the skin also makes an impact on the perception of trustworthiness. Individuals with smoother skin were rated as being more trustworthy and attractive.[177] Photographs of women smiling were perceived to be more trustworthy than when they were not smiling, with a more intense smile garnering a higher perception of trustworthiness. [178]

Women were found to be more attuned and sensitive to untrustworthy faces, perhaps as they face more danger from untrustworthy individuals. In this study, both male and female untrustworthy faces had slightly narrower, more upturned noses, showing more nostril than did the trustworthy faces. The trustworthy faces had slightly upturned corners of the mouth while mouths of the untrustworthy faces turned down slightly. The trustworthy faces looked directly into the camera, giving the impression of them looking you in the eye, while the untrustworthy appearing faces seemed to look as if they were looking at the forehead or nose.[179]

In a study of male faces photographed with the eyes open and again with the eyelids partially lowered, giving the "bedroom eyes" look, men were asked if they would trust the faces as a business partner or neighbor. Men preferred the guy with the eyes open and lacked trust in the faces with the eyes partially closed. Women were asked how attractive they found the men for short or long-term relationships. The bedroom eyes were rated just a bit less attractive as open eyes for a short-term fling, but unattractive for long-term relationships. The photos of men with lowered eyelids were perceived to be less trustworthy. They were considered to be sexually promiscuous, having short-term mating strategies, more likely to challenge authority, and more likely to poach mates.[180] Thus, sleepy eyes appear untrustworthy.

Untrustworthy or dominant faces are perceived as more threatening, angry, and dominant, and threatening faces are associated with the perception of criminality. Of course, this can be a bias that creates reality, as an individual with a stereotypic "criminal" appearing face is more likely to be suspected, arrested, picked out of a police line-up and convicted than a person with a trustworthy, smiling face.[181] These implicit appraisals give us reason to curate our faces.

Who are you going to trust? Me or your lying eyes?
Groucho Marx

Generally, a more juvenile appearance is judged to be more trustworthy. However, in another series of studies, boys from lower socioeconomic status households that had baby-faces were more likely than their more mature-faced peers to be delinquent, and the baby-faced delinquents committed more numerous crimes.[182] Perhaps having an innocent face allowed them to get away with more infractions, so they learned that they could. Alternatively, baby-faceness is associated with a higher fWHR, and thus with more untrustworthy behavior.

In a study where the assessment of trustworthiness from the heuristic perception of the face was correlated to actual behavior, *only four percent* of the variance in trust behavior was accounted for.[183] Thus, the heuristic perception of trustworthiness is of questionable trustworthiness.

The concept of trustworthiness may not be specific enough, especially when making implicit assessments of leadership. Is trustworthy just being passive rather than hostile or dangerous, or is it more? The evaluation of trustworthiness appears to be dominated by interpretation of happiness (more trustworthy) versus anger (untrustworthy and threatening).[184] Thus, the heuristic for trust may be related to the perception of physical danger rather than honesty or reliability.

There are several behavioral aspects fall within the broad definition of trustworthiness, and they include:

- A person that is *dependable* will be trusted to act consistently. For example, they can be trusted to show up for work on time.
- A person that is *reliable* can be trusted in what they say. A reliable witness will correctly report what they saw, and not be easily biased.
- An *ethical* person of integrity holds to a moral code of behavior and can be trusted to act in accordance with those precepts.
- A person that is *altruistic* will not exploit the weakness of others for their personal gain.
- A *caring* person is helpful and supportive.
- A *conscientious* person will do their best to accomplish what they are asked to and agree to do.
- A *faithful* spouse does not stray in a relationship or poach mates.
- An *honest* person does not steal.
- A *truthful* person does not lie.
- A *responsible* person can be trusted to try to get things done.
- A *chivalrous* person can be expected to help others in times of need.
- A *loyal* person does not betray his or her friends or country.

Meanwhile, a *guileless* person may simply be naïve, and *delicate, frail,* or *cowardly* persons may appear unlikely to pose physical threats. Certainly, the traits of innocent or childlike appearance should not be confounded with responsibility or integrity.

Thus, the term trustworthy is too broad for use as a single trait. Studies of implicit recognition of trust need to clearly define what aspects of trust are incorporated into the heuristic evaluation. Competence is by far the most important trait in voter preference. Several of the traits in the list above are likely components of the unreflective inference heuristic of competence rather than being judgments of trustworthiness.

The implicit judgment of trustworthiness is likely closer to being an absence of threat, hostility, and non-reciprocating highly self-serving behavior. When the face is at rest, slightly upturned corners of the mouth give a less threatening appearance. Appearing relaxed and happy makes people look more trustworthy.

When we meet someone and we are happy to see them, we make eye contact, smile, give a small upwards nod of the head, and an upwards flick of the eyebrows that lasts about a sixth of a second. This is a social signal that we are not a threat.

Chapter 10: More than Appearance

Beauty is what beauty does

~Anonymous

Society is a shallow place. We make snap judgments about each other based on superficial information. Xenophobia and other prejudices emanate from the subconscious, instinctive urges befitting coddled childish minds. There are all sorts of prejudices, and our success in life is often influenced by things that have nothing to do with our abilities, character, or quality of our work.

On a primal, instinctual level, we make several near instant judgments about people when we first see them:

- What is their gender?
- Are they healthy?
- Are they fertile?
- Are they from our tribe?
- Are they hostile?

First, if we don't recognize a person, we assess their gender and if they are a danger to us. Next we assess to see if they are from our tribe and if they are potential mates. Pretty primitive isn't it? Living in society, most of us have learned to override some of our natural biases; however, they largely remain until we get to know the person.

Two of these subconscious judgments, health, and fertility, correlate with physical attractiveness. In a primitive world (like ours,) hanging out with a diseased individual is risky. So, we avoid and are less comfortable being around individuals we perceive as being unhealthy. Another genetic imperative is the selection of mates likely to provide healthy offspring. Our subconsciously determined visual assessment of physical attractiveness is largely an assessment of health and fertility. Smell is also used, especially by females, in mate selection.

When Darwin spoke of survival of the fittest, he was referring to the reproduction of individuals that were best adapted to the environment. We humans also select mates on the basis of reproductive fitness, and what we find attractive is generally that which is fit. The hip to waist ratio of 0.7 that men find most attractive in women is the one that correlates best with fertility. An attractive face is a healthy one.

In terms of evolutionary survival, our species has also evolved to detect health, and we make implicit judgments of health just as quickly as make inferences of mood and temperament from faces. We make bitter, sour, or disgusted faces if we taste foods that are bad, as it may be toxic or putrid, and it tells those around us to avoid the food. When infectious diseases are a major cause of death, as it has been for most of human history, it is a survival imperative to recognize and avoid those who are diseased. As with fertility, we choose healthy mates in order to increase the survival of our offspring. We also pick leaders that appear robust and healthy. Appearing haggard is not a good look for a leader.

We interpret health and vigor on several clues. They include unblemished skin; a symmetrical face and body; an elegant, even gait; and a relaxed mien; as these are all signs of health. Men who appear muscular and fit and women with a narrow waist give the appearance of fertility and thus fit the evolutionary precepts for beauty.

Appearances affect how we are perceived. If I walk into a room to see a new patient and their clothes are disheveled and their hair straggly and unkempt, part of my assessment as a doctor will be to assess their mental health and social situation. I need to determine whether the person is able to take care of themselves; are they mentally ill, do they have resources to get their medications, do they live in a stable environment where they will be able to get and take medications properly? I spend less time focusing on these issues for patients that present neatly dressed and well-groomed.

Attractive individuals are assumed to be more intelligent, healthier, and more resilient. Physical attractiveness increases access to success in our society. In high school, the more popular and well-liked students are usually attractive, well-groomed, and well-dressed. Attractive people earn more and achieve better positions at work. Implicit physical clues, especially that of competence determine who gets elected and influences who gets hired and promoted.

It may seem unfair that outward appearances have such a great impact on our ability to succeed. Nevertheless, except for the truly unfortunate, being attractive and appearing competent depend considerably more on nurture than nature. We are stuck with our genetics and our past, and may never be strikingly beautiful or movie star handsome, but most of us can modulate our appearance to a level of physical attractiveness that serves us well, providing us access to success. It does take an investment of time and intent to enhance our attractiveness.

When I watched a class of graduating high school seniors, those graduating summa cum laude stood out from most of their classmates as being particularly attractive. But, these successful students were selected by their GPA, not by their looks. The health and spirit of these young people was notable. It seemed obvious that they were loved and cared for by their families, that they had self-confidence and composure, and were eager to take on challenges. When I visited Stanford University and saw a crowd of new students on the first day of their school year, I was struck by how attractive, healthy and well-cared-for this set of young people was. But photos are not part of the application process; test scores, essays and grades are.

Physical attractiveness has its roots based in health, and so does academic competence and ascendance. One can manipulate attractiveness with makeup and surgery, but you can't fake health or being alert and energetic so easily.

A panel of 500 people rated digital images of young adults in a study designed to determine what factors were associated with attractiveness. The images included the digitized images of 64 young women and 32 young men aged 17-29, and from these, additional morphed images were created. Images of young beauty queens without makeup were also rated. In this study, there were several features that were consistently associated with highly attractive faces, and these are listed in Table 10-1, below.[185] Many of these features associated with attractiveness are controllable; better health, control of weight, and with the use of cosmetics. Several other features associated with attractiveness; narrower face, less pudgy face, upper-face wider than the lower face, and lack of nasolabial folds, are features that change with adiposity or aging.

Table 10-1: Some Determinants of Attractiveness

Attractive for Women	Attractive for Men
Health-related	
✪ Thicker, longer and darker eyelashes	Thicker and darker eyelashes
Thinner eyelids	Thinner eyelids
✪No circles under eye	No nasolabial folds
✪Darker, thinner eyebrows	✪Darker eyebrows
Less pudgy face	Less pudgy face
✪An even complexion	✪An even complexion
Prenatal/Age/Weight-related	
✪Higher cheekbones	Higher cheekbones
Narrower facial shape	Narrower facial shape
Hormonal	
✪Rosy complexion	✪Browner skin
✪Narrower nose	Prominent lower jaw
✪Slightly wider distance between eyes	Upper half of the face broader in relation to the lower
	More prominent chin
Youthful	
✪Fuller lips	Fuller and more symmetrical lips
	Lack of receding hairline
White sclera*	White sclera*

* Visible in study morphed images but not discussed.
✪ Determinants that are amenable to makeup

Pebble: Although increasing skin contrast does not make men more attractive as it does for women, cosmetics that even the complexion, and mask skin lesions, and give a healthier skin color can be used by men to appear more attractive.

Pearl: Even better than makeup ais a diet high in lycopene and other carotenoids that not only improve the appearance of health, but actually improve health and also protect the skin from UV damage and aging. It takes several weeks of a diet with adequate carotenoids to fully improve skin tone.

Chapter 11: Beauty Sleep

One of the most important components in maintaining health and attractiveness is beauty sleep. In a Swedish study, researchers presented pictures to untrained observers of individuals who were either mildly sleep-deprived or who had sufficient sleep. These observers ranked the sleep-deprived individuals as less attractive and less healthy.[186] The lead scientist concluded, "Sleep is the body's natural beauty treatment. It's probably more effective than any other treatment you could buy."

In a later study performed by the same research group, 25 healthy students with normal sleep patterns averaging 7 hours and 35 minutes per night were photographed, and then photographed again after two nights of curtailed sleep, in which they only slept 4 hours for two nights in a row. This gave a 7-hour sleep deficit, a typical sleep deficit seen in many adults who short-sleep by about one hour each night and accumulate a deficit similar to one night's sleep. This amount of sleep deficit usually allows people to function without feeling tired, however not functioning at their best. This level of sleep deficit is so common, in fact, that *more than half* of the students that had volunteered to participate in the study were rejected because they were determined to be already sleep deprived.

Over 100 observers, (65 females and 56 males) aged 18 to 65 rated the photos of each subject. Only one photo of each subject (either before or after sleep deprivation) was shown to the raters. The raters scored each photo on a scale of one to seven for sleepiness, attractiveness, health, and trustworthiness, and were asked: "how much would you like to socialize with this person?"

The sleep-deprived subjects were rated as appearing sleepier. As in their previous study, the sleep-deprived subjects were rated as less attractive and less healthy. There was a non-statistical tendency to rate the sleep-deprived students as less trustworthy. The observers were clearly less interested in socializing with the subjects that were sleep deprived. In effect, they were voting not to hang out with the less healthy, less attractive, less trustworthy, sleep-deprived individuals.[187]

The Need for Sleep

Sleep is essential to health. If lab rats are completely prevented from sleeping, they eat more but lose weight; their heart rates accelerate, they develop skin ulcers, and die within a few weeks. Sleep is required for survival. Even tiny nematodes sleep. If sharks stop swimming, they suffocate. Porpoises need to come up to the surface to breathe, and sharks need to keep swimming to get water to flow through their gills, but these animals need sleep. Birds that migrate long distances across vast oceans also need to sleep but must stay awake to survive. Therefore, these animals sleep half of their brain at a time. Although some of us appear only to be half awake, this trick does not work in humans; we need sufficient, quality, whole-brain sleep.[188]

Humans sleep about one-third of their life away, or at least, we are healthiest and perform best when we do. When we get insufficient sleep, reaction times slow, attention lapses, the mood becomes labile, cognition foggy, and memory suffers. Decision-making can become faulty, and logic blurred.[189] Nineteen hours of sustained wakefulness creates performance impairment equivalent to a blood alcohol level of 0.05%; the level at which it is illegal to operate a motor vehicle in most jurisdictions. After 24 hours of sustained wakefulness, the performance deficit is equivalent to a blood alcohol level of 0.1%,[190] a level sufficient to impair reaction time and gross motor control.

In addition to the need for sleep, our bodies have circadian cycles that tune the metabolism to daytime activity and nighttime quiescence. These cycles do much more than entrain the sleep cycle to help us wake and sleep coincident to dawn and nightfall. The circadian cycles are intimately tied to the release of at least a dozen hormones that control the body's energy use, activity, appetite, digestion, immune function, growth, and healing. Disrupting the circadian cycle can throw these hormonal cycles into disarray.

The various sleep stages make different contributions to learning. In the first part of the sleep cycle, SWS (short-wave sleep) helps to stabilize visual and declarative memory ("Just the facts, ma'am"). Stage 2 sleep helps reorganize the content that has been learned during the day and helps with learning motor sequencing and automaticity skills, such as playing a musical instrument or coordinated movements such as used in sports, dance or operating machinery. Throughout the night, REM (rapid eye movement) sleep enhances the memory, adds insights, explores interrelationships and helps reorganize information into associative networks.[191] These repetitive sleep cycles throughout the night allow for the iterative creation of memory and learning, and for winnowing the salient from the inconsequential. The brain is not relaxing during sleep – it is actively processing information. It may take two to three nights sleep to organize complex information into a gestalt. Adults that are actively engaged in learning have creative demands or require peak attention and reaction times need to dedicate eight hours per day to sleep. When sleep is disturbed or of poor quality, we do not learn efficiently.

Normally, the thyroid hormone T3 is released at night during sleep, and T4 form of the hormone is released in the morning. T3 is geared more for supporting growth and repair while T4 is more supportive of activity. T3 stimulates the wrapping of nerves with myelin by oligodendrocyte precursor cells,[192] and thus, is important for neurological development, learning, and repair after injury. Sleep deprivation inhibits thyroid stimulating hormone release.

Sleep Deprivation

Chronic sleep deprivation usually only causes a mild decline in *subjective* functioning. Nevertheless, it can cause a severe decline in attention and reaction times. So when people are severely and chronically sleep deprived, they don't feel much worse than when they are only mildly sleep deprived. Regardless, their functioning can be seriously impaired. Maintenance of peak reaction times requires just over eight hours of sleep each night.

Many adults make do with much less sleep time without obvious problems. Even when sleep is restricted to only four hours a night, most adults will not complain of feeling fatigued or impaired, even after two weeks of curtailed sleep. It appears that there are different thresholds for feeling sleep-deprived for different individuals.[193] Nonetheless, those who feel well when sleep is limited are impaired by sleep deprivation as are those who feel exhausted; they just don't feel it. They still suffer just as severe performance deficits as those who do feel bedraggled.

Peak functioning, as measured by attention measurements, actually does not depend on sleep, but rather, on avoiding excessive wakefulness. Being awake too long diminishes focus. The effect of time awake is cumulative. Being awake an additional hour each day for 8 days in a row diminishes the level of focus and attention equivalent to missing one night's sleep; staying awake one extra hour daily for 16 days in a row will cause the difficulty in focus and attention that missing two night's sleep would. Performing at full attention and focus proscribes being awake for more than about 16 hours per day on average,[194] resulting in our need for about 8 hours of sleep.

The excitatory neurotransmitters, such as glutamate which keep us active and alert, are neurotoxic when they over-accumulate; they can damage the brain. Sleep provides an opportunity for the brain to detoxify, replenish antioxidants, and repair itself. During sleep, the glymphatic system flushes wastes from the cerebral spinal fluid to help recover from the toxins and metabolites that accumulate during wakefulness.[195]

Energy Balance

Individuals sleeping fewer hours are more likely to become obese. Children who sleep less than ten hours a day are 89% more likely to be obese than children who get more sleep, and adults who get less than six hours sleep are about 55% more likely to be obese than adults who get more than six hours of sleep. The association between short sleep time and obesity has been found in more than 30 studies performed on six continents; this effect is not limited to the North American or Western lifestyle.[196]

Obesity is also associated with longer sleep time as obesity greatly increases the propensity for snoring. When snoring becomes severe, it can disturb sleep and is often associated with sleep apnea. In obstructive sleep apnea, the person's breathing becomes obstructed momentarily, disturbing the sleep and preventing deep sleep. Heavy snorers may be unaware of their dozens of semi-awakenings occurring throughout the night that result in poor quality, non-restorative sleep. In a vicious cycle, the sleep deficits from sleep apnea promote inflammatory substances (cytokines) that increase appetite and thus obesity that worsens snoring and sleep apnea.

Obviously, a lack of sleep leads to fatigue. It is not only the lack of sleep, especially short wave sleep, but disruption of the diurnal cycle of thyroid hormones, growth hormone, and cortisol, and the increase in inflammatory cytokines that cause fatigue. The fatigue, lack of energy, and decrease in muscle function act to dissuade many short sleepers from exercise; this leads to another vicious cycle of obesity and poor health. Lack of and poor quality sleep is a risk factor for cancer, including breast, prostate, colorectal, and brain cancers.

Children and adolescents need more hours of sleep than do adults. These extra hours support growth and learning. The optimal sleep time for adults is about 7 hours and 45 minutes. This is about the length of time that adults will sleep if they have no impediments to sleep, a quiet, dark place, no appointments or scheduling imperatives or night-time disturbances. Most healthy people take another 15 minutes to fall asleep and spend 15 minutes lying awake in the morning before arising. This is reflected in the 7.7 hours average sleep time, and 8.3 hours average time in bed observed in studies of healthy Americans.

Table 11-1: Typical daily hours of time in bed needed for sufficient sleep[197]

Age	Hours of time in bed
Newborn	16.5
3 months	15
9 months	14
2 years	13
3 years	12
5 years	11
9 years	10
14 years	9
17	9.6
22	8.9
30	8.6
40	8.3
50	8.3
60	8.2
70	9

When adults feel sleepy during the day, it usually indicates an accumulative sleep deficit of over 7 hours. Sufficient sleep is required for learning and memory consolidation. Even small sleep deficits slow reaction times. Adults who get sufficient bed and sleep time, yet still feel sleepy during the day, often have sleep problems that require medical attention.[198]

Sleep deprivation changes our appearance. Photographs of ten young men and women were taken before and after sleep deprivation and the effect of sleep deprivation on appearance was studied. Use of makeup was not allowed for these photos. Forty adults were recruited to rate the 20 photographs. They were shown the photos in random order on a computer monitor for 5 seconds, and rated them on 12 different criteria; thus each rater made 480 separate evaluations. The raters were not comparing pairs of photos, but rather rating each photo on the various criteria independently. Table 11-2 gives the percent of the sleep-deprived subjects that were rated significantly different from their well-rested photo on the following criteria:

Table 11-2: Visible signs of short-term sleep deprivation:[199]

Droopy eyelids	90%
Swollen eyes (thicker lids)	60%
Pale skin (especially in men)	60%
Dark circles under eyes	60%
Fine lines around eyes	60%
Droopy corners of mouth	60%
Red eyes	40%
Rash/eczema	30%
Tense lips (only in men)	30%
Sadness	70%
Fatigue	70%

When people are sleep deprived, it shows on their face. Sleep-deprived individuals are perceived as appearing fatigued and sad. When people are sleep deprived, it shows on their face. Sleep-deprived individuals are perceived as appearing fatigued and sad. Several facial traits induced by sleep deprivation are identical to the characteristics associated with appearing less attractive, less competent, and of having lower intelligence in studies of implicit perception.

Skin pallor was more evident in men than in women. Three men had tense lips, while women were more likely to have drooping corners of the mouth when sleep deprived. Three of the ten subjects had facial rash or eczema present with sleep deprivation that was not apparent in their well-rested photo.[200]

Pearl: Don't short-change your sleep. Getting a full eight hours in bed every night allows the opportunity to get the sleep that makes you appear, and likely feel, more energetic and happier. It makes people more attractive and to appear more competent, trustworthy, and likable.

Pearl: If you have daytime sleepiness, you likely have a large sleep deficit. If you have daytime sleepiness and are getting sufficient sleep time, you likely have poor quality sleep or a sleep disorder.

Pearl: If you take vitamin D_3 supplements, take it mid-day, the time you would naturally make it in the sun, to help strengthen the circadian rhythm. Adequate vitamin B12 is also needed for a healthy circadian cycle.

Pearl: Vigorous exercise early in the day helps reset the circadian clock to nighttime sleep cycles for better sleep but heavy exercise in the evening can delay sleep onset.[201] [202]

Pearl: Caffeine has a six-hour half-life for most people, and it is longer for many. This means that more than half of the caffeine will still be present in your brain five hours after your last dose. Chocolate contains theobromine, a molecule that acts as a stimulant similar to caffeine, and has an even longer half-life. Avoid these after 2 P.M.

Pearl: The purchase of a well-made, new car, with proper maintenance, care and luck should provide about 4000 hours of service; 4000 hours at an average of 50 MPH gives 200,000 miles, costing about $25 per hour, accounting for typical expenses. A good mattress provides about 30,000 hours of comfortable service at the cost of about six cents an hour. Comfortable bed and bedding are an inexpensive luxury and an investment in health and productivity.

Pearl: The bedroom temperature should be pleasant and several degrees cooler than the daytime room temperature to promote sleep. The body temperature needs to fall about 3° F (1.7° C) to help initiate sleep and a bedtime room temperature cooler than the environment in which the person spent their day is conducive to this. The room should be dark, and quiet, without distractions. There should not be a TV or computer in the bedroom; reserve those distractions for a different location.

Pearl: Old pillows are uncomfortable and downright nasty, as they accumulate saliva, skin, and dust mite feces. Doctor's orders: replace them. Polyester pillows should be washed every three months and replaced after six to nine months. Memory foam pillows can last from 18 months to three years. [203]

Pearl: Fluorescent lights, televisions, computers, and smartphones have high levels of light in the blue spectrum that impedes the onset of sleep. Even electronic-paper readers project a great deal more blue light into the eye than is encountered reading a paper book with room light. Do you like to read a few pages of a book before falling asleep? Reading an eBook around bedtime reduces sleepiness, increases sleep delay time, decreases melatonin output, and reduces next-morning alertness compared to reading a printed book.[204] If you like reading at bedtime, get this book in print or as an audiobook. If you feel the need to use a screen before sleeping use apps that decrease the amount of blue spectrum light from screen devices in the evenings.

Pearl: Alcohol use impedes deep, restorative sleep stages and causes fragmentation of rapid eye movement (REM) sleep. Alcohol consumption desynchronizes circadian rhythms, thus making regular sleep more difficult.[205] Alcohol also prevents light from resetting the circadian clock.[206] A nightcap may help a person get to sleep, but causes an increase nighttime awakening a few hours later as the blood alcohol level falls.

Pearl: If you have evening events, or are on the road away from home, interviewing or campaigning, be sure to plan and get sufficient sleep time. If these plans include naps, make sure that your caffeine intake does not interfere with napping. If you want a brief early afternoon nap – a cup of coffee just before a nap should kick in about 30 minutes later and help you get moving again.

Chapter 12: Skin Tone and Character

An important clue to health is skin color.

In an experiment, healthy Caucasian volunteers were injected with nanogram doses of the bacterial endotoxins, LPS. LPS (lipopolysaccharides) are a component of the cell wall of anaerobic bacteria. I would not have volunteered for this experiment, as LPS is one of the things that make you feel ill when you have an infection. A spectrophotometer was used to measure the skin color of the subjects before and several times over the ensuing hours. In the first hours, the skin of the face became paler, less yellow and less red. After three hours the levels of carotenoids in the blood began to fall. Carotenoids are a class of antioxidants that we get from vegetables in our diet, which give the skin a healthy yellow-orange glow. Thus, the LPS caused a depletion of carotenoids and decreased blood flow to the face, making these volunteers pallid.[207]

Healthy faces have a yellowish skin tone that comes from certain carotenoids. The yellow tone suggests the person is healthy and eating well. Having a reddish skin tone, from hemoglobin in the blood, also suggests health and fertility, rather than anemia that can be the result of blood loss or parasite infestation.

Faces that lack yellowness look unhealthy. We generally find faces with less adiposity to be more attractive, but not if the face is pallid. This may be because we associate pallid faces with infectious or other disease,[208] or with times of famine. Neither famine nor pestilence bodes well for survival or reproduction. The carotenoids provide a skin tone associated with immune competence, and thus, health, attractiveness, and competence.

Another facial cue to health is adiposity. Facial adiposity is highly correlated with body mass index. When associated with being overweight, facial adiposity is negatively correlated with the perception of health and attractiveness.[209] As men's body fat level rises above 12%, their faces become less attractive to women, and this increase in facial and whole body adiposity is associated with lower immune competence, and lower testosterone levels.[210] Having inadequate facial adiposity is also associated with poorer health. Facial symmetry is associated with better health.[211]

The pigment melanin also gives some yellowness to the skin in Caucasians, and brownness to the skin in darker races. Both carotenoids and melanin increase skin yellowness, attractiveness, and perception of health. This is why having a "healthy tan" is associated with a healthy appearance. Men have more melanin and darker skin than women as a result of testosterone. In women, an increase in yellowness from carotenoids is found to be more attractive and a better signal of health than is melanin. More melanin gives a perception of masculinity,[212] as testosterone increases melanin production in the skin. In dark-skinned peoples, adult male siblings generally have darker skin color than their sisters.

Anemia, a lack of healthy red blood cells, is an unfavorable condition for survival and fertility. Especially for women, a rosy complexion is a sign of fitness and health. This does not apply to faces red with anger or embarrassment. Otherwise, redder, rather than paler, faces are perceived as healthier and more attractive. The redness shows adequate oxygenation, cardiovascular fitness, and a lack of anemia. Skin redness also increases with estrogen levels in women, and this acts as a sign of fertility.[213] Blushing also occurs during sexual arousal. Aerobic training increases the skin redness, and thus, fitness increases facial redness and attractiveness.[214] The cosmetic use of blush mimics blushing, and thus increases attractiveness by increasing redness in the face. Alcohol also causes facial blushing, and this blushing may be perceived to be sexual arousal and receptiveness.

In men, however, facial redness is associated with aggression. When different women adjusted the color of men's photos to maximize perceived aggression, dominance, or attractiveness, women associated the aggression with a redder face, dominance with an intermediate amount of redness, and attractiveness with the least redness.[215] High levels of aggression may be associated with mating success, but also with danger.

Skin coloration is not only a clue to health but also to age. In a study of 160 British Caucasian male faces, aged ten to seventy, 300 participants rated the faces for age, attractiveness, and health. They also rated an isolated area of the cheek skin for these criteria. An isolated area of skin showing color homogeneity and condition was sufficient to predict age, health, and attractiveness.[216] Having an even distribution of melanin was a stronger clue of younger age, whereas an even hemoglobin distribution was more strongly associated with the perception of health and attractiveness.[217]

Facial redness from small broken and dilated blood vessels in the skin of the face (*telangiectasis*) gives an aging appearance. So does a blotchy distribution of melanin. Telangiectasia occurs when small blood vessels in the skin become enlarged and visible. These dilated vessels can break and leak blood into the skin. Although it is often a hereditary tendency, telangiectasia is also caused by exposure to temperature extremes (cold weather) and UV exposure. Wearing a scarf over the face in cold weather and sunscreen to prevent UV damage can prevent injury to these veins. Alcohol causes flushing and dilation that causes these veins to break, thus avoiding excess alcohol may prevent it.

The skin disease rosacea is an important cause of blotchy red skin on the face of adults, and it is often accompanied by telangiectasia. Rosacea is an inflammatory condition that is often caused by *Demodex* mites that also cause blepharitis (inflamed eyelid margins) and ocular rosacea. Rosacea can be treated, so early treatment can prevent damage to the skin and veins and allow healing, and decrease unattractive facial redness. (See *Demodex* and Facial and Eye Redness in Chapter 13). Vitamin C and the amino acid lysine strengthen the capillaries and help prevent them from breaking. Misuse of topical steroids can also induce rosacea. *Demodex* mites feed on the sebum in the skin, and since men produce more sebum as a result of testosterone, men are more likely to be affected by rosacea.

Telangiectasis can be treated with a laser to coagulate the veins. An alternative treatment is a topical, 10% witch hazel lotion, which is anti-inflammatory and decreases redness of the skin.[218]

Lighter skin color (less melanin) is a sign of fertility in women. Skin darkens with age, during pregnancy, and during the second half of the menstrual cycle, after the days of fertility during the cycle. Additionally, injury, including injury from UV damage, tends to darken skin and becomes another sign of aging. There is also a loss of homogeneity in the skin coloration with aging, a sign of cumulative damage. Acne and post-inflammatory changes decrease the homogeneity of the skin and decrease attractiveness.

In a study of dietary intake of fruits and vegetables in mostly Caucasian participants, fruit and vegetable intake was followed over six weeks, and the skin color was measured throughout the study. Participants that consumed at least three servings of vegetables a day had noticeably yellower skin and higher levels of β-carotene and lycopene in their skin at the end of six weeks. Participants with a daily consumption of at least 2.9 servings of fruits and vegetables were perceived to be healthier, and those consuming more than 3.3 servings a day were perceived to be more attractive.[219] A similar study among Asian university students found visible increases in skin yellowness and redness after 4 weeks of dietary intervention.[220] Beta-carotene is found in many green, yellow, and orange vegetables, and lycopene is found in tomatoes, pink guavas, and watermelons.[221] Both accumulate in the skin. There are several other carotenoids found in foods as well that are important for health including lutein, and zeaxanthin. Dietary polyphenols such as those in green tea may also protect the skin from UV damage.[222]

Thus, facial yellowness is a sign of a healthy diet containing fruits and vegetables and redness is a sign of fitness, especially for women. Both colors are perceived as indicators of health and attractiveness in studies of Caucasians, Asians, and Africans.[223] [224]

Even within dark-skinned racial groups, darker skin color within the group is generally considered less attractive.[225] If we consider that yellower skin is a sign of health, then seeing yellower skin as more attractive is part of natural selection of more fit individuals. Carotenoids do not only make the skin yellowish; they also act as a natural sunscreen that protects the skin from UV damage,[226] and in doing so, may decrease the development of excess melanin in the skin. Thus, genetically similar individuals with a similar propensity to form melanin with sun exposure may have different pigmentation depending on the quality of their diet. Those consuming more vegetables may have lighter, yellower skin, reflecting better health and appear younger and fitter. Additionally skin darkens with aging and accumulation of skin injuries.

Lycopene, principally found in the western diet in tomatoes and tomato products is a more effective UV quencher than is β-carotene, but β-carotene, lutein, and dietary flavanols found in fruits also provide UV protection.[227] [228] Thus a diet high in these natural compounds not only increases attractiveness, but it also protects the skin and eyes from photoaging and skin cancer[229] and may prevent high-level melatonin deposition in the skin. Lycopene is poorly absorbed from raw tomatoes and is only slightly better absorbed when cooked. Adding some olive oil to either raw tomatoes (in a salad) or cooked tomatoes (in pasta sauce) greatly increases the amount of lycopene absorbed into the bloodstream, and thus, into the skin.[230] [231] The amount of olive oil used in one of these studies works out to about half a teaspoon of olive oil for one cup of raw tomatoes, two tsp. of olive oil per cup of tomato juice, ¼ cup of olive oil per cup of tomato paste, and ¼ tsp. of olive oil per tablespoon of catsup. It is probable that eating tomatoes in a meal with other fats similarly aids in absorption.

Pearl: Consume at least four servings of vegetables a day for more attractive and healthy skin and let at least one of those be tomato with some olive oil! Other studies have shown that those eating 6 to 7 servings of fruits and vegetables have the best outlook on life.

Overall skin yellowness is more closely associated with the perception of health than is red coloration. The perception of health from facial redness is limited to redness in the cheeks and around the eyes. Luminance around the eyes also contributes to the perception of health. In women, increased facial contrast increases the perception of health and attractiveness.[232] [233]

In women, the luminance contrast of the eyebrows decreases with age and the lips lose much of their redness. The area around the eyes also loses color contrast, becoming less yellow and less red.[234] Young women with higher facial contrast are perceived to be more feminine, healthier and more attractive. With aging, facial contrast has been found to decline in Caucasian, Hispanic, Asian and African women.

In a matched pair selection of faces of women from various ethnic groups, female participants were asked to select the younger appearing women. For each photo, a second version was manipulated to raise the contrast around the lips and eyes.. High and low contrast images of two different women were paired, and participants were asked to select the younger woman. The women chose the high contrast image as the younger subject 79 percent of the time.[235] When the facial contrast of women was tested for age perception within 10 year age groups, the face with the higher contrast was selected as being younger over 90 percent of the time.[236]

Pearl: A principal effect of makeup for women is to increase facial contrast and decrease variation in skin color; this provides a healthier, more youthful and feminine appearance.

Pearl: Sleep deprivation increases fine wrinkles and bags under the eyes, and promotes eczematous rash in some individuals.

Chapter 13: Scleral Health and Attractiveness

Don't' vote until you see the whites of their eyes!

Humans are the only animal in which the sclera, the white of the eye, is visible any time the eye is open. The anterior sclera is visible in humans as our iris covers a relatively smaller area of the globe of the eye than it does for most other animals. Seeing the sclera allows us to observe where other people are looking. Visible sclerae allow human infants to follow their mother's gaze to look where she is looking. This does not occur in chimpanzees or other primates.[237] Visible sclerae also let us know when people are rolling their eyes in disbelief.

The whites of the eyes not only help communicate what we are focusing on and our emotional state, but also are a clue to our age and health. With age, the whites of the eyes tend to lose their whiteness. It is the white of the eye that gives the high contrast that makes people, and especially women and children, more attractive.

Inside of the eyelids and over the sclera is a thin layer of mucosa called the conjunctiva. The conjunctiva is home to numerous, tiny mucous glands that help lubricate the eye, spread the tear film evenly, and keep the eye moist and shiny.

White sclerae reflect youth, health, and thus attractiveness, where dark, yellow, or red may indicate disease and loss of vitality. There are several things that cause the sclera to lose its whiteness. The conjunctiva is highly vascular and has many tiny blood vessels. With irritation and inflammation, these blood vessels enlarge and become visible. When we do not get enough sleep, our eyes get red. The sclerae tend to get yellowish with age. The conjunctiva can also get pigment spots, (melanosis), and this occurs more commonly in dark-skinned individuals. Chronic vitamin A deficiency results in dry eyes and also causes discoloration of the white of the conjunctiva called Bitot's spots. Jaundice from liver disease, such as from hepatitis, causes yellowing of the eye. Much of the aging and discoloration of the white of the eye results from sun damage. These and other conditions cause the loss of scleral and conjunctival whiteness and loss of contrast with the iris and skin.

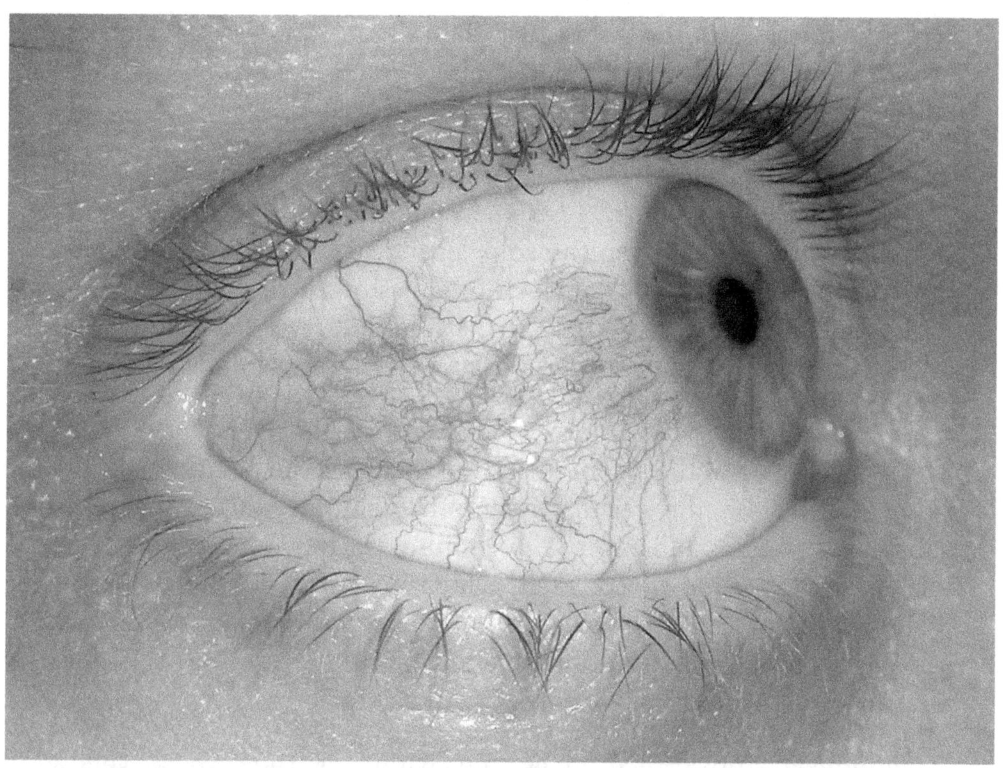

Figure 13-1: Conjunctival injection.

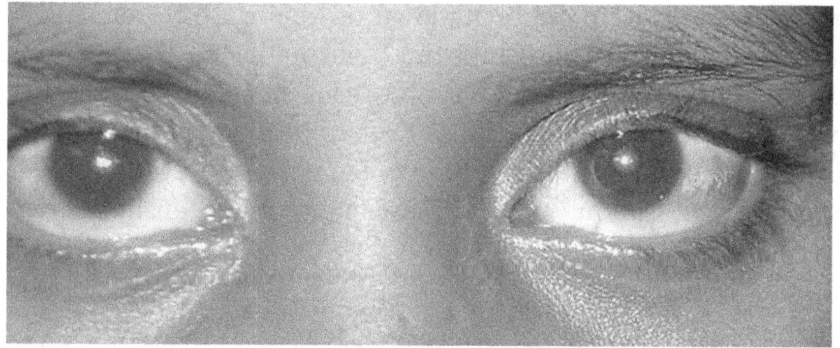

Figure 13-2: An adolescent with Bitot's Spots indicating a history of vitamin A deficiency. As many as half a million children die, and a similar number go blind each year from vitamin A deficiency. If you would like to make a difference, donate to UNICEF at www.unicefusa.org/help/donate.

The sclera thickens during adult life, at least to the age of 70.[238] This thickening, however, does not likely cause changes in the appearance of the eye. The conjunctiva decreases in thickness after the age of 20 but is stable through midlife. It then begins to thicken after the age of 60.[239] Throughout life, with age and injury, we lose goblet cells in the conjunctiva that are needed to help lubricate the eye and spread the tear film. By the age of fifty, 14.4 percent of Americans suffer from dry eyes, with higher rates among women.[240]

Much of this loss is the result of inflammatory processes which are exacerbated by poor quality tear film,[241] and a lack of sufficient antioxidants in the tears.[242]

As we age, the sclerae lose luminance and get redder and yellower. This causes a loss of contrast between the iris and the sclera and the skin and the sclerae. When the color of the sclerae was manipulated in photographs of women between the ages of 20 to 70, both young and older women were judged to be healthier, younger and more attractive when the sclerae were less red, less yellow and the whites of the eyes were brighter.[243] [244]

The yellowing of the sclerae does not appear to be a natural part of aging but maybe the result of cumulative injury or exposure to substances such as bilirubin. The conjunctiva may also yellow from increased deposition of collagen, which occurs with injury. Excess dietary carotene can cause a condition called carotenemia, which will cause carotenoderma, an orange/yellowing of the skin, but this does not cause yellowing of the conjunctiva or sclera.

Jaundiced appearance gives the white of the eye a yellow discoloration, and when severe can also cause the skin to yellow. Jaundice occurs from the breakdown of hemoglobin, released from dying red blood cells, into bilirubin. Normally the liver gets rid of bilirubin quickly, but this does not occur in liver disease such as hepatitis. Bilirubin is what causes bruises to turn yellow before they clear up. Thus, faces that are too yellow may indicate liver disease. Bilirubin discoloration, however, is usually only seen in the sclerae unless bilirubin levels are quite high.

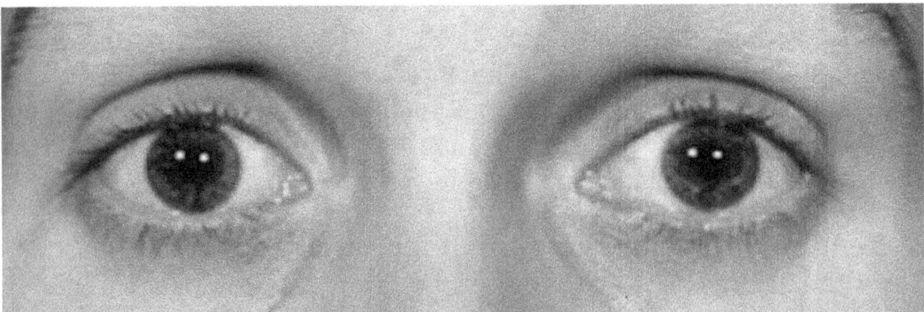

Figure 13-3: This photo shows yellow sclera and skin from jaundice (visible in the ebook edition). Notice also the deep recess above the eyelids indicating the loss of normal fatty tissue.

Reddened Eyes

Eyes get red when we cry. Photos of individuals with reddened sclera are perceived to be sadder, less healthy and less attractive.[245] Red eyelid margins make people appear weak, tired, or sick.

Reddening of the sclera can be caused by irritation, inflammation, allergies, dry eyes, lack of sleep, and exposure to smoke and dust. The principal cause, however, is the loss of properly functioning tear film that protects and lubricates the eyes.

The tear film is composed of a thin layer of tears, overlaid with a thin layer of phospholipids (predominantly phosphatidylcholine) that protects the aqueous phase of the film from evaporation. The tear film is like a sandwich with a mucin layer at the surface of the eye produced by goblet cells in the conjunctiva, an aqueous layer made of tears, and a very thin lipid layer over the top. The surface tension and hydrogen bonding have a much greater force than gravity, so the tear film does not fall off.

In about 80 percent of patients with dry eyes, the cause is not a lack of tears, but rather from a deficit in the lipid layer of the tear film. The lipid layer lowers the rate of tear evaporation by 90 to 95 percent. If the lipid layer is disturbed, then the aqueous layer can easily evaporate, and the salty tears become overly concentrated. This leads to irritation and inflammation that bothers the eye.[246] Antioxidants in the tears can also quickly oxidize when the lipid layer is disturbed.

The loss of antioxidants in the tears, oxidative stress over a lifetime and the drying of the eyes depletes the goblet cells in the conjunctiva that produce mucin that anchors the tear film. This causes irritation and thickening of the conjunctiva. With irritation, the tiny blood vessels in the conjunctiva enlarge, causing bloodshot eyes. The loss of goblet cells furthers the inflammation[247] and redness. This damage to the conjunctiva may explain some of the loss of whiteness of the eye.

The source of the lipids in the lipid layer is the Meibomian glands, also known as tarsal glands. There are about 50 glands in the upper lid and 25 somewhat larger glands in the lower eyelid. These glands can be seen on the inner surfaces of the eyelids and the glands open along the border of the eyelids, just inside of the eyelashes. These glands secrete meibum, a phospholipid-rich secretion. Meibum helps seal the eyes while we sleep and this keeps the eyes moist at night. Additionally, small amounts of meibum are slowly deposited into the eye during the day, and this creates the thin film over the aqueous layer of the tear film.

Infection of Meibomian glands causes blepharitis. When this occurs, bacteria can ferment the meibum causing the formation of fatty acids that irritate the gland and cause a loss of the phospholipids that protect the eye. Additionally, the secretions may become waxy and thick, and block the glands. As the tear film becomes unstable and begins to evaporate, the tears become more concentrated and oxidized, causing irritation and inflammation. With continued inflammation, the Meibomian glands become keratinized, and obstructed, causing further decreases in meibum; creating a vicious cycle of dry eyes and loss of Meibomian gland function.[248] Dry eyes can lead to keratitis (corneal injury). With chronic blepharitis, there is lid redness and swelling, loss of eyelashes, and dilation of the blood vessels on the skin of the eyelids.

Warm compresses may help treat inflammation of the Meibomian glands, but medical treatment may be required.

Demodex and Facial and Eye Redness

Demodex are tiny, nearly microscopic, ectoparasites that inhabit human skin. Most adults have them in our skin, and they are nasty little buggers! Humans become infested with two species of *Demodex*; *D. brevis* which inhabits sebaceous glands and *D. folliculorum* which favors the hair and follicles. They enjoy living in the skin of the face on the cheeks and nose and in the eyelashes and eyebrows of adults, especially during middle age. By adulthood, almost all adults are infested;[249] however, not everyone has a significant infection.

At night, while we sleep, the parasites crawl out and emerge from our eyelash follicles and have sex on our eyelashes right in front of our eyes! Commonly there are five or more of these bugs living in a single eyelash follicle, and they have a 14-18 day life cycle. [250] And if that were not enough, not only do they live in our pores but even more disgustingly, they lay their eggs, and then die there. These little critters don't have an anus, so they fill up with poop, and when they die, the feces is released all at once.[251] Just as with any feces, *Demodex* poop contains bacteria. These bacteria include *Bacillus oleronius that cause an inflammatory reaction and induce aberrant wound* healing.[252] [253] Some people, perhaps those most affected by leaky gut, mount especially strong inflammatory reactions to these bacteria, and as a result, have strong inflammatory reactions in the skin.[254] Avoiding food sensitivities and a healthy diet high in fiber may decrease the inflammatory reaction in the skin.[255]

These are the same ectoparasites that are responsible for papulopustular rosacea. *Demodex* and inflammatory reactions to them and their bacteria are a major cause of rosacea,[256] blepharitis, meibomian gland dysfunction, dry eyes, and keratitis.[257] *Demodex* is also implicated in acne.[258] The finding that 1% topical ivermectin, an anti-parasitic medication, is somewhat more effective in treating rosacea than is the anti-bacterial agents, metronidazole (topical) or tetracycline drugs (oral),[259] underscores the importance of controlling or eliminating Demodex in the treatment of rosacea, blepharitis, and meibomian gland dysfunction.

The diagnosis of Demodex may require the use of a special confocal microscope, which is not usually available in a doctor's office.[260] You may be able to see evidence of the parasites as tiny cuffs of "dandruff" at the base of the eyelashes, especially in the morning before face washing. Many doctors remain unaware of the impact of *Demodex* on the skin and eyes, so you may need to ask about it if seeking treatment.

There are over the counter treatments for Demodex; the best well known is tea tree oil. Never use full strength tea tree oil on, or around, the eyes as it will burn. Generally, 5% to 50% solutions are used. Begin with a weaker solution, as one can increase strength with time. Tea tree oil (TTO) can be diluted with olive or coconut oil to make a 10% to 50% tea tree oil solution, but be cautious as it stings the eyes. Also, some people can develop allergic reactions to it. Ophthalmologist Dr. Lora Cremers recommends applying a drop of tea tree oil to a clean towel moistened with warm water, and then gently stroking the eyelashes with the eyes closed. Wash the eyelid off if there is any burning sensation, or let it air dry if there is not.[261] A 10% dilution of TTO is likely not strong enough to eradicate Demodex,[262] but 25 to 50% solutions do. One of the things TTO does is to cause the Demodex mites to leave the follicles so that they are less likely to die within them. It takes about four weeks of treatment to eradicate Demodex, as the youngest ones are the most susceptible; they are the one most likely to be killed by TTO. Washing bedding and pillowcases weekly and drying them in a hot dryer, and treating spouses that may also be infected, was done in the eradication protocol to prevent reinfection.[263] TTO can also be used on the face to treat rosacea.

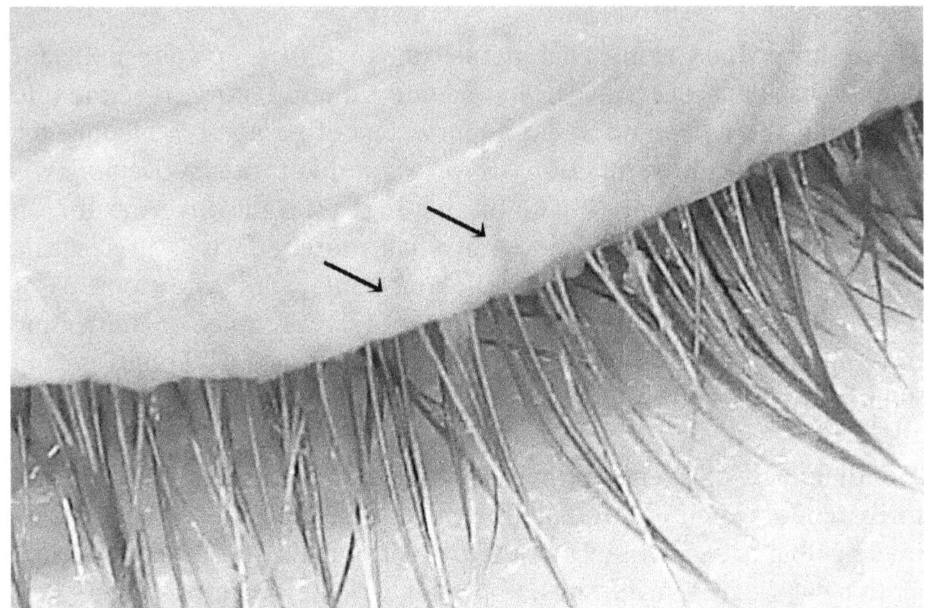

Figure 13-4: These eyelashes show mild cuffing "dandruff" at bases, typical of *Demodex*. Note also mild telangiectasia of eyelids (arrows).

Contact lens use decreases the number of functioning Meibomian glands. Contact lens wearers with an average age of 31 were found to have the Meibomian gland function typical of persons in their 60's.[264] This appears to be much worse among contact lens wearers with allergic conjunctivitis.[265] People who wear contact lenses and glasses are more likely to have significant eyelash *Demodex* infestations than those who do not use them.[266] [267] Thus, Meibomian dysfunction in contact lens users may cause, or at least be worsened, by *Demodex* infection.

Individuals who wear contact lenses should avoid sleeping with them, even when labeled safe to do so, and should only use the lenses when clean and in good condition, as contact lenses can easily cause eye irritation. Individuals with allergic conjunctivitis should think twice about using contact lenses or restrict their use.

There are eye drops that will get the red out, but the over-the-counter eye drops such as Visine® don't last much longer than a few minutes and cause a rebound increase in swelling of the tiny blood vessels, making the situation worse. They can help for a photo shoot, but so can digital editing of the photos. These drops disrupt the tear film and should be avoided. Carbomer containing eye drops should only be used when prescribed by a doctor for treatment of eye disease, as carbomer is toxic to corneal cells that cover the clear part of the eye.[268] Benzalkonium chloride is a preservative used in many eye drops and in some cosmetics that causes tear film instability and damage to the goblet cells of the conjunctiva.[269] It should be avoided.

Brownish pigment in the conjunctiva may be associated with high exposure to UV light from the sun. These spots are not uncommon in dark-skinned individuals. Sunglasses may help prevent them.

Small thickened bumps in the whites of the eye, called pinguecula, may be yellow or reddish when irritated. They are caused by protracted exposure to the sun and irritation from dry or windy environments. Using a wide brim hat and sunglasses can help. A pterygium is a similar but more severe growth, sometimes called "surfers eye," that may require medical treatment. These too are caused by sun and other environmental exposures, and they may be prevented or mitigated by the use of sun protection, as well as with eye drops from a doctor. Wrap-around sunglasses of those with side protection are recommended for those with, or at high risk, of pterygium.[270] Surfers may be at increased risk from the saltwater washing away the tear film, or even from skin lotion that may get into the eyes. Sweat running into our eyes during exercise also disrupts the tear film. Headbands that prevent sweat from running into the eyes can help prevent this.

Pearl: Swimming, especially in chlorinated, indoor pools causes red, inflamed conjunctiva and can cause asthma. It is not the chlorine, but rather *chloramine* formed from the reaction of chlorine and urine and sweat (but mostly urine) in the pool that causes eye and lung irritation. Swimmers should wear swimming goggles to protect their eyes, and of course, never pee in a pool.

Wind can be very drying for the eye especially with low humidity. Having the air-conditioner vent in a car directed at the face can dry the eyes, especially for those wearing contact lenses. In dry, dusty areas, wind can blow fine dust and sand particles that can irritate the eyes. When we are outdoors, and our eyes tear and our nose may run, it is often because our eyes are responding to the disruption of the tear film.

While UV radiation is at its greatest from two hours before and after solar high noon, exposure of UV radiation to the eye is highest earlier and later in the day, when the sun is lower on the horizon. UV damage is not just from light directly entering the eye, but as well as from light hitting it laterally, or light that is reflected off of the back of lenses. This is why sunglasses that shield light from the sides (wrap-around sunglasses) should be worn for those at high risk.

Photokeratitis—commonly called "snow blindness" is UV induced inflammation of the cornea (the clear area over the iris, from UV exposure. Snow reflects about 90 percent of the UV that hits it, explaining snow associated UV damage especially at high altitudes, such as in ski resort areas. However, it also can occur among those spending time at beaches such as in Florida and California.[271] Snow blindness is also a problem in the icy north.

Warning: Conjunctivoplasty is a medical procedure sometimes done as cosmetic surgery. It is done under the name "Ibrite" by one clinic. In this procedure the visible conjunctiva is removed, giving the eye a white and younger appearance. A review paper from Wills Eye Institute in Philadelphia found that this procedure has an unacceptably high complication rate even in young, healthy adults. Over 40 percent of those undergoing this procedure have severe long-term complications, and many will require lifetime medical treatment; nearly a third will require additional surgeries. The author strongly advises that this cosmetic procedure is avoided.[272]

Pearls: To keep and help recover white sclera and conjunctiva

☞ Get plenty of sleep.

☞ Avoid removing meibum from the lid margins when washing the face. Keep makeup off the lid margins.

If you use contact lenses – don't sleep with them, even if they are extended wear lenses. Never wear lenses that bother your eyes and remove lenses as soon as your eyes feel dry or irritated. Discard contact lenses that are worn out, damaged or that irritate your eyes.

☞ Take breaks from the use of computer monitors. Get a glass of water and look around so that you don't spend hours fixing your gaze straight ahead. The same goes for watching TV.

☞ Avoid excess alcohol. Drink plenty of water.

☞ Eat plenty of vegetables and fruits with β-carotene. The body converts β-carotene to retinoic acid, a form of vitamin A that helps with the health of the Meibomian glands that keep the eyes lubricated. A diet high in antioxidants or substances such as raw garlic and broccoli that increase antioxidant enzymes may increase the tear production and improve tear film stability.[273]

◉ Eat a diet with a low n-6 to n-3 fatty acid ratio. The long chain n-3 fatty acids found in cold water fish are anti-inflammatory and have a lower melting temperature and thus help produce a better quality meibum and tear film. Several studies have demonstrated that omega-three fat supplements can help with dry eyes. In most of these studies, two to four capsules containing 180 mg of eicosapentaenoic acid and 120 mg of docosahexaenoic acid were used a day. Tear film quality and eye dryness improved after about six weeks.[274] [275] [276] [277] Although omega three capsules work, it takes large doses to get the n-6 to n-3 ratio low enough to decrease the pro-inflammatory actions of n-6 fats in the diet. A healthier choice is a diet low in n-6 polyunsaturated fats combined with eating cold water fish, which are high in n-3 fats, a few times a week. It is having a low ratio of n-6 to n-3 fats that prevents inflammation, rather than the amount of n-3 fats alone. Preventing the loss of Meibomian glands is a much better strategy than trying to cure their loss.

◉ Avoid allergens or get treated for allergies. You may love that cat, but… that cat dander may not love you back. Cat dander remains present in a house for many months after the cats have moved out.

◉ Use wrap-around, UV-protection sunglasses especially in bright and windy environments.

◉ If there is ocular rosacea or blepharitis, consider treatment for *Demodex*. Facial rosacea should also be treated.

◉ Isotretinoin, (Accutane) a medication used for acne should never be used near the eyes as it can cause eye irritation and dryness as it causes dysfunction of the Meibomian glands. Isotretinoin treats acne by inhibiting sebaceous lipid synthesis and is thought to act similarly in the Meibomian glands.

Chapter 14: Fitness and Exercise

When people are overweight or out of shape, it is not just the increase in girth that alters the way they are perceived by others. Increased weight alters the posture, affects skin color, and the shape of the eyes. People can see these features and have an implicit heuristic reaction to them. Exercise not only makes us healthier, more attractive, and less overweight, it makes our brains work better. Like sleep, exercise and cardiovascular fitness correlate with tests of working memory and executive function; it improves function in areas of the brain used in problem-solving. One does not need to run marathons, but we all need exercise. The *minimum* exercise required for brain health is equivalent to walking 20 minutes per day; about one mile. Good health requires more. Vigorous exercise of sufficient intensity to cause sweating several times a week is required to reduce the risk of cancer and to maintain optimal brain health.[278]

Upper body exercise can help develop strong shoulders that add to the perception of robust health and competence.

Clearly, diet is associated with health, vigor, and attractiveness. Most Americans do not get enough green vegetables in their diet, and they eat excessive fatty, fried and preserved foods. Polyunsaturated n-6 fats that are found in most cooking oils (corn, sunflower, safflower, peanut, and soy oils) promote inflammation and raise the risk of chronic diseases including obesity, diabetes, heart disease, Alzheimer's disease, and cancer. Extra virgin olive oil does not. Avoid high fructose corn syrup; your brain cannot use fructose as fuel, but the liver turns it into fat.

Acne: The foods best documented to cause acne are certain dairy products high in lactose. Skim milk is two to four times as likely to cause acne as compared with whole milk. Cottage and cream cheese also increase acne. Hard cheeses are not high in lactose and are not associated with risk for acne. This suggests that lactose and lactose intolerance are associated with acne. The reason is likely their effect on the microbial balance of the gut.[279] Emotional or physical stress can also cause dysbiosis (pathologic changes in the balance of gut bacteria) that promote systemic inflammation.[280] A diet rich in plant fiber can help diversify and normalize the bacterial biome of the intestine and help prevent inflammation and acne.[281]

> Good health prevents acne: Avoid junk food; get sufficient sleep and exercise. To lower the risk of acne, shampoo at least 3 times a week, gently wash your face twice a day and change your pillowcase at least once a week. Medical treatment can prevent acne and scarring. Women with cystic facial acne should ask their gynecologist if they may have polycystic ovary syndrome, which often causes severe facial acne, irregular periods, weight gain, and depression. It is a treatable medical condition, which may further respond to a healthier lifestyle.

The two nutrients most commonly deficient in the American diet are magnesium, which is found in the center of every chlorophyll molecule in green leaves, and vitamin D_3, from sunshine during your 20-minute daily walk. If you live north of the South, however, you live too far north for the sun to make vitamin D_3 in your skin during six months of the year. People living north of San Francisco, St. Louis, or Washington, D.C. get too little sunshine to make vitamin D_3 from October to March. Even in southern latitudes, if you don't get out much, or have dark skin, you may need a vitamin D_3 supplement.

With age the skin thins and adults spend almost all of their time indoors; thus most adults make insufficient Vitamin D in their skin. We get some, vitamin D3 from eating fish and eggs, but not enough. Also, some people with digestive problems waste vitamin D3 from their intestines.. We get some, but not enough vitamin D3 from eating fish and eggs, but not enough. Also, some people with digestive problems waste vitamin D3 from their intestines. Low vitamin D3 levels can cause bone and muscle pain, muscle fatigue, lack of energy, and depression, and it puts one at higher risk for diabetes and osteoporosis. Individuals with darker skin may require 25 times as much sun exposure as fair-skinned persons to make the same amount of vitamin D3. Women, especially those with dark skin or that do not spend a lot of time outside commonly have inadequate vitamin D levels. A young man can make 10,000 units of vitamin D3 by spending 15 minutes in the sun, so taking 2,000 to 5,000 units a day is not going to cause a problem for an adult. Another nutrient commonly in short-supply in the Western diet is choline,[282] a B-vitamin-like compound. There are sufficient amounts of this nutrient in whole foods, but little is present in most processed foods, such as those made from wheat flour, starchy tubers, fats and sugars. Health is an essential element in appearing competent, attractive and trustworthy. Consuming a healthful diet and getting sufficient exercise that one looks and feels well, are essential components to looking the part.

Chapter 15: Eyelashes and Eye Makeup

Thicker, longer, and darker eyelashes are an important aspect of attractiveness. While the simple answer is mascara, allow me to do my thing and complicate it.

Humans typically have about 400 eyelashes; about 100 to 150 in each upper eyelid, with the lashes two or three rows thick, plus about 75 to 80 lashes in a single row on the lower eyelid. It took me several tries to count them all. The upper lashes are usually longer and curve upwards in Caucasians and Africans, but may be straight in Asians. Unlike scalp and other hair on the body, the eyelashes do not typically gray with age.

The eyelash growth cycle ranges from five to eleven months. The lashes grow quickly during an anagen phase, about 0.15 mm a day for about 45 days reaching an average length of about 7 mm, and then stop growing in the catagen phase. The follicle then takes a break from growing (telogen) for four to nine months. The eyelash gets pushed out when the new anagen phase begins. Thus, on average, one eyelash falls out each day. This cycle is considerably different than for the scalp where the anagen growth phase can last for several years.[283] [284]

The hairs in the eyebrows grow for about four to seven months and then stay put there around for three to four weeks before they fall out. The follicle then rests for about nine months. The eyebrows are lazy growers, as half the follicles have no hair at any one time. In comparison, the scalp hair has about 90 percent of its follicles in the anagen growth phase of the cycle at any time.

With age, the hairs of the lashes and eyebrows become less dense, decrease in length, and lose their pigmentation making them less visible.

Mascara and eyeliner can enhance contrast with the sclera and give the perception of youth and health. Healthy skin, replete with carotenoids and with rosy cheeks, adds to color contrast, making the sclera to appear lighter.

Eye Cosmetics

Eye cosmetics are not the eye's best friend. It is not only cosmetics but also eye cosmetic-removers that cause problems. Waterproof cosmetics are more difficult to remove. Oil-free makeup-removers contain surfactants (mild detergents) that also remove meibum, and thus disturb tear film formation, as well as drying the skin of the eyelids. Oil based cleaners are efficient at removing mascara, but oils often end up in the eye and also disrupt the tear film. Micelle-based cosmetic cleansers may cause fewer problems. Contact lenses should be removed prior to removing makeup to avoid spoiling the lenses.[285] Contact lenses should also be removed before an evening shower or face washing, as washing makes it more difficult to remove the lenses.

Cosmetics can cause immediate irritation, and of course, any cosmetic that does should not be used. Eye cosmetics can also accumulate within the tear ducts and conjunctivae over the years. Powdered eyeshadow used above the eye is particularly likely to get into the eye and cause irritation. Some types of mascara contain nylon fibers to elongate the lashes and these fibers can fall into and irritate the eye.

Mascara use is associated with the dreaded disease milphosis. Milphosis is the loss of eyelashes. Milphosis was experienced by 30% of female medical students who used mascara, but only 13.6% of those who didn't. Sixty percent of those using mascara reported mostly minor eye problems while only 27% of those not using mascara did. It may have been the vigorous removal of waterproof mascara that caused the loss of eyelashes that was observed among women in this study. Women who used oil or tissue to remove waterproof mascara had a greater loss of lashes.[286] Also, curling of lashes, after the application of mascara, causes milphosis, as the lashes tend to stick to the curler.

Pearl: If you curl your eyelashes, do it before applying mascara to avoid the loss of eyelashes.

Pearl: A marked loss of eyelashes can result from thyroid disease. If you notice a distinct loss of lashes, it may be time to see your doctor.[287]

Cosmetics and skin creams can spoil contact lenses, creating irritation and causing them to need to be discarded. Skin creams may also affect the glands of the eyelids causing problems with the eye and tear film.[288]

Cosmetics can become easily contaminated with bacteria. Avoid sharing makeup with others and discard makeup that you suspect may be contaminated with bacteria. Eye makeup does not offer a cosmetic advantage if it causes red eyes.

Pearl: Less expensive makeup is easier to throw out and replace with new, uncontaminated makeup than is the expensive stuff. This is a scientific fact.

Pearl: Bedtime application of castor oil to the eyebrows with a mascara brush can enhance the appearance of the brows, making them appear fuller, apparently by increasing their luster.[289]

Chapter 16: Other Cosmetics

Wearing makeup is associated with higher earnings potential and higher job status for women. Thus, it is easy to conclude that women benefit from the use of makeup. While true, however, makeup if not appropriately used, can also cause difficulty for women.

Women are considered more attractive when wearing make up by both men and women. Men also perceive women to be of higher prestige when they wear makeup. [290] I think that in this case prestige may mean "out of my league" for these men.

Female faces with more luminous contrast, larger eyes, and redder lips are considered to be more feminine and more attractive. Another feature is smoother, more even skin. As we age, the contrast in the face declines. Adding contrast can thus give a more youthful appearance. All these are easily achieved with makeup.

When men and women rate the attractiveness of women using cosmetics, there is agreement in the amount of makeup that is found to be optimally attractive. However, when people were asked what amount of makeup they thought other people would find most attractive, they overestimated the amount, especially when estimating the amount that men would find attractive. *When women applied their own makeup to optimize attractiveness, they applied it in amounts far in excess of what others considered to be optimal.*[291]

Pearl: Less is more with cosmetics; most women over apply makeup. Avoid applying makeup for what you think others will prefer. Find a cosmetologist that makes other people look good, and have them teach you what works best for you.

Professionally applied makeup has been found to increase attractiveness more than self-applied cosmetics. It has also been found that for highly attractive women, there is a smaller increase in attractiveness from the use of makeup and that less attractive women have a higher incremental gain from its use. Thus, women of average attractiveness get a greater boost in attractiveness from cosmetics. This is especially true when they are personally trained on how to apply it by a professional. In a study that compared female models that were considered slightly more attractive than average university students with supermodels, makeup increased the attractiveness of the supermodels by about two percent, but increased attractiveness in the more ordinary models by 33 percent.[292]

Heavy makeup makes women less recognizable and decreases the amplitude of brain-waves when faces are flashed on a screen compared to light makeup. Using light makeup increases recognition and brain-wave amplitude.[293] [294] More attractive faces are also more easily remembered.[295] Thus, use of light makeup can make a woman's face more easily recognized and easier to remember than if the woman uses either no makeup or heavy makeup.

Pearl: when meeting someone new for the first time, using light makeup will make a woman more easily remembered.

Contrast

The luminance contrast between facial features has important impacts on the perception of attractiveness of the face. For women, an increase in contrast between the skin and the lips and eyes increases attractiveness. A higher contrast between these features reduces the perception of masculinity and increases attractiveness.

Women have more luminance contrast between the lips and eyes and the surrounding skin than do men, and this contrast influences the perception of gender. Androgynous faces can be made to appear more feminine by increasing contrast and less feminine by decreasing it. Cosmetics used by women increase facial contrast and thus increase the perception of femininity. [296]

Men, while having an overall lower contrast in their faces, have a higher contrast between the eyebrows and surrounding skin. Men have a more prominent upper orbital bone and thicker eyebrows. These features make a face appear more masculine as it accentuates the heavier brow of a masculine face. As people age, there is a decline in facial contrast among all races.[297]

This difference in contrast provides the appearance of health (fertility), and thus attractiveness. The perception of health and attractiveness is increased by:

- ❖ A greater luminance and yellowness contrast between the skin and the eyebrows
- ❖ A greater luminance, redness, and yellowness contrast between the skin and sclerae of the eyes

❖ A greater luminance and redness contrast between the skin and lips.[298]

One of the ways that cosmetics increase attractiveness in women is that it increases the luminous contrast of the face, particularly between the facial skin and the eyes and mouth. This luminance contrast enhances femininity and attractiveness in women and can be used to give women a more youthful and feminine appearance as they mature. Makeup that increases contrast reduces masculinity and attractiveness in the faces of men and is thus not often used by men.

Figure 16-1: Makeup increases attractiveness by increasing contrast. The image on the right has been modified; the skin is smoothed, sclerae whitened and the lips have been contrast-enhanced lips.

The eyebrows thin with age and lighten, thus darkening the brows can add contrast and give a healthier and more attractive appearance. As we age the lips thin and lose their rosy color and become duller; lipstick protects the lips from sun damage and increases the appearance of health and attractiveness.

Pearl: Prevention: Both lipstick and SPF 15 UV protection lip balm can prevent UV exposure that accelerates aging of the lips. Smoking accelerates aging of the lips. Dietary carotenoids, discussed in Chapter 12, also protect the skin and lips from sun damage.

Eyeliner and Mascara

Larger eyes give a younger and more attractive look, and eyeliner and mascara can make the eyes look about six to seven percent larger in area. However, while this illusion works for either eyeliner or mascara; there is no additional gain by adding one to the other. Eyeshadow can also create an optical illusion of larger, slightly wider eyes. Perhaps the most surprising findings in a study of this illusion from makeup are just how little eyeliner, mascara or eyeshadow is needed to maximize these effects. Lightly applied mascara to the upper and lower lashes was just as effective as heavier mascara and eyeliner in giving the illusion of larger eyes. In this study mascara and eyeliner were used mostly on the lateral two-thirds of the upper lid to give the eyes a wider and more juvenile appearance.[299] In the eyeshadow experiment, only a subtle amount of eyeshadow, blended in, applied to the upper, outer orbital area was used. The illusion relies on fading the eyeshadow lighter away from the eye. [300] When properly applied, even a small amount of eye makeup can give large effects.

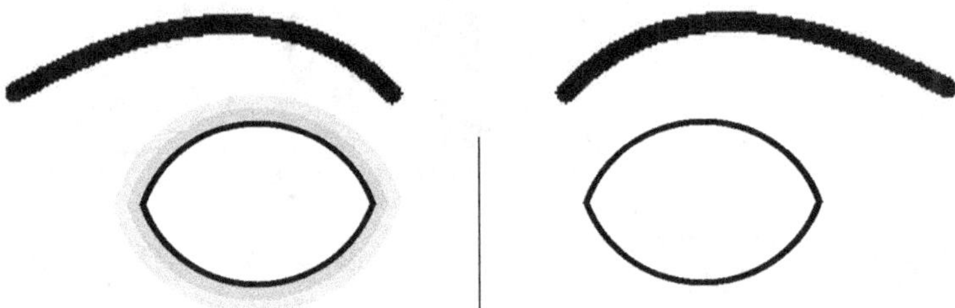

Figure 16-2: A ring of shading around the eye-shape makes it appear bigger, but closer together to the midline.

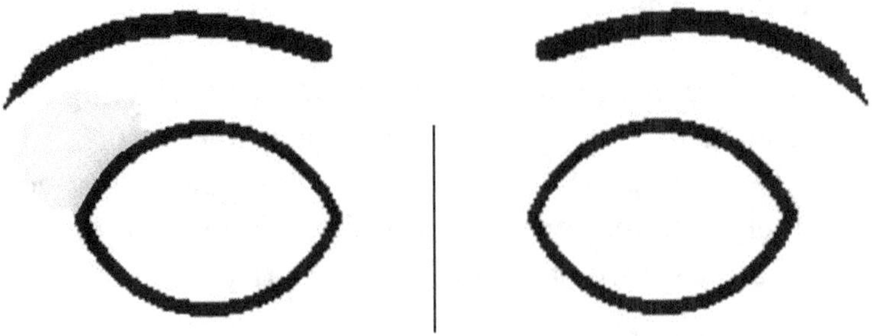

Figure 16-3: The eye-shape on the left appears slightly larger, farther away, and closer to the "brow-line" as a result of the shadow around it. Only a small shadow is needed for this effect. Lateral placement of the shadow also gives the perception that the eye is slightly moved outwards, and upward. The shadow should fade away from the eye to have a full effect.

Eyeliner can be used to make the eyes appear larger and add contrast by adding a border. If eye liner is used, it should be applied to the outside of the eyelashes, never on the lid margins where it will mix into the meibum. Fast-drying liquid eyeliner should mix less with the meibum than wax pencil eyeliners.

As with most cosmetics, using small amounts gives a better effect than using more; eyeliner to the outer eye makes the eye appear larger. For a light, professional look, use a thin line on the upper lid beginning above the medial edge of the iris and tapering to get slightly thicker at the lateral edge of the eye. If you want to line the lower lid, begin below the center or the outer edge of the iris, and bring it to meet the line of the upper lid, and add a line to create an extra outer upper eyelash. Thus, eyeliner for the lower lid should be thinner and only to the outer third to half of the lid margin.

Pearl: Use dark brown eyeliner rather than a black one as it will give more natural coloring.

YouTube is a great resource for learning how to apply makeup. Look for tips on how to get a natural and professional appearance, but avoid glamorous or sexy makeup for professional situations. "Aly Art" has several excellent YouTube videos on the use of light makeup.

Pearl: If using mascara, eyeliner is not needed. Properly applied, either one makes the eyes look larger. Using two together does not add to the effect. Mascara generally looks more subtle and natural.

Pearl: With age, the eyebrows fade in color. Use an eyebrow pencil just lighter than your natural color. Also, use a hair color a shade or two lighter than your youth color to dye your hair.

Pearl: Moisturized daily, gently exfoliate two to three times a week. Using an eye cream or skin cream to the face at bedtime decreases the appearance of fine facial lines.

Eyeshadow

With aging, the outer corners of the eyes sag just a bit, the eyelids may droop a tad, and the eyelashes thin and become less apparent. It makes the eyes less open and makes older people appear less energetic.

The common use of eyeshadow to increase attractiveness may seem surprising in light of the fact that it decreases the contrast between the eye and the surrounding skin. Furthermore, younger, healthier skin around the eye is both redder and yellower in youth and health, yet women commonly use greenish and bluish eyeshadow. What's up with that?

The use of eyeshadow trades away a more youthful appearance for one that is more sexual. The darkening of the region above the eye decreases brow contrast and thus enhances this masculine aspect.[301] At the same time, it increases the contrast with the white of the eye. Eyeshadow also lowers the perceived distance between the brow and the eye, giving a more assertive appearance. This may act as a clue of sexual intent. Indeed, just as women perceive other women wearing red to be more sexually promiscuous, and have more feelings of jealousy towards them (See Chapter 23) they also view women wearing glamorous makeup as more attractive to men, more dominant and promiscuous. Women also experience more jealousy toward women wearing glamorous makeup.[302] Heavier eye makeup makes younger women appear more mature, another cue that suggests fertility and sexual readiness.

Pearl: Eye shadow can be effective for evening use, for increasing the perception of beauty, fertility and availability. It is not such a good lure for voters, especially female voters. Although it can increase the perception of dominance, in a professional setting it does not increase the perception of competence but decreases the perception of likeability and trustworthiness, and can act as a distraction.[303]

If used in a professional setting, limit eyeshadow use to just the upper outer area as shown in Figure 16-3 to increase the apparent width and size of the eyes, and use natural skin tones. Keep it subtle.

Foundation and Blush

As discussed in Chapter 12, having an even and glowing complexion is a sign of health, youth, and attractiveness. Using a foundation evens the skin tone and hides many blemishes and inhomogeneities of the skin. Blush adds redness to the cheeks and can be used to shape the face, giving it the appearance of higher cheekbones and even a thinner face.

When facial photographs were manipulated to smooth the appearance of the skin, it increased not only the attractiveness and perception of the health of the person but also increased the perception of competence and trustworthiness.[304]

With aging, there are many changes in the skin. The clues people use most in estimating age are changes to the skin in the eye area and the loss of skin color uniformity in the rest of the face. Additionally, younger people associate dark circles under the eyes, a deepening nasolabial fold and brown spots with old age estimates, while older adults notice the loss in lip border and a decrease in eye openness.[305]

Many years worth of skin damage can be avoided through the use of sunscreen and a diet high in carotenoids and polyphenols. For those who find themselves with damage, mitigation can be done with cosmetics. Even for older persons, a diet high in lycopene and carotene will give a healthier appearance and color to the skin. Foundation should then be matched to this healthy color rather than the pallid color of poorly nourished sun damaged skin. Caution needs to be used to avoid overuse of foundation in older women as it can settle into wrinkles accentuating them.

Lipstick

The implicit goal for the traditional use of lipstick is to show health and reproductive fitness, but as well as to mimic sexual arousal. When people are sexually aroused, there is increase blood flow to the face and lips. Bluish, pallid, or grey skin suggests anemia or hypothermia. A darker (brownish) lipstick will make a younger woman appear older. A lighter, pinker lipstick can give a more youthful appearance. Women have the same average thickness of the upper lip as do men but have a slightly thicker lower lip. Women wearing lip gloss or glossy lipstick are considered to be more attractive.[306]

As we age, our lips become less prominent. The upper lip (the area between the base of the nose and the top lip) lengthens, the volume of the lips decreases, and the red area of the lips rolls inward, exposing less color. The lips also become wider and the lateral tips bend downwards with aging. As the skin ages, the lips also lose color. This causes lips to be less prominent, thinner and have less color with age.[307] It can also give older people a slight permanent frown, making them look grumpy. Also, by the time people are in their 40's, the philtral columns, the two ridges in the center of the upper lip, collapse, and with it, the M-shape cupid's bow of the top lip begins to disappear. Lipstick can thus be used to make the lips look more feminine, younger, or older.

In an experimental setting, participants were asked to manipulate the color of the lips of men and women on a computer screen to increase attractiveness. The participants increased the redness of the lips of Caucasian women and reduced the redness in the lips of Caucasian men and reduced blueness more in women than men.[308]

Thus, lipstick increases attractiveness for several reasons:

- ❖ It increases the contrast between the lips and the skin.
- ❖ Redder lips look healthier
- ❖ Redder lips can show sexual arousal
- ❖ Wet appearing lips also show health and arousal
- ❖ Fuller lips look more feminine and youthful
- ❖ Lipstick can be used to give a more youthful or more mature appearance.

As in other areas of cosmetics, the goal in choosing a lipstick to enhance professional appearance of competence, attractiveness, and gravitas, is to increase contrast and appearance of health, without appearing sexually aroused or vulnerable. For women with light skin, this means choosing a lipstick color that is somewhat darker and redder than their natural skin color, without going too bright red that gives a sexual appearance. Women with very dark skin may increase lip contrast by going lighter and rosier.

Pearl: The natural youthful color of one's lips can usually be found just inside of the lower lip, where the lip has not been exposed to the sun, but outside of the pale buccal mucosa. Using lipstick that matches this color can give a natural, youthful appearance.

An experiment was conducted in a carefully controlled laboratory setting to determine the effect of lipstick color; it was done in a popular bar on the Atlantic coast of France. The average delay-time before a young woman was approached by an unfamiliar man when she was not wearing lipstick was 27 minutes, with brown lipstick it was 24.83 minutes, for pink it was 23.35 minutes, and for red lipstick the delay was only 19.78 minutes before the woman was approached.[309]

Pearl: Steer clear of fire-engine or candy red lipstick in professional and other settings where an overtly sexy look is not the objective.

Younger women can take on a more mature look by using a darker colored lipstick. Wine, burgundy, and brown lipsticks make women look older.

Older women can thicken their lips slightly by using a makeup pencil, thus, adding contrast to the lower borders of the lips. The lip liner should be applied before the lipstick, and the color either that of the lipstick or the natural color of their lips, and then blended in with the lipstick. The lower lip can be made to look fuller by adding a millimeter wide line to the natural lower border of the lip. No more than about one millimeter is needed to give the lips a more youthful appearance. Women can also narrow the apparent width of the lips and give them the appearance of a pleasant upward curve using a lip liner pencil.

Pearl: Use a lip liner the natural color of your lips and blend it into the lipstick you are using. A lip liner pencil can be used to subtly recreate the peaks on the M of the cupid's bow of the upper lip.

For professional situations, a lipstick that can be put on while on the go and that lasts for six hours has a great advantage over ones that come off in a couple of hours and will not make it through a lunch meeting. Also, the carefully applied lipstick and liner that take 10 minutes to apply and look great for a photo session, are likely not the same as a lipstick that can be applied in the rear-view or restroom mirror before walking into a meeting. As women age, it becomes helpful to use lipstick that does not migrate or bleed into lip wrinkles.

Pearl: "Wet n Wild Mega Last Lip Color ™ ($1.99) has been highly rated as a superior choice for long-lasting easy-to-apply lipstick.[310]

Pearl: To avoid lipstick migration, apply it with a brush or your finger rather than applying it directly. Top it with a gloss or balm.

If a person has not grown up in a home or community that placed value on outward appearances, stylish clothing, make-up, and hairstyling can seem to be nothing other than vanities. Certainly, considerable wealth may be spent on clothing and accessories, or plastic surgery. Nevertheless, looking fit, healthy and attractive does not need to be expensive. Most people can make marked improvements in their appearance with a moderate effort. It does, however, take attention. Many people, especially young people, are naturally beautiful. Nonetheless, most of the people others perceive to be beautiful, put effort into their physical appearance. No one should feel obliged to wear makeup. The goal for use of makeup in this context is not to appear sexy or to try to conform to a hegemonic standard of beauty, but rather to increase access to leadership roles. Makeup can be used to enhance the appearance of health and competence

At the time of this writing in 2022, there are 24 women in the US Senate. Their ages range from 45 to 74, with the exception of Diane Feinstein (age 88). In their official portraits, all are using lipstick and appear to be wearing foundation and blush. Almost all are using mascara, and many use an eyelash pencil to darken their eyebrows. Only two are clearly using eyeshadow. Only one is using eyeliner, and she would have been better off without it. Almost all have a good healthy color and appear bright, vigorous and competent. None has gray or white hair, although, in many photos, roots are evident but not pronounced. Thus, most if not all these women color their hair.

The United States Army Code of Conduct prescribes dress and grooming codes. The Army dress code makes good, general, professional advice for anyone seeking professional or leadership positions. Here is what it says about the use of cosmetics.

Army Regulations on the use of cosmetics

AR 670-1 Chapter 3, paragraph 2b. *b. Cosmetics*

(1) Standards regarding cosmetics are necessary to maintain uniformity and to avoid an extreme or unprofessional appearance. Males are prohibited from wearing cosmetics, except when medically prescribed. Females are authorized to wear cosmetics with all uniforms, provided they are applied modestly and conservatively, and that they complement both the Soldier's complexion and the uniform. Leaders at all levels must exercise good judgment when interpreting and enforcing this policy.
(2) Eccentric, exaggerated, or faddish cosmetic styles and colors, to include makeup designed to cover tattoos, are inappropriate with the uniform and are prohibited. Permanent makeup, such as eyebrow or eyeliner, is authorized as long as the makeup conforms to the standards outlined above. Eyelash extensions are not authorized unless medically prescribed.
(3) Females will not wear shades of lipstick that distinctly contrast with the natural color of their lips, that detract from the uniform, or that are faddish, eccentric, or exaggerated.

Although the army's take on cosmetics is not exactly what makes a woman appear most attractive, sticking with lipstick colors that are near natural for the woman is not a bad idea. The complete text of the Army Regulation 670–1: *Wear and Appearance of Army Uniforms and Insignia* can be found at:

https://www.army.mil/e2/c/downloads/337951.pdf

. It is worth repeating: The goal as a candidate for leadership is not to look like a sexy 26-year-old fashion model, but rather to appear healthy, engaged, competent, and adult.

Pearl: Makeup is the most effective when it is the least obvious.

Chapter 17: Faux Pas

What Not To Do

A survey of 2800 human resource managers revealed the major reasons qualified candidates were passed over for jobs they were otherwise qualified for. They were:

- Body piercings
- Bad breath
- Visible tattoos
- Wrinkly clothing, and
- Messy hair [311]

Body Piercings

Other than a single piercing for earrings, avoid visible pierced jewelry for interviews. For men, if you don't think it will help with an interview, leave it off. This also applies to photographs, which might be seen on a Facebook page by a prospective employer or elsewhere you wish to present yourself in a professional light.

Halitosis

Halitosis, bad breath, is a professional liability. It is mostly caused by bacteria that release volatile sulfur compounds. It can be caused by lung, tonsil or sinus infection, so if cleaning the mouth does not work, see your doctor.

Halitosis can be caused by poor dental hygiene, so attend to that. Most halitosis, however, is caused by food residue and bacteria on the tongue and between the teeth. Thus, it is not enough to brush one's teeth; the tongue should also be brushed to remove any coating so that the tongue is pink. Dental flossing is essential.

Much of the bad breath comes from the bacterial fermentation of food particles and other detritus that accumulate in the mouth. The detritus that adheres to the tongue can be removed by holding water in the mouth and brushing the tongue when the teeth are brushed. Waterpiking and flossing also helps get rid of foodjatives and criminal plaque. When you are done, the tongue should be dark pink, not white, yellowish, or any other color.

Sinus and lung infections can also cause foul breath. If you eat garlic, it will stay on the breath for a day or so; avoid it before interviews. Don't smoke.

In a systematic review of the medical literature, zinc citrate containing toothpastes were one of the most effective treatments for bad breath other than halitosis caused by infections.[312] Zinc in the toothpaste appears to either prevent or neutralize the volatile sulfur compounds that give morning mouth its reek. Zinc in toothpaste, along with fluoride may also help remineralize the teeth,[313] a good thing, as it hardens the teeth and may help fill tiny defects. The zinc also helps prevent plaque accumulation.[314]

Pearl: Toothpaste containing zinc citrate decreases bad breath. Tom's of Maine® toothpaste contains zinc citrate without fluoride. Colgate Sensitive Toothpaste (Multiprotection)® contains 2% zinc citrate and fluoride. Many forms of Pepsodent® toothpaste also contain zinc citrate.

NOTE: if you live in an area with high levels of fluoride in the water, excess fluoride from toothpaste can cause mottling and softening of the teeth. In areas where the water is fluoridated, African American children are especially susceptible to fluorosis of the teeth. Fluoride consumption can cause or exacerbate thyroid dysfunction. Fluoridated toothpaste should be avoided, especially if the water is fluoridated. I advise avoiding fluoridated toothpaste during pregnancy and in young children.

Pearl: If you fill your mouth with water and close your lips around the toothbrush, it makes it much easier to brush and float debris off the tongue while decreasing the gag reflex at the same time.

Your Pearly Whites

A healthy smile with white teeth is an important aspect of attractiveness and for the perception of competence and self-confidence. Studies with functional MRIs show that subjects have increased activity in the medial orbitofrontal cortex of the brain when shown photos of people smiling. This is a reward area of the brain that is also stimulated by pleasant music, tasty food, and monetary gain. Thus, when someone smiles at us as if they are happy to see us, it makes us feel good. It even works when seeing photos.

A study compared photos of political candidates for the lower houses of Japan (180 seats) and Australia (150 seats), which are similar to the US House of Representatives. Photos were taken from campaign posters or voting materials. Thus, they were a photo that had been selected by the candidate for their campaigns. Using computer software for recognition of facial expression, each candidate's photo was scored from zero to 100 percent full smile. A smile that did not show the teeth fully, or in which the mouth but not the eyes smiled was recognized as a partial smile and given a percentage score. Even in Japan, where smiling without showing the teeth is considered polite, full smile campaign photos were associated with getting more votes. After controlling for many other potential influences, a candidate with a full smile in their photo enjoyed a 2.3 percentage point boost over no smile, and in Australia, with a culture more similar to America's, there was a 5.2 percentage boost in votes, enough to swing most elections. The effect appears to be linear, with the benefit increasing with the size of the smile, from no smile to a full, pleasant, toothy, natural smile.[315]

Make sure your teeth are in good repair and white. As my daughter's Boy Scout master would tell the kids, "You only need to brush the ones you want to keep." (Old Larry had more daughters than sons, and didn't see much reason not to have girls as part of his scout troop). Floss and Waterpik daily.

Braces are a gift from parents to children who need them, as they give a lifetime boost in appearance, and function.

Most people can successfully use the fairly inexpensive, over-the-counter Crest® whitening strips. Most dentists offer professional whitening or home whitening kits.

> Note: orthodontic braces are generally associated with a lifetime commitment to wearing a retainer at night to keep the teeth in place, as they tend to migrate back with time. But a great smile is worth it.

Pretty much anything that stains cotton will stain your teeth. Coffee and wine come to mind. Nursing a cola is a great way to stain and rot your teeth, as slowly sipping it over an extended period repeatedly feeds bacteria in the mouth, and does not give time for the saliva to wash it away.

Pearl: Try Oral-B Glide Pro-Health® deep clean floss, in the silver-gray pack. It is the most comfortable and effective floss I have found, and that encourages regular use.

Orthodontic braces or other medical intervention may be appropriate for improving physical appearance. The pearly white smile is not only a sign of health and vitality; it is a sign of non-aggression, one of the primal, instinctual clues. Poor dentition gives the impression of a sick, effete individual.

Pearl: Smile. Make eye contact and smile.

Tattoos

Although a tattoo may only cost $100, its real cost may be thousands of dollars per year in lost salary. Removing a tattoo can easily cost $10,000. Individuals with exposed tattoos are perceived to be less educated, less acquiescent, more intransigent and vagarious, thus more difficult to manage and work with.

Even though tattoos are much more common in recent years, and thus more accepted in a variety of workplaces, they do not add credibility, particularly for women. For men, they are perceived as a bit of risky bad-boy behavior which is often acceptable. Not so much for women, especially for women in positions of authority.

Women with tattoos were judged harshly. They were rated by both men and woman their age as being less physically attractive, to be heavier drinkers and to be more sexually promiscuous, with an increasing rating of these attributes by the number of tattoos.[316] In another experimental study, temporary tattoos were used so that the same model could be used with, and without tattoos. Men were more likely to approach women on a beach reading a book when they had a tattoo on their lower back than when they did not. The men reported that they felt more likely to get a date with the tattooed woman and more likely to have sex on the first date.[317]

Another study looked at the attractiveness and credibility of both men and women with tattoos. Although in this study, as with other recent studies, individuals with tattoos were not considered to be less attractive, however, they were judged to have lower credibility.[318]

Pearl: Visible tattoos should be avoided. Although much more accepted now than in the past, tattoos can still be a detriment to employment and to attaining leadership positions. The owner of "Body Electric" tattoo and piercing studio in Hollywood California, advises clients against tattoos on the hands, neck, and face. He calls tattoos on the face "job stoppers" adding "if you don't want to get employed, tattoo your face."[319]

Pearl: Tattoo removal can be done by laser; however, it is painful, expensive, difficult, and only partially effective. Better to use tattoos that wash off! With temporary tattoos, you can appear reckless when it suits you and can make them go away tomorrow.

If you want to express yourself with body art, do it with a radical haircut, dyed fluorescent green, and clothing styles, or a henna drawing. When you tire of these, you can let your hair grow out, pick a new hair color, change your fashion, and wash the drawing off. How confident are you that you will still admire the body art you think is cool today, in 10 or 20 years, when it is blurring? Ask yourself, would you choose the same tattoo today that you thought was cool when you were 12?

Warning: Black Henna temporary tattoos (illegal in the U.S.) contain para-phenylenediamine (PPD) a chemical also found in black hair dye. Tattoos with PPD cause allergic sensitization in many of people that later cause allergic reactions with the use of black hair coloring or even to new clothing dyed with this agent.[320] In children with G6PD deficiency, skin contact with natural henna can cause life threatening breakdown of red blood cells.

Wrinkly Clothes

Iron your clothes for interviews and other occasions when you will be judged (everywhere). Use permanent press clothing to look sharp.

Since physical attractiveness is closely tied to success and improves self-esteem, efforts to improve appearance may be an astute investment into your future, rather than an indulgence in vanity.

Messy Hair

Messy hair is another common reason cited for not hiring otherwise qualified job candidates. Healthy primates, such as macaques normally groom each other, but those who suffer social defeat do not; they are left to groom themselves. Thus, when a primate is well groomed, it means that they are cared for by members of their group. When a primate is poorly groomed, it suggests that he or she has been rejected by their troop. When we see someone with wild, unkempt hair, we wonder if they are crazy or dangerous. Only Bernie Sanders could get away with that look, and it may not have helped him.

The primal first impression of someone with well-groomed hair is that they are healthy, loved, cared for and valued. The instinctual reaction to someone with messy hair is that the individual has been subjugated, rejected by, or lost its family, perhaps due to disease. Such individuals are implicitly considered risky.

Clean, groomed hair provides the perception of youth and vitality. Using a good conditioner adds body and sheen to hair, giving it a more youthful healthy appearance. In youth, when hair is clean and healthy, it is shiny and full, and lies nicely.

But when we have a fever, hair may become matted and sweaty. When malnourished, hair becomes dry, frizzled and thin. As we age, the hair does not grow as long, thins out, loses color, and becomes dry. As adults age, aside from losing hair, hairs on the scalp become about 20 percent finer. This results in limp, flat looking hair that can easily blow in the wind and appear unkempt. When hair has not been washed, it also appears limp and flat. Thus hair reflects an individual's health and vitality.

Hair needs to be well groomed and in place in order to appear competent. It should be clean and shiny. Hairstyles that look easy to care for give the impression of being practical and busy, rather than vain and leading a life of leisure. The army code regulations for hairstyle give a professional look that is appropriate for most situations. The code was revised in late 2014 to accommodate hairstyles for African-American women.[321]

Keep your hair clean and neat. If you have difficulty maintaining neat hair, consider a hairstyle that demands little care.

The woman with the longest hair in Congress is Tulsi Gabbard of Hawai'i, also one of the youngest members. Her hair rests on her shoulders. (She does not hide her scattered grey hairs, perhaps to add gravitas to her look.) As women get older, having shorter hair gives a younger look.

Hairstyles frame the face and change the perception of the person. A study by a professor of Women's Studies at Yale University found that hairstyles influenced observers' perceptions of the person in a blink. Women with styled hair (any style) were perceived as sexier, but less intelligent. Women with very short hairstyles were seen as more confident and outgoing, but less sexy. Women with long blond hair were seen as more affluent, but more narrow-minded. Women with medium length casual styles were seen as good-natured and intelligent.

Longer hair is an indicator of health and provides an impression of better health and youthfulness in women. Long hair makes a stronger impact on the perception of health and attractiveness in less attractive women, but only slightly raises the attractiveness in the perception of health in very attractive women.

Men with front flip back hair were perceived as confident and sexy, but self-absorbed. Men with long hair were perceived to be less well off, but more open-minded. Men with hair parted to one side were perceived to be more intelligent, but narrow-minded. [322]

Hair Parts

The "hair part theory" suggests that parting the hair on the left side accentuates the perception of left brain dominant activities, such as logic and reasoning, stuff of a more masculine domain, and that parting the hair on the right accentuates the appearance of right brain activities associated with intuitive and artistic pursuits, and attributes that are more associated with the feminine. According to this theory, men are perceived to be more gender-normative with a left-sided part and women who part their hair on the left are perceived to be stronger, but perhaps less feminine. The originator of the theory, John Walters points out that actor Christopher Reeves when playing Clark Kent parted his hair on the right, looking hapless and weak, but had his hair parted on the left as Superman, and looked super-manly. As far as I can find, there is no academic research on the topic, only secular findings.

For example, only six U.S. presidents parted their hair on the right. Three of these are considered among the worst presidents (Buchanan, Andrew Johnson, and Harding), and two of the others (Tyler and Arthur) are considered to have been inconsequential. Hilary Clinton and Margaret Thatcher both wore left sided parts, and both were considered strong and unfeminine. The decision on how to part their hair likely resulted from how they perceived themselves rather than the image they were trying to create with their hair.[323]

According to the statistics available on the HairPartTheory.com website, 66 percent of the members of the 110th U.S. Congress parted their hair on the left, 19 percent on the right, 16 percent had a part in the center, no part or were bald. Also, 57 percent of CEOs were found to have left parts, and only 12 percent had right parts. Women CEOs and members of Congress, however, were about equally likely to have their hair parted on the right. When a series of portraits of writers was examined, 27 percent parted their hair on the left, and 32 percent did on the right.

The actual determinant of the side that hair is parted on is likely the direction of the scalp whorl at the crown of the head. If the hair spiral grows clockwise, the part more naturally falls on the left, and the hair will have more volume combed to the right. If the whorl is counterclockwise, the part is more natural on the right. The formation of the hair whorl occurs at 10 to 16 weeks of fetal development and is then fixed for life. Over 90 percent of Americans have clockwise hair whorls, while in Japan it occurs in about half the population. The whorl can be hard to detect in people with long or thin hair. About five percent of the population has double whorls.[324] Triple whorls may be associated with things gone wrong during fetal development.

There is some evidence that the direction of the whorl may be related to cerebral language dominance.[325] Most people are right eye and right hand dominant. Less common is left hand and left eye dominance. And then some people are hand-eye cross dominant. Not only are cross-dominant persons less accurate in shooting baskets and guns, but cross-dominant men may also be at higher risk of schizophrenia[326] and are more likely to suffer from migraines with auras.[327] Subtle differences in cerebral dominance may be reflected in the way that the hair lays and thus how it is parted, and this may be included in the heuristic assessment of faces. Thus, the hair part theory is ever-so-slightly plausible.

There are some evidence-based conclusions that can be counted on when it comes to parting the hair. The first, is that a left part is more common among American men; the second is that parting the hair against the natural lie adds more volume as the hair tends to stand up more. This can give a healthier appearance. It is also fairly certain that changing the direction the hair is combed will not alter brain function significantly.

Pearl: Parting against the natural lay of the hair may give more volume as the hair will not lay down as much as when it is parted in the direction that the hair lays.

Pearl: Perhaps because it is more normative for men to part their hair on the left, some observers consider a left-side part to be perceived as more dynamic. Those who would like to be perceived as more thoughtful, creative, and caring, but less dominant may try parting their hair on the right to see if it works for them.

Pearl: Women who wish to appear more feminine can try parting their hair on the right; those who wish to accentuate their intelligence and appear more dynamic can try parting their hair on the left. More attractive women are said to appear more dynamic with a left part without detracting from their femininity. Of course, this theory may not hold any water.

Pearl: Remember that what you see in the mirror is the reverse of how other people see you. Use a photo to see how others see you. Ask independent observers to give unbiased feedback comparing photos with parts on each side, as to which appears dynamic, approachable, competent and attractive. Assume that your own appraisal will be biased.

Pearl: The typical place for a side part is above the center of either eye, and it thus draws more attention to that eye.

Pearl: No matter what side you part your hair on, directing the part so that it angles towards the crown of the head, distributes the hair more evenly, and make the hair and head appear more balanced.

Select a hairstyle that projects the image you want for yourself. The most important component of hair is that it appears well groomed: that the hair is clean, shiny, not dull, matted, or lifeless. On a primal, subliminal level, this will provide an image of health, vigor, and vitality. It suggests that you have people that care about you and that you are valued.

The single most important thing about hair is that it looks well groomed and neat, without flying cowlicks, or looking like you have been on a bender or sleeping in your car or on a park bench. Pick a style that looks good even when you are not in front of a mirror, and that does not need a lot of maintenance throughout the day.

Pearl: While thick hair on a man gives the appearance of health and vigor, noticeably fine, thinning hair can cause men to look weak or waning. Men with shaved heads are perceived to be more dominant, confident, masculine, an inch taller, and 13 percent stronger than men with hair, but are considered less attractive and appear about four years older. Men with thinning hair are perceived to be less attractive, dominant, confident, and masculine, and physically weaker than men with either thick hair or shaved heads. Men with thinning hair also had a non-significant decline in the perception of their leadership rating.[328] Men with thinning hair may consider shaving their heads to be seen as stronger and more attractive. A toupee may also work.

Other Hair

I remember as a small child being terrified of old people. They looked like witches and goblins to me. Looking back, I'm convinced that those old folks were much uglier than the contemporary elderly now are. It was not the wrinkles or even the long earlobes and nose, or saggy jowls that got to me. What was frightening to me was their bad breath, skin lesions, and worst of all, the whiskers growing out their noses, bristles coming out of their ears, and old ladies with mustaches and chin hair.

As men age, not only does the scalp hair thin, but they get more nose and coarse ear hair, bushier eyebrows, and even hair growing on the tip of the nose. As women get older, there is often a testosterone effect that causes thinning of the hair on the scalp, and an increase of facial hair, especially on the upper lip and chin. Aging is a process in which less hair grows where one wants it and more grows where it is unwanted.

Part of impeccable grooming associated with competence is not having visible nose hair, whiskers sprouting from the ears, or odd bristles on the chin.

Pebble: Men with clean-shaven faces are perceived to be less dominant, and with light stubble, heavy stubble, and bearded faces they are perceived to be increasingly dominant.[329]

Men can shave their mustache and beard, but women generally only have sparse hair and shaving creates unsightly stubble.

Pebble: Most nicks during shaving are slices from pulling the razor along the wrong angle. Always pull the razor straight in the direction of the handle. A closer shave comes with shaving against the lay of the hairs.

Contrary to folk wisdom, plucking and shaving do not cause hair to grow back darker or coarser. The best solution to unwanted stray hairs is plucking and other forms of epilation. Tweezing removes one hair at a time, and is the best solution for removal of limited numbers of hairs. Waxing, sugaring, and threading pull out many hairs from an area where there is a denser growth. With each treatment, generally 2 to 5 weeks apart, the regrowth will be lighter and finer. Laser hair removal only works on dark hairs and can cause inflammation and permanent darkening of the skin area, especially in persons of color. Electrolysis is appropriate when only a small number of hair follicles need to be destroyed. Vaniqa® is a prescription cream that is FDA-approved for use in reducing the growth of unwanted facial hair in women. Over-the-counter hair removal products should not be used on the face and do not give good results.

Pearl: Sugaring is generally considered a less painful method of hair removal than waxing, as it is applied at room temperature and adheres less to the skin than does wax. It is less likely to cause skin injury than does waxing

Peach fuzz: Women commonly develop fine peach-fuzz on their faces as they age. If it is not visible from arm's length in the mirror, or from four feet away by another observer, it is likely not noticeable to anyone the person is not intimate with. Its visibility depends on the color of the downy peach-fuzz and the skin. Bleaching can greatly decrease the visibility of these fine hairs.

Nevertheless, even if it is not noticeable, the peach-fuzz can cause difficulty with makeup, as foundation and powder may stick to the tiny hairs. When applying foundation to a fuzzy area, rub it in and let it dry. Later buff off the excess foundation with a cloth or a clean, slightly dampened makeup sponge. If using a powder foundation, after applying it, mist the face lightly with water to settle the powder, and then gently pat it dry.[330]

Nose Hair: Nose hair helps filter the air, so it is best not to remove them. Plucking is not only painful but can lead to infection. Additionally, if you have ever attempted plucking them, the pain likely had you quickly realize that trimming nose hair is the solution of choice. Well designed water-resistant, battery-operated trimmers work nicely.

Pearl: While hairs can be plucked from the outer ear, do not tweeze hair that emerges from the ear canal, as this skin is easily injured and it can lead to infections. Hairs emerging from the ear canal can be trimmed with an electric trimmer but never use scissors, as they can nick the ear. Ear hair can also be treated with laser by a dermatologist or cosmetic surgeon. Ear hair removal is easier done by a trusted accomplice than by oneself.

Although completely acceptable and considered trendy and even sexy among Millennials, a female candidate's underarm hair is probably not what she wants the conversation to be about. No one will notice or comment on shaved underarms on a woman wearing a sleeveless top or dress. Since it is not a thing a candidate wants to be noticed for, make it and any conversation about it disappear.

Pearl: With weight gain and age many people become insulin resistant. This causes the pancreas to release more insulin to control blood sugar. The increased insulin raises sensitivity to androgens such as testosterone. This insulin resistance and increase in androgen activity also underlies the pathology of polycystic ovary syndrome, which also causes and increase in facial hair. Exercise and a healthy diet can help avoid insulin resistance and unwanted effects of testosterone such as facial hair on women.

Pearl: Use of a boron supplement (6 mg chelated boron daily) can increase the conversion of testosterone into estrogen and help prevent the development of some hormonal effects from testosterone.

"Men and women range themselves, into three classes or orders of intelligence. You can tell the lowest class by their habit of talking about nothing else but persons; the next by the fact that their habit is always to talk about things; the highest by their preference for the discussion of ideas."

Henry Thomas Buckle

Chapter 18: Dress for Authority

Leadership is imbued with authority, and authority with leadership. We follow the advice of our doctors and lawyers based on two important assumptions; firstly that they are considerably more knowledgeable, experienced, and objective than we are in their area of expertise, and secondly, they are honest advocates on our behalf.

Social power gives authority. Police are granted an incredible amount of power, and if we decline to defer to them, it puts us in great peril. When we put ourselves in the hands of a surgeon, dentist or lawyer, we acquiesce our future to their competence and good faith. We defer to our bosses as it allows us to continue to earn our livelihoods. And when we vote for politicians, we assent to give the keys of our government to them. These grants of power and authority in a democracy are part of an implicit social contract based on the two premises outlined above; that the person is a legitimate expert and they are acting on our behalf. We make these assumptions and hope for the best.

There are various hallmarks of authority; one is a title. America does not use heritable titles, – or do we? We may not use princes, countess, duchess, duke or lord, but how many politicians gain access to power based on their family name? Three generations of Bushes, plenty of Kennedys and numerous political dynasties at the state and local level have controlled high government offices for generations.

Another form of title is a job or professional title. My personal favorite is doctor; others include professor, CEO, CFO, executive secretary, sheriff, general, major, or inspector. There are academic and professional certifications, such as MBA, PE, and many others. These titles are meant to give an objective certification of competence in an area.

Another important clue to role and authority in society is clothing. The guy in the chef's hat and garb likely works as a cook and the ones in the orange pajamas on the side of the road are likely conscripted. An important means of evincing authority is to dress the part. We follow the directions of those nice people in uniforms directing traffic and hope we are white when they pull us over. We assume that people are who they dress to be and how they present themselves.

Like many of our decisions, we make implicit choices based on the costume of the wearer.

I recently saw an excerpt from a TV show in which the host was wearing surgical scrubs and was interviewing a doctor about a medical procedure. The implicit message was that the host was a doctor and thus a knowledgeable and credible medical expert. However, it backfired for me, as I see wearing surgical scrubs outside of the hospital as unprofessional. Most often, when I see them worn outside the hospital, it is by non-professional med-techs or orderlies. Seeing this person wear scrubs caused a dissonance; rather than my making an automatic assumption of his expertise, I questioned it. I realized it was an attempt to manipulate the audiences perception. Although he may have been a doctor, it broke the illusion, and he lost credibility.

Most of the time, however, we trust our eyes and assume the cues are correct. Professors may wear tweed. The business suit is the uniform of an administrator or leader, with more expensive, well-tailored ones associated with higher status and more power. It has been said, however, that women do not have a power suit as men do.

Hillary Clinton, especially later in her career and campaigning for the presidency wore bright, solid-colored pantsuits, red, yellow, blues, green, orange, purple, browns and white, usually with a knit shirt of identical color. This was her power suit. Meanwhile, the male politicians were wearing nearly identical business suits. In one Republican primary in 2016, the eleven male candidates wore nearly identical dark suits, and most of them used a red power tie. The largest variation among them was that one outlier wore brown rather than black shoes.

If Clinton's pantsuit look had been effective, it would have been emulated by other women across the country. She had many supporters, but they were not following her lead on style. This lack of emulation should have been taken as a sign that her clothing was not delivering the message she intended. Instead of serving to project leadership and authority, her clothing became a humorous meme.

In contrast, consider the fictional TV Secretary of State Elizabeth McCord, whose work attire is modern, elegant and feminine. The apparel she wears is becoming, and projects dynamism, competence, and professionalism while being sophisticated, sensible, and modest. There are blog sites dedicated to the clothing shown on her show. She appears at times in a button-up shirt with her sleeves rolled up, ready for work. Her style was crafted to portray power in a feminine form, and it pulls it off.

For men, the classic business attire and a red or blue tie are easily recognizable symbols of authority and power. Let's examine why.

Sports coats and suit jackets have padding that squares the shoulders, giving the impression of strength and vitality. It provides a formal look of professionalism that works equally well for men and women. A man's red tie sends the implicit message of vitality. A blue tie is cooler and may send the message of being reason-based, cautious and deliberative. The V-shape of the shirt under the jacket and tie also gives vertical shapes that give the illusion of height.

It has usually been assumed that the square shoulders from shoulder pads make a man appear more muscular. I suggest the effect is just as much to make the wearer look more optimistic and in control, as opposed to rounded shoulders giving the appearance of a person that may be depressed or defeated. If you look back at the picture of the macaques in Illustration 21-1, you will see the rolled, depressed shoulders. Posture that projects success and resilience is essential to the implicit assumption of competence and authority.

The long sleeve-button down solid color blouse that mirrors a man's button-down oxford can be elegant and feminine, but also practical and professional. On men and women, a button-down shirt can add structure, especially when fitted, rather than a "classical" cut. It can be made of silk or satin to add a more feminine appearance. Top male administrators aren't often seen wearing plaid shirts. Women may benefit by underplaying prints and sticking to solid colors for professional attire.

In place of a tie, women might wear a simple necklace. For women, a vest is not recommended in an attempt to mimic a three-piece suit. Vests are also not suggested for men of less than average stature, as they can make a person look shorter.

Pearl: Keep a change of clothing with you in your car or office in the case of a spaghetti sauce emergency during a business meal. Women are advised to keep a change of shoes so that they can switch into tennis shoes or heels when appropriate.

Pearl: Avoid black clothing, especially for the upper body and neckline; it is aging, and can cause wrinkles to appear deeper. Dark earthy colors are more attractive and can be used in place of black when darker tones are wanted.

Dress the part you want to play. People mostly assess each other at face value. If someone is wearing a police uniform, most people assume the person has some civil authority. If they dress in business garb, suit, and tie, they assume a different type of authority (e.g., expertise or control of capital.) The way a person dresses, their costume, tells others their station in life. The costume you choose will determine how people see you and your role in society. You will get more respect and will more likely be accepted as a legitimate authority when you are dressed for the part, clean and well groomed, even when you act as a firebrand promoting change.

Pearl: Ruffles, bows, hair ribbons, and cute prints can make women appear juvenile and less competent.

Style

Some of us lack a sense of style, don't care, or don't perceive themselves to be attractive, and thus, don't make an effort. Most of us can use the eye of an expert in improving our appearance. Don't be shy about asking a friend with a sense of style, or asking a professional in the field, how you might improve your dress, hairstyle, and other components of your physical appearance.

When clothes don't fit correctly, it can look like something is wrong. A person who is overweight and wearing well-fitted clothing may look big, but if they wear clothing that is too tight, it looks like they are rapidly gaining weight, and out of control. If clothes are too loose, it looks like the person is losing weight, which on a primal level sends a subliminal message that they may have a wasting disease, perhaps infectious, and that they should be avoided. Well-fitted clothing provides an air of competence, while poorly fitting clothing suggests the use of cast-offs.

Look for clothes that fit you well. Dressier clothing comes in many sizes and cuts; however, you may not find these in stock at most retail outlets. Most men's dress clothing comes in a "classic cut" which looks stodgy and baggy on young and slimmer men but is the cut most available in stores as it accommodates the highest number of body shapes. Thin men might look for fitted, modern, slim, or athletic cut clothing. Young women may prefer modern, curvy, petite, or junior clothing styles to get the best fit for their body.

Find the size and cut which suits your body best, then look for them online, rather than trying to make do with what may be in stock at your local store. There will likely be better selection and prices online. If you order clothing from an online store with a nearby retail outlet, there may be no shipping charges to pick them up and try them at the store. Change clothing size when your body changes so that you look your best.

Pearl: Clothing should be close fitting and comfortable, but never tight or baggy. If the fit is too tight the fabric will buckle or pinch and the clothes will be uncomfortable. If the clothes are too loose, they will look baggy, and will likely buckle and look wrinkled. Well fitted clothing should have smooth, unbroken lines.

Pearl: If the clothes are uncomfortable the wearer is likely to look uncomfortable. As a leader, you want to look comfortable, relaxed, and in control.

Pearl: The back of the jacket should fall over the curve of the buttocks so that it does not ride on top of it. A double vented jacket is less likely to hike up when sitting than a single or unvented jacket and better accommodates a curvy tush.

Pearl: The lapel width should be less than the distance from the lapel to the shoulder seam. The arm length for men should allow a half inch of the shirt cuff to be visible when standing.

Pearl: It is far better to have a small wardrobe that makes you look good than to have many pieces that don't flatter. Don't buy off the discount rack just because of lower prices. Any clothing that does not fit correctly, no matter the price, is a waste of money.

Pearl: A tailor or alteration shop can help fit your clothes.

Pearl: Keep a safety pin in your purse for fashion emergencies, to adjust how open a blouse is or for the loss of a button.

Chapter 19: Jewelry and Accessories

US Army Regulations 670-1; 3-4:

Soldiers may wear a wristwatch, a wrist religious or identification bracelet, and a total of two rings (a wedding set is considered one ring) with Army uniforms, unless prohibited by the commander for safety or health reasons.

Females only are authorized to wear earrings... Earrings may be screw-on, clip-on, or post-type earrings in gold, silver, white pearl, or diamond. The earrings will not exceed 6 mm or 1/4 inch in diameter, and they must be unadorned and spherical. When worn, the earrings will fit snugly against the ear. Females may wear earrings only as a matched pair, with only one earring per earlobe.

For a professional setting and as a candidate, jewelry should be a simple and elegant adornment. Like with other implicit impressions, you want to be perceived as attractive and competent, without having the observer realize what has influenced their perception. Being attractive, appearing successful, and valued by your family, supports an aura of competence.

A small amount of quality jewelry gives a more elegant and sophisticated look than does wearing several pieces. The piece or pieces should be a simple adornment, rather than a show of wealth. Use of very expensive, showy jewelry, may be seen as a flaunting of wealth and may cause resentment and jealousy from women. Thus, flashy jewelry should be avoided during campaigning. Expensive jewelry should also be left at home for job interviews. Employers may perceive women wearing expensive jewelry and expensive outfits to be "high maintenance," and as such, a woman who interviews wearing jewelry might cost more to maintain as an employee.[331]

Pearl: Dress for work for an interview, dressing slightly better than you expect to dress on a normal day on the job. It makes it easier for the employer to imagine you in the position. The same holds true for political candidates.

Watches: A timepiece is fine if it is not a distraction. A smartwatch can easily be a distraction for the wearer.

Pebble: Men should limit their professional accessories to a practical watch and a wedding ring if he wears one. This is in line with the Army code. The more formal the clothing, the more formal the watch should be.

Pearl: It is far better to check your wrist-watch for the time, than to check the time on your phone, and have people think you are distracted. If people see you checking the time, they may think you want to be somewhere else.

Earrings: Be subtle. As in compliance with Army regulation 670-1, use only one earring per ear, and use a matched set. However, small hoop earrings and medium-sized studs are fine. Avoid large hoops or large dangling earring. They do not communicate a professional and competent appearance. The impression you want to present is that of success, so wear high quality, but not ostentatious earrings. Stones should be small. If a colored stone is used, it should match the attire. Keep it simple. If your earrings attract notice, you have likely over done it

Pearl: 7.0 to 8.0 mm diameter pearl earrings give a classic and understated, elegant but casual, every day look, while 8.0 to 9.0 mm pearls are a bit dressier. Pearls larger than this become increasingly expensive and more appropriate for special events, something that might be worn with an evening gown, but not for professional situations.

In their official photos, most female senators are wearing earrings; most commonly, simple pearl earrings or a small gold loop. About half wear a necklace.

Necklaces:

A necklace for a woman, like a tie for a man, helps bring attention to the upper body. Necklaces and pendants should be simple, elegant, and not distracting. A string of pearls or of other beads may be used, or alternatively, a chain with a small pendant, that fits the rest of the attire. Heavy gold chains or bling that denotes wealth should be avoided.

Pearls: A 17 to 19 inch string of pearls is simple and elegant. Larger women might want to go to the upper length of this range or use an extension. Beads that are 7.0 to 8.0 mm are elegant but remain casual. Beads 8.0 to 9.0 mm are more formal and more often used by women over thirty. Beads over 9.0 are luxury items, and send a message of privilege, and should be avoided by job and political candidates

Figures 19-1, 19-2: Senator Dianne Feinstein often wears a large bead necklace. This may be appropriate for a senior senator, as it infers dominance, but would not likely be helpful to a new candidate. Senator Catherine Cortez Masto appears to be wearing 7-8 mm pearls. As a senator, Kamala Harris often wore what appeared to be a 36 inch string of pearls looped twice

"The pearl is the queen of gems and the gem of queens."

Natural pearls, and especially perfectly round pearls, found in the wild in oysters are exceedingly rare. All pearls in retail commerce for the last 100 years have been farmed (cultured). There are three types of saltwater pearls, South Sea, Tahitian, and Akoya, with the Akoya being the least expensive. An Akoya necklace of reasonable quality may be found on sale for just under $1000, but typical prices are multiples of thousands. Freshwater cultured pearls are grown in mussels rather than oysters and are far less expensive, being priced in the hundreds of dollars. Doing a quick search, I found that Macy's had a regularly priced $200 18" strand of 7.0 to 8.0 mm freshwater pearls on sale for $29. This likely reflects the wholesale cost of this cultured pearl necklace.

Pearls marketed as "shell pearls" are man-made beads from crushed mother of pearl and are perfectly sized, round, smooth, shiny, and identical to each other, and the necklaces sell in the 10's of dollars, typically less than $30. Tahitian, freshwater and shell pearls come in a wide variety of colors. Only about 40% of Tahitian pearls and two percent of freshwater pearls are spherical and smooth. The "baroque," "rice," "biwa" and other irregular shaped pearls are used in less formal, and generally, considerably less expensive, but still beautiful jewelry.

Pearls are delicate and can be easily damaged. They should be stored in a soft silk bag or velvet-lined box, and not stored in the same container as other jewelry that can scratch them. Pearls should be put on last, after makeup and any sprays, and taken off first. Perspiration can damage them, so clean them with a soft, lint-free cloth after using them each time. They can be cleaned with a soft damp cloth. Some experts recommend an occasional cleaning with a small amount of mild detergent, a quarter teaspoon in a cup of water. Then rinse them and lay them straight to dry. Do not hang pearls as this will stretch the string.

Rings: The Army regulations allow a soldier in uniform to wear a total of two rings, with a wedding set considered as one ring. I recommend limiting rings to one ring or one wedding set when in professional situations.

Pearl: Class rings: there is no time or place where a class ring rewards the wearer.

"Wearing a high school class ring tells everybody, "My life peaked at 17 and I'm going to die in the same town I grew up in. Wearing a law school class ring should be like putting a magnet on your hand that is irresistibly attracted to your face so you can't stop punching yourself. A law school class ring is like a singularity of douchiness: an infinitely dense accessory where the laws of normal human behavior break down."

Quote from Elie Mystall[332]

Engagement Rings: Avoid wearing a flashy engagement ring to an interview, or any other large rock ring in most professional settings, including while campaigning. A large diamond is a flash of wealth and can cause jealousy and resentment. Secondly, engagement is often a time of distractions from one's career. An employer might suspect that your head will not be totally in the game while planning a wedding and romantic honeymoon. A new marriage is a time of change. The employer may also wonder if you will move or quit after getting married.

A wedding ring is entirely different, as it suggests stability and fewer nights out drinking. A wedding ring suggests that you have roots in the community and have committed to a long-term relationship; and that you are less likely to see the position as a short-term job. The wedding ring can be seen as a sign that a person has settled down, made commitments to family and a stable adult lifestyle. At least, that is a general perception. A wedding band may also be seen to decrease the risk of destabilizing office romances.

Broaches and Pins: Lapel broaches are not currently in style, and thus, for an older woman, they may increase the perception of age or non-contemporary styles. However, especially for younger women, it is not a reason to avoid wearing one. Broaches and pins may also be worn in a more contemporary use as a scarf pin. When broaches and pins are used, it should be to make a statement, and not a fashion statement. Avoid cute or feminine pins (kittens and flowers) when seeking a leadership position. Rather use the pin to make a statement. Whether it is an American Flag, a bald eagle or breast cancer awareness ribbon, a pin can be an elegant way to show your support and convictions in a campaign. A symbol of strength, such as a stallion or lion, may also be appropriate for non-political situations.

Bracelets: Avoid jewelry bracelets in professional settings or as a candidate. Bracelets are usually delicate and don't convey active engagement in work activities, but rather prestige and leisure. They also make noise when they hit a table that can be distracting.

The silicon "support this idea" wristbands are too pervasive to be persuasive, but may curry favor with supporters of that issue, and thus can be used for this reason. For me, however, they just remind me of my grandfather and how he used to put a rubber-band on his wrist for each thing he needed to remember to do, but would then forget what those things were.

Pearl: Avoid excess or overly expensive jewelry as a job or political candidate. Elegant jewelry is a marker of success and privilege. Success suggests competence, but be modest and don't rub it in. Women may resent other women wearing displays of wealth, interpreting it as unearned prestige, leisure, and an assumption of superiority, whether it is intended this way or not.

Pearl: If you wish to use a showy piece of jewelry or other accessory, let it be the centerpiece and avoid any other jewelry other than simple earrings and a wedding band. Heavy or excessive jewelry is inelegant.

Chapter 20: Contemporary Appearance

Older adults, in spite of being reliable workers with years of experience often have a difficult time finding new employment. After the ideal age for candidates, it also becomes more difficult to get elected. As adults get older, it is important to choose clothing and hairstyles carefully that present them well.

Ageism in the job market may arise less from bias against older workers than from an implicit bias against the perceived loss of competence and contemporary skills. (It is illegal to ask age during a job interview but is easy to figure out. Google your landline telephone number to see how old you are and find other info you would rather have private.) If a late middle-aged professional appears for an interview wearing a hairstyle from the 1980's, eyewear from 1970's, and thirty-year-old clothing styles that look somewhat worn and perhaps don't fit quite perfectly, it would question how successful they are and how well they keep up with their professional knowledge. It also raises the question of how engaged they are in contemporary society and how tolerant they might be to values held by their coworkers.

It may be simpler for men. Men's professional clothing and hairstyles change slowly and less dramatically than do women's. All a man may need is a new shirt and tie and to get a haircut to appear contemporary. However, since there is less difference, a man may also not notice the less obvious changes in style. For men, having clothing that fits his body shape well and appears comfortable is most of what it takes to look contemporary. One thing that does change is tie style and usage.

Part of the perception of competence is appearing up to date; thus, clothing and hairstyles that are both classic and contemporary support the appearance of engagement and action. Conversely, wearing older appearing clothing, whether it is because they look worn, have lost their shape, do not fit perfectly, or are just vintage in style, gives the impression that the wearer may not be successful enough in their current position to afford new clothing.

Pearl: A well-cared-for image is attractive. If your appearance seems to show that you have let yourself go, others may treat you in the same way.

Pearl: Clothing should fit well, but not be tight. Vertical seams can give a slimmer appearance.

Rough woven and thick sweaters often give a shapeless baggy look. Thick, textured fabrics will give a more voluminous appearance. However, very fine fabrics that lack form may follow the body too closely. Medium to lightweight fabrics can add structure and give form.

Avoid bell-shaped jackets. Women with wide hips may look fitter and more feminine using a fitted jacket or one that has its lower edge above the hips.[333] Other than on slim women, a pleated skirt adds unwanted volume. Pleated pants do the same for men.

Pearl: If you have been using the same hairstyle for a decade, it may be time to consider something new. Use a contemporary adult hairstyle that is appropriate for professional situations

Pearl: Although dark colors may make people look thinner, dark clothing to the upper body creates more contrast, and can make wrinkles and expression lines more evident. Avoid dark clothing at the neckline. Women can wear a scooped top or light blouse to avoid this.

Pearl: Rather than black, use fundamental hues that are natural to your skin, hair, and eye color.

Pearl: As with cosmetics; wearing fewer and less noticeable accessories has a greater impact than wearing more.

Pearl: The goal is not to look young, but rather healthy, alert, energetic, reliable, successful, and competent.

Chapter 21: Stature and Posture

"We must straighten our backs and work for our freedom. A man can't ride you unless your back is bent."

~Martin Luther King

The larger animal has an advantage in a fight and wins more often. Cats arch their back and bristle their fur, birds puff up their feathers, and fish extend their fins to look bigger when confronted, so that they appear larger and thus less easy a target, in hopes of avoiding the challenge. Perhaps the aggressor will think twice, and back off. For millennia, humans have deferred to bigger and stronger individuals, and people still conflate physical size with authority and leadership.

Posture not only changes how people see us, but how we perceive ourselves. There is evidence that our hormones respond to our posture. Poor posture can be an important giveaway of low self-esteem and low power. When a person is beaten down or has low social standing, they tend to slouch, making themselves smaller and shorter. Slouching causes one to look disengaged, and rolled forward shoulders give the appearance of weakness and defeat.

We look up to our leaders, and this is natural when they are taller than us. A person that is considerably taller may look more robust and undefeated even when their posture is imperfect. A person with a correct, erect posture may assume a leadership stance even when they are not taller than average, especially for non-supreme-leader roles. A more erect posture gives a candidate an air of confidence and capability.

Non-human primates that suffer social defeat exhibit behaviors similar to human depression. These animals display slumped or "collapsed" posture with the spine rolled forward, shoulders slumped, and head and eyes facing downwards when they have been bullied or lost ranking in their troop at the hands of a more dominant animal. They become less active and self-groom rather than interact in normal, mutual-grooming behaviors. Lower rank monkeys cower and make themselves appear smaller to avoid aggression from the more dominant animals. Thus, this posturing makes them appear smaller and unthreatening, decreasing the risk that they will be seen as a challenge to the alpha male and be attacked.[334]

Figure 21-1: The two macaques (Macaca fascicularis) on the right manifest social defeat, with huddled posture (head down, less alert; they stay alone and lack interest in interaction), analogous to human depression. The animal on the left shows normal posture. Photo by Dr. Fan Xu.[335]

This social defeat posture is the opposite of a dominant or leadership posture. We rightly do not want depressed leaders, but rather looks for leaders that project confidence, are outgoing, have the capacity to adapt to new situations, and will not surrender or give up when faced with adversity. It may be an implicit assumption that taller individuals are not suffering from social defeat. Posture is likely as, or more, important than stature in our selection of leaders. Thus, women, even though smaller than men, can still be seen as competent leaders.

Self-affirmations can improve our posture, and improved posture projects power. When we perceive that others see us as having power, we feel more confident, and others can see this, reinforcing it.

Poor posture is endemic in high school students. Although postural problems may require medical evaluation and treatment, the most common problem seen in adolescents is slouching, (nag, nag, nag.) This postural predicament results in part from spending many hours seated each day. The muscles of the upper back become weak. Also, when we spend much of our day seated, we learn to set our posture using our eyes rather than the inner ear, which is the main sensor of balance for the brain. If you have poor posture, trying to stand straight feels uncomfortable and unnatural. The muscles that should be used to stand can become imbalanced and weak. Additionally, walking while wearing a backpack that weighs over 10% of the body weight, throws off the posture and balance, and trains the wearer to slump.

Proper postural alignment, when looking at a standing profile, should have the opening of the ear canal directly above the mid-shoulder, the trochanter prominence of the hip bone, the center of the knee, and the ankle.

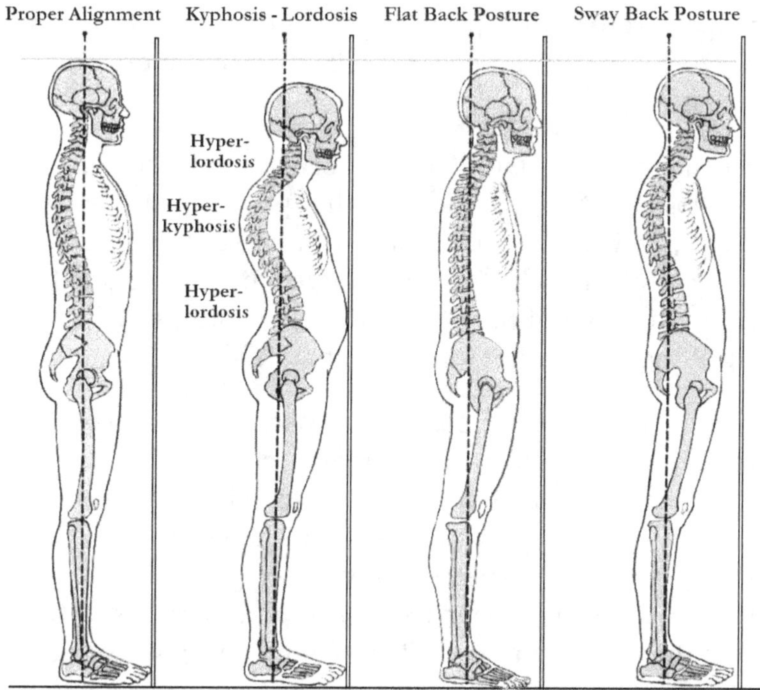

Figure 21-2: Correct and common postural faults

The most common problem with posture seen in Western society is a "head forward" position, usually accompanied by hyper-kyphosis and rolled-forward shoulders.

Men have thicker vertebral bones and more muscular necks than do women. Women's necks are 9-16% smaller than men's although the difference in head mass is much smaller.[336] This puts women at greater risk of whiplash injury in car accidents. Long necks may be seen as elegant, while a thick, muscular neck appears shorter. In ancient physiognomy, a thick neck was associated with a strong, bull-like will, and a thin neck, timid and cowardly, like a deer. The pejorative "pencil-neck" refers to a timid or person. When wearing clothing, the shape of the neck usually remains visible, and it allows for the implicit assessment of muscularity that is associated with physical strength and dominance.[337] [338]

A head-forward position causes a lengthened view of the anterior neck, causing it to appear long and thin, and thus, weak, and causes the shoulders to look A-shaped rather than square. It also lowers the neck in relation to the shoulders and causes a loss in perceived height and vigor. Thus, head-forward posture causes a person to be perceived as weak and effete, while correct posture gives the perception of strength, control, and competence. With a head forward posture or other postural deviations, the head may not be level. Having a level head may actually give the impression of level-headedness.

A second postural fault, one especially common in women, is hyper-lordosis of the low back. In this posture, the pelvis is tilted downwards, and the low back has an increase in its concave shape. This also causes the belly to appear larger. If you imagine headlights attached to the front of the pelvis, in this posture the lights would be pointing at the floor rather than straight ahead.

Dancers have beautiful posture, in part because they depend on balance. Try this: stand with your eyes closed, and dance around (without running into things) for 15 seconds. With your eyes still closed, stop, and stand with your feet shoulder-width apart, eyes straight forward, with 90 percent of your weight resting on your heels and 10% on the rest of your feet for several seconds until you feel balanced; then open your eyes. This should give good posture. If you stand with your toes against a wall, unless your nose is four inches long, it should not touch the wall.

You can also try standing with feet together and curl your toes up. This should shift the weight back so that you are standing with most of your weight on your heels. If these maneuvers cause a large shift in your posture, your posture likely needs work.

To maintain posture, people need to maintain muscle and bone mass, especially as they age. This requires good nutrition with at least 0.8 grams per kilogram body weight of quality protein in the diet daily and sufficient exercise to maintain muscle mass. Many older and overweight adults require more than one gram of protein per kilogram of body weight to maintain muscle mass, as more protein is required when there is insulin resistance. Increasing muscle mass requires more than one gram of protein per kilogram. Avoiding bone loss also requires adequate protein, vitamin D_3, and vitamin K_2. Most American women can benefit from taking a Vitamin D_3 supplement.

Devices and Support

If your posture is less than perfect, as it is for many of us, especially those of us that work seated, there is help from devices. A posture support can not only improve one's appearance during "public performances," but can also serve to train the posture. Many can be hidden under clothing.

A "posture brace" is not the same thing as a "back brace." which typically supports the low back. Posture braces are designed to provide support to prevent the slumping of the shoulders and may help decrease excessive kyphosis (forward bending) of the upper back. When shoulders are back, and the upper back has a normal amount of kyphosis, it helps decrease "head forward" positioning.

A postural brace is not a fix, but rather a tool. Inappropriate use of this tool can actually worsen posture. It should not be used to replace musculature, but rather to help build it. The proper use of a posture brace is as a training device to gain awareness of correct posture, form better postural habits, and to strengthen postural muscles.

Generally, the postural brace should not be worn for more than a total of one hour each day during the beginning of postural retraining. As the muscular strength improves and better postural habits develop, the brace may be used for four to six hours. The user should see lasting results within the first 12 weeks of use, and then no longer need to use it on a daily basis, as long as they stay fit and don't fall back into the habits that led to the poor posture.

Maintaining a healthy posture is a continual process. It does not get fixed and then stay fixed. Exercise and awareness of standing and sitting posture are needed to maintain correct posture.

If you work at a computer, make sure you have a large enough monitor and typeface, and correct visual acuity, so that you are not leaning in, with neck forward, while working. Make sure that your workspace and tasks do not encourage poor posture. Your keyboard and monitor should be placed at ergonomic heights so that you are not leaning forward to use them.

Some highly rated postural braces include the SheerPosture® and the ShoulderBack Lite® by EquiFit. A different type of device is the "Posture Medic" which is an exercise device that doubles as a shoulder brace. Note that some, but not all postural braces can be worn and hidden under the clothing. Posture braces may be more comfortable when worn over a form-fitting T-shirt to avoid chaffing. The website PostureBraceGuide.com has reviews and descriptions of many different braces and advice for their use.

Posture assisting bras are available for women. These can be comfortable and hidden under the outer clothing. For men, a posture T-shirt preferably with a V-neck so that it is hidden when not wearing a tie, is the most comfortable posture assist for use in men. These can be worn all day without discomfort.

There are also electronic posture minders. These devices attach to the upper body and vibrate to let one know when the wearer is slouching, reminding them to straighten up. The "Upright" is designed to only be worn while sitting and only for short periods of time. The "Posture Master" vibrates when slouching for more than 60 seconds. The "Lumo Lift®" is the best known of these devices. Rather than adhering to the skin, the Lumo Lift uses a magnet to attach to the clothing. It has various settings so that the time-to-vibrate can be controlled. All these devices claim to improve posture in three months.

These posture correction devices work for most people, but they must be used correctly to get good results. To repeat, these devices do not fix posture; they help the user correct their own posture. It takes several weeks to strengthen the slow twitch postural muscles. Trying to do too much too quickly will cause more soreness and may decrease your commitment to progress.

Even though most of these posture improving devices focus on the shoulders and upper back, this is usually enough to improve balance for the entire body. When the shoulders are upright, the head moves back as well. Try standing with dropped shoulders, hyperkyphosis/

hyperlordosis, head-forward, pelvis tilted forward position. Now raise your shoulders up and hold them there for ten seconds. You will probably notice that your entire balance shifts backward, and posture improves.

Exercises for hyper-lordosis are shown in this chapter below the section on high heels.

Pearl: The breasts are subject to gravity, and with age, the mass of the breasts sits lower on the chest. Breasts that rest low on the chest make a woman appear older and less dynamic as they also mimic the appearance of social defeat as when the shoulders are rolled forward. Bras should be fitted and adjusted so that the breasts are held up at the position where they lived when they were young. One method to correctly adjusting a bra is to get on hands and knees so that the back is parallel to the floor and the breast hang straight down. The breast should fit and fill the correct cup size in this position. Then have a confidante adjust the straps to remove slack.

Pearl: Purchase bras that fit correctly using the loosest set of hooks. As the elastic gets stretched, use the tighter hooks. Replace the bra when those get loose.

High Heels

Although almost exclusively worn by women, much of the behavioral effect of high heels is on men. Men rated pictures of women as being sexier; more youthful, good-looking, and elegant; and having prettier legs and buttocks when wearing high heels, even though the shoes were not shown in the photographs used in the study. Men, but not women were more likely to interact with women and be helpful to women wearing high heels. At least five studies have provided evidence that both men and women find women wearing high heels more attractive, and women consider themselves to be more attractive when wearing high heels. [339]

An experimental study assessed how men responded to women wearing flats, medium (two-inch), or tall (3½-inch) high heeled shoes. Men were fifty percent more likely to participate in surveys when invited by women in medium-high heels and twice as likely to participate if the woman conducting the survey wore tall high heels. When a woman wearing flats dropped her glove, 38 percent of men failed to help, but only seven percent of men did not respond to women wearing tall high heels. Men were more likely to approach a woman in a bar if she was wearing tall high heels but not more likely to approach her if she was wearing medium heels than if she wore flats.[340]

Thus, research has verified that women wearing tall high heels get men's attention, but this research has focused on sexual attention. The question remains open as to whether the added height given by tall heels improves a woman's stature in a way that gives her non-sexual power. Men may perceive women wearing tall high heels as more approachable, but this may also mean that men perceive them as being more easily dominated or sexually receptive.

Thus, tall high heels may not increase the perception of leadership, and it suggests that very tall heels may, in fact, lower it some. Keep in mind that height has less effect on the perception of power for women than it does for men. Nevertheless, it does not mean that high heels are not useful. When in social situations and gatherings, heels can make it easier to meet and interact with men. Tall heels make it more likely that an attractive woman will have an opportunity to meet male voters, men in positions of power, make contacts, and state her case for her candidacy, or sell her issue.

Pearl: Round-toed, shapeless shoes and those with low, thick heels make the legs appear shorter and heavier. Slightly higher heels make you look taller and slimmer.

It has been estimated that 11,200 women seek emergency room care each year in the United States for injuries related to wearing high heels, mostly sprained ankles.[341] This statistic falls greatly short of describing the pain caused by wearing them. The most prevalent injury from high heel is likely *hallux valgus* deformity, commonly called a bunion. Additionally, when high heels are chronically worn, it can cause tightening of the Achilles tendon and cause foot problems; it's best to limit their use and wear flats most of the time. High heels also cause low back pain. This results especially from long hours of use, causing anterior pelvic tilt and weakening of the abdominal muscles. This weakening causes poor posture and back pain.

Almost all women develop abdominal diastasis recti during pregnancy, but it is also not uncommon in middle-aged men and women who are overweight, even after weight loss. In this condition the muscles of the abdominal wall weaken and separate, causing a bulging of the belly. This can be seen and felt as a vertical bulge along the center of the abdomen during a partial sit-up (crunches). This weakness will cause the belly to bulge. The diastasis (separation) increases the waist circumference even after weight has been lost.

Strengthening exercises can help bring the abdominal muscles back together and narrow the abdominal girth. The exercises that have been used in most studies are abdominal crunches, kegels, posterior pelvic tilt, and the Russian twist. More recently, plank exercises, isometric contractions of the belly, and curls (partial sit-ups) are being investigated as treatments.[342] [343] [344] The exercise treatment program likely requires 16 weeks, exercising at least three times a week. During this time, a progressive decrease in waist measurement should begin after about six weeks. Finding the optimal exercises is an area of ongoing research. Plank exercises and crunches appear to be promising exercises for the treatment of diastasis recti.

"If you want people to think you're strong, you have to look strong."
Lady Barbara Judge

Posture Exercises

Strengthening of the abdominal muscles through "bridge" and "plank" exercises can prevent and help correct the excessive pelvic tilt, decrease lumbar lordosis, and prevent back pain associated with high heel use.[345] These exercises also help to improve low back posture and bulging belly. Adding isometric belly contractions, and curls can help corrects diastasis recti and decrease the waistline in those with it.

Plank exercise: Lay down on the floor supine and then support your body resting on your forearms and toes, lifting the body off the floor, straight like a plank, and hold this position for 20 to 30 seconds, rest, and repeat two more times.

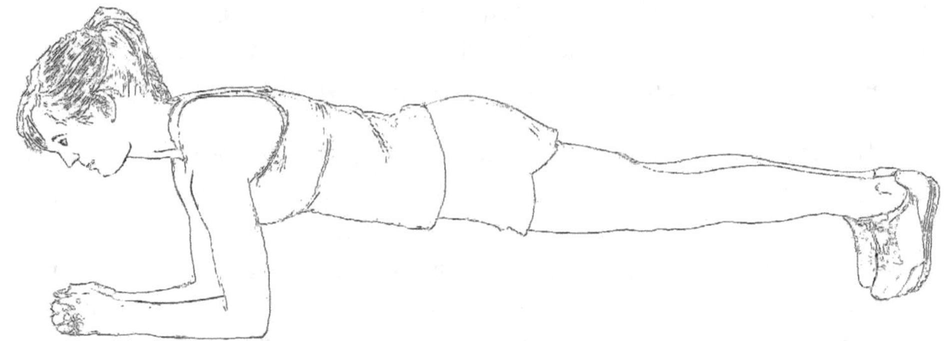

Figure 21-3: Plank exercise. Hold for 20-30 seconds. Release and repeat 2 more times.

Bridge Exercise: Begin, lying face up with the knees bent 90 degrees, so that the feet are flat on the floor. Raise the pelvis off the floor with the weight of the body distributed between the feet and the upper back and shoulders so that the hips are straight and hold this position for 15 seconds, and then return to rest for 30 seconds. Repeat this three times. As you strengthen your body, increase the hold time of the exercise to 30 seconds. To do further strengthening, extend one leg into the air in line with the body during the bridge, and increase to four cycles so that each leg extension is done twice.

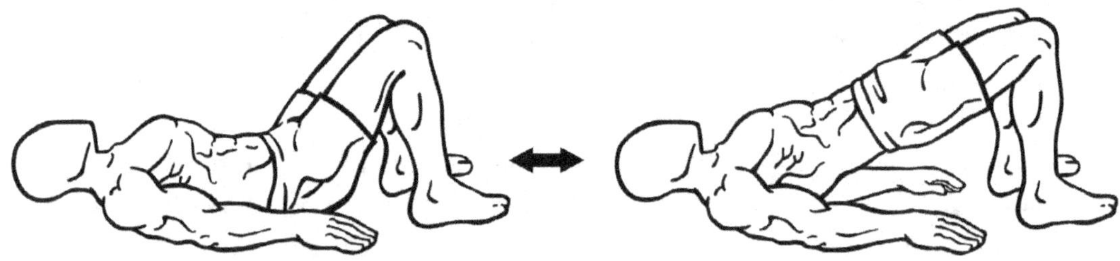

Figure 21-4: Bridge exercise.[346]

Isometric Belly Contractions: While seated, place the hands on the abdominal muscles. Now, contract the abdominal muscles, pulling the stomach in, straight back towards the spine and hold it for 30 seconds, while breathing in and out with small controlled breaths and then relax. Do ten repetitions.

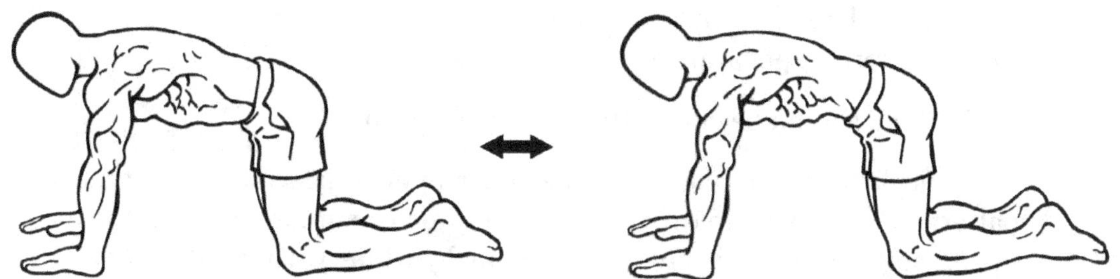

Figure 21-5: Alternate isometric Belly Contraction method.

Crunches: Curls are a partial sit-up in which the upper back comes off the floor, but the lower back stays on the floor. Raise the shoulders and shoulder blades off the floor, hold for 5 seconds, relax and rest 5 to 10 seconds and repeat. Gradually increase the number of repetitions to 20.

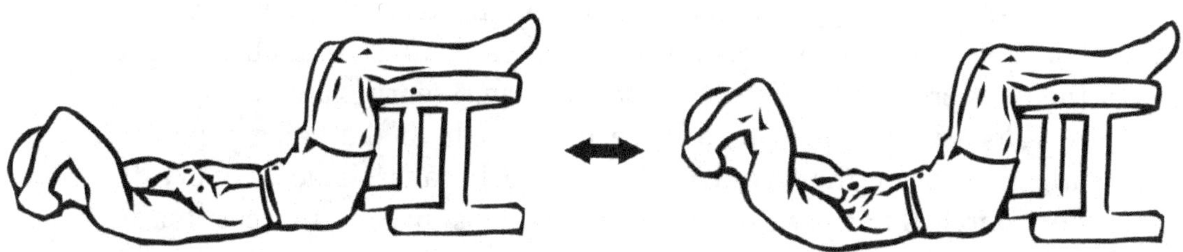

Figure 21-6: Crunches.

Pearl: Get sufficient exercise so that not only do you look healthy, but you feel healthy and attractive.

Clothing and Perception of Stature

Through careful selection of appropriate clothing, one can appear taller. Since the perception of leadership is often aligned with stature, this is especially important for women and men who are not tall.

A String of Pearls:

Clothes that fit properly give a taller appearance than do loose or baggy clothing, especially for clothing above the waist. Dresses and other clothing that fit at the waist give a thinner and taller appearance. Loose or bulky clothing, such as loose blouses or heavy sweaters give a heavier and shorter appearance. A thinner waist gives a taller look. A tucked in shirt gives a taller appearance than one left out especially when wearing a top that is fitted. For shirts that are not tucked in, the lower hem should not go past the trochanter of the hip, (not more than halfway down the pant zipper for men), to avoid giving a shorter appearance.

Clothing should be close fitting, but never tight.

Monochromatic clothing gives a taller appearance than do large patterns or mixes of color. Wearing the same or similar color on the upper and lower body gives a taller look, while wearing different colors on top and bottom divide the body into two, shortening the vertical appearance. This may be one of the reasons that wearing a suit projects power. If different colors or shades are worn, use a darker shade on the bottom half of the body and a light one on the upper half to move the eyes upward and give a taller appearance. Although darker colors may give more perception of mass, wearing all black makes one look smaller and older.

Vertical lines give a taller look and horizontal lines a shorter, wider appearance. This is not only for patterns in the fabric but for the lines created by the cut of the clothing. Wearing a belt, especially a wide belt or one with a large buckle can make shorter persons appear shorter than going without one because it accentuates the horizontal. A narrow belt, however, can be slimming by accentuating a narrow waist, giving a taller appearance. The placket on an oxford style shirt is an example of a subtle vertical line that promotes a taller look.

V-neck dresses and tops can give a taller appearance than a square or round neck. When wearing a button-down shirt, leaving a couple of buttons undone can create a V-neck.

Sleeves that expose the wrists give a taller appearance than those that cover the wrists. However, short sleeve shirts give a shorter appearance than do long-sleeved shirts. Wearing a long-sleeve shirt and rolling up the cuffs a bit can give a taller look. A shorter skirt will give the appearance of longer legs; however, very short skirts are not appropriate in professional settings. Slimmer sleeves and trouser legs will give a longer, taller appearance.

Waist high pants can give a taller appearance to women than those that ride low on the hips. The pants should fit the crotch rather than being baggy in this area, to give the wearer longer legs. Pants that come close to the floor also give the appearance of longer legs. Be sure, however, that the pants don't touch the ground or sag on top of the foot as this will give the perception of being shorter. If socks are worn, their color should match the pants so that they do not draw attention and decrease the perception of stature. For casual wear, fitted denim pants (skinny jeans) for women should generally come to the top of the ankle when socks are not used.

A jacket or blazer with slimmer sleeves is slimming and gives a taller appearance. The jacket will build up the shoulders giving a taller, stronger presence.

Typically, suit jackets are long enough to cover the buttocks, but this will cause shorter individuals to look shorter. Jackets that have their lower edge at the hips and expose more of the trouser rise give a taller appearance than those that extend below the hips. The trouser rise is the vertical distance from the crotch seam to the top of the trouser. A waist jacket can give a taller look, but these are not currently in style nor are they part of professional attire.

Keeping a well-fitted suit jacket or blazer buttoned will give a slimmer waist and V-shaped torso as well as a taller look than wearing it unbuttoned. Using the top button of a two buttoned jacket is traditional. The button used to close the jacket should be just above the belly button, at the narrowest part of the waist. This creates slimming and gives a taller appearance.

Showing more vertical area of the shirt (and tie) above the waist when using a jacket gives a longer V and a taller appearance. This relies on the blouse or shirt having visual contrast from the jacket.

Heels and shoe lifts can increase apparent height. Pointed toe shoes add to the appearance of longer legs.

Using accessories in the upper third of the torso brings the eyes to the upper body, and aids in the perception of height. This can be done with a lapel brooch or pin, necklace, or another accessory. Hats, sunglasses, and scarves can be used to increase the illusion of height, by drawing attention to the upper body.

A large handbag will make a woman appear smaller.

Long hair can make people look shorter.

Pebbles: For men, slim, fitted, or athletic cut dress shirts can give a taller appearance than "classic cut" shirts do, which tend to be baggy.

Avoid using vests as these prevent the lengthening effect of the jacket. They also give a stuffy appearance.

Off-the-rack clothing is designed to fit as many people as possible and thus made boxier to accommodate a wider range of people. This is particularly a problem for suits, especially for men. The shorter or thinner a person is, the more likely they will need a tailor to get a suit that fits well and looks good. A suit that is large in the shoulders or waist or that has baggy trousers will make a person appear smaller, shorter and less dynamic.

When funding precludes the engagement of the services of a tailor, rather than buying an ill-fitting suit and having it modified to fit, it may be easier and less expensive to purchase a sports jacket or blazer that fits well and purchase well-fitting trousers separately, matching the pants to the color and fabric of the jacket. This also allows the purchase of several pairs of matching pants rather than one pair that comes with the suit, for easier cleaning.

While a big guy with broad shoulders may look silly with a skinny tie, as a slim person, I feel like a circus clown if I wear a wide tie. Tie width styles change with time; so stay contemporary. For slimmer men, a tie that is 2¾ inches (7 cm) wide at its widest point is sufficient, and ties more than 3 inches (7.6 cm) wide should be avoided. Wide ties with thick fabrics will create larger knots that make the neck appear smaller. The tie should ideally come down to the mid-belt line, never below the belt.

If using a patterned shirt use a plain tie. A patterned tie can be used with a plain shirt. The four-in-hand knot is recommended for men with smaller frames because of its symmetrical, elongated shape that directs the eye upwards. If the tie is too long, the narrow end can be tucked into the shirt.

Suit pants (other than tuxes) generally have pleats and cuffs. As a rule, double pleated pants have cuffs, while they are optional for single pleated, and unusual on flat front pants. The cuffs are considered dressier and of higher quality. The cuff adds weight that allows the pleated pants to drape better. Pleated pants usually have a higher trouser rise, are worn on the waste and give more room and comfort for heavier men. Flat front trousers have a lower cut and lack of pleats that cause the belly of a person with a belly to look larger, and thus are unhelpful for heavier people.

Slimmer men do not need the extra room afforded by double pleated pants, and the double pleated pants will look baggy on them. Although not traditional for use with a suit, flat panel pants look good on slimmer men, and are generally worn on the hips rather than the waist, and thus have a lower trouser rise. Pants with a shorter trouser rise give men a taller appearance. Cuffs also break the visual line of the pant above the shoe and cause the wearer to appear less tall. Thus, for slimmer men and those who wish to appear taller, use of pants without cuffs gives a taller appearance.

For men, the hem of dress pants is usually long enough so that the pant leg "breaks" when it hits the shoe, folding the pant slightly. Slightly shorter length pants that just barely rest on the front of the shoe, giving a "quarter break" or less, give a taller appearance. Slenderer pants will give a taller look and expose more shoe, giving a longer line, especially if the shoe is a similar color to the pants.

Pants which can be worn without a belt can give a taller appearance as the belt creates a horizontal line that is shortening.

Pearl: A belt and buckle that match the color of the trouser or outfit are less apparent and thus give less shortening effect than a belt that contrasts with the other clothing.

Standard men's dress shoes add about three-quarters to one inch to the height. Standard western boots (cowboy boots) have a 1.5-inch heel. Riding heels are a bit taller at about 2 inches and are tapered. Western boots with roper heels are larger to give more contact with the ground and used for walking long distances; they are only about one inch high.

Marco Rubio wore Florsheim Duke Bike Toe Boots with a 1.75-inch heel during his campaign to add height, and Ted Cruz added about 2 inches by wearing cowboy boots with riding heels. Giorgio Brutini Men's Pointed-Toe Dress Boots have a 2-inch heel.

Shoe lifts can add an additional inch or more to the apparent height without being as visible as heels, and even higher lifts can be added to boots for men or women. Elevator shoes are shoes designed with lifts inside, and thus can accommodate higher lifts than regular shoes can, while camouflaging the fact that one is using a lift. Elevator shoes generally increase stature from 2.5 to 3.5 inches.

Shoes that add height can give a taller appearance; however, any height over about two inches is likely to cause back and foot pain and may throw off the posture. Posture is more important in giving the appearance of confidence, competence, and health than is an extra inch in height.

Chapter 22: Finger Nails

The army code of conduct has a few things to say about fingernails. Not only that, they seem pretty serious about it.

AR 670-1 Chapter 3, paragraph 2c. Fingernail Standards and Grooming Policies

*Fingernails. All personnel will keep fingernails clean and neatly trimmed. Females will trim nails shorter if the commander determines that the longer length detracts from a professional appearance, presents a safety concern, or interferes with the performance of duties. **Females may only wear clear polish** when in uniform or while in civilian clothes on duty. Females may wear clear acrylic nails, provided they have a natural appearance and conform to Army standards.*

Note: This paragraph is punitive with regard to Soldiers. Violation by Soldiers may result in adverse administrative action and/or charges under the provisions of the Uniform Code of Military Justice.

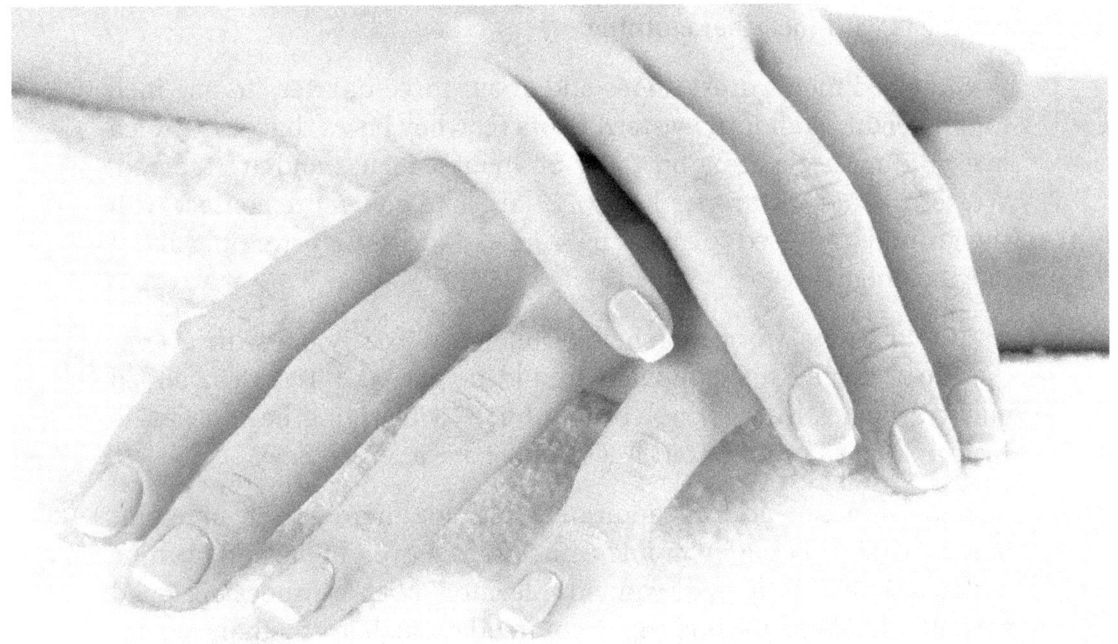

Figure 22-1: Nails that appear natural, healthy, well groomed, and likely not to be noticed.

According to a study published in the journal, Behavioral Ecology, while fingernail varnish increases the attractiveness of the female hand, nail length does not. Hands with reddened or damaged skin near to the nails were found to be unattractive in both men and women.[347]

After a thorough review of the literature, I came up with nothing on studies examining the relationship of fingernail shape and color on voting patterns or on entry to higher levels of corporate and organizational hierarchy. I then did an extensive opinion study (subjects = 1 (me), p-value = 1.0), that guides much of the following discussion.

Fingernails should reflect competence, health, vigor, and engagement in activity. They should be practical. They should reflect the prestige of a leadership position, rather than appearing to have suffered the damage which occurs to the fingernails of those engaged in menial labor. The nails should not call anyone's attention; they should be subtle.

Thus, the fingernails should not appear unkempt, dirty, damaged, or diseased. At the same time, they should not shout that the person has the luxury of spending an hour a week in a nail salon buffing their vanity. The fingernails should not be showy or sexy and should not be decorated except perhaps for celebrations.

Color: The natural color of the nail bed is the best. Thus, a clear polish is preferable other than when an opaque polish is required to hide damage to nails. If an opaque polish is used, it should be close to the natural nail bed color or slightly pinker, as this promotes an impression of health. Avoid the use of multiple colors or other nail ornaments for a professional appearance. An advantage to clear polish is that it does not leave a noticeable gap along the nail bed as the nail grows.

Pearl: A drop of pink or red nail polish mixed into a clear polish can give a healthy rosy tinge to the transparent polish that still looks natural.

Shape and length: The Army got it right; nails should be no longer than ¼ inch beyond the fingertip, and preferably half that or less for a practical professional appearance. A bit of extra length beyond the nail bed can give the impression of longer, thinner fingers, which is associated with maturity.

The leading edge of the nail should be rounded and smooth, not filed to be pointed or flat. If you are running for office or interviewing for a job, you may be shaking a lot of hands. You don't need your nails to scratch or impale your constituents or your prospective employer.

As a nervous habit, nail-biting gives the appearance of anxiety and lack of confidence. Biting and tearing of the skin around the nails should be avoided. Nail biting is a common cause of paronychia, an infection of the skin around the nails that causes redness and inflammation.

Use of detergents, such as washing dishes, dries out the nail and can cause them to split and crack more easily. Wear gloves for washing to protect them. Avoid exposing the hands to bleach or bleach water. Nails should also be moisturized with a thick skin cream to help keep them healthy. A clear nail hardener can improve nail strength and appearance.

Pearl: Dipping the fingertips into hydrogen peroxide for a few seconds and pulling the fingertip back so the peroxide can get under the free nail while cleaning them will turn the exposed under-surface white.

Note: Although I have recommended the Army grooming standards as guideline – there is no need to take it further. Use them as guidelines and starting points, not as rules, unless you are in the military.

People are like stained-glass windows. They sparkle and shine when the sun is out, but when the darkness sets in, their true beauty is revealed only if there is a light from within.

~ Elisabeth Kübler-Ross

Chapter 23: Sexual Attraction

In a discussion of the perception of physical attractiveness and social power, it would be remiss not to discuss the implicit traits that men and women perceive to be sexually attractive.

Both men and women have different criteria for what is attractive depending on the situation. Women prefer strongly masculine appearing men while in the fertile phase of their menstrual cycle for short-term trysts but prefer men with more average masculinity for long-term relationships. A mate that is more masculine and physically stronger and more robust, increases fitness and survival of a woman's male offspring. The male offspring of these pairings are more likely to exhibit masculine traits and behavior, and thus, will probably have more sexual partners and spread the woman's DNA more broadly. That's what we're here for, right?

Women find highly masculine faces to be more attractive during the 2 – 3 days around their ovulation when they are fertile, and women are more likely to engage in impulsive liaisons during these days. This helps with the survival of the species. Thus, the days around ovulation, in the middle the menstrual cycle, may be a risky time to explore new liaisons when looking for a long-term partner.

Males have a nearly unlimited capacity to mate and reproduce their DNA at minimal cost, while females are limited to a relatively small number of offspring, and each comes at high physical, resource, and time commitment and costs. Thus, the selfish DNA strategy for reproduction favors women having at least one male child with high masculinity. This child and his children can spread the woman's genes at little or no cost or danger to her.

These highly-masculine mates are, however, less desirable to women for long-term relationships.[348] Men with higher facial width-to-height ratios (fWHRs) are perceived to be more masculine and dominant and are more attractive to women for short-term, rather than long-term relationships.[349] Men with more average masculinity are perceived to be more social, trustworthy, and youthful, kinder, and more willing to stick around and raise children.[350]

This perception is not misguided. Men that produce more testosterone are less likely to form stable marital relationships and have a lower quality of marital interactions. These men are more likely to engage in extramarital liaisons (perhaps as a result of greater opportunity for brief relationships), and there is a higher danger of physically abusive behavior from these men.[351] Highly-masculine men are perceived as being more dominant. They have greater muscular strength, and thus may be considered more dangerous in a domestic situation. During harsh environmental situations, women living in adverse conditions prefer men with less masculine faces as long-term partners than do women living in more favorable conditions.[352]

Even though societal norms and birth control moderate the actual impact of these reproductive forces in modern life compared to our ancestral environments, the instinctual imperative continue to impact our preferences and behaviors.

Men's perceptions of a woman's attractiveness also vary considerably depending on the situation. When the potential for a brief liaison arises, the features that evoke a gestalt of attractiveness for men differ from those features valued by men seeking a long-term relationship. For short-term relationships, men's focus is heavily influenced by physical characteristics that portend fertility, rather than on facial appearance.[353] In a study that tracked the eye movement of men asked to evaluate how attractive various pictures of women were, men looked more often, and spent more time looking, at the breasts, and not much time focusing on the face.[354]

Men consider women with a waist-hip ratio of 0.7 as being the most attractive female shape,[355] as this ratio correlates with health and fertility. This is constant for both short-term and long-term relationships. In situations offering possible short-term relationships, however, men are attracted to large breasts. In an experiment, a 20-year-old woman stood by the side of a road in France, where hitchhiking is common, and changed the cup size of her bra, to observe the number of ride offers from 1200 motorist. As her bust size increased, so did the percentage of ride offers from male drivers, but bust size did not alter the number of female drivers that offered her a ride.[356]

Dress also affects men's perception of a woman's receptivity to sexual advances. In experiments similar to those above, men were more likely to approach a woman in a bar when she increased the cup size of her bra.[357] In another French hitchhiking experiment, wearing makeup increased ride offers from men, but not from women.[358] Men were found to approach a woman in a bar more quickly if she was wearing red lipstick (Chapter 21),[359] or tall high heels (Chapter 21)[360] and men considered women with a tattoo on the low back to be more promiscuous (Chapter 17).[361]

As noted above, women prefer men with more masculine faces for short-term relationships, but perceived men with less masculine faces a better choice for long-term relationships. Surprisingly, men also prefer women with more masculine faces for short-term relationships, but not when seeking long-term relationships.[362] Women with more masculine features may be perceived to be more willing to participate in risky or short-term relations, and to be less selective in choosing sexual partners.

In another hitchhiking experiment, 18 percent of men stopped to offer a ride to a woman wearing a blond wig, but only 14 percent did when she wore a brown or black wig.[363] In a separate experiment, a woman dyed her hair blonde, brunette or red, and visited several nightclubs on different evenings. She was approached by men more frequently when her hair was blonde. However, when men were asked to assess images of this woman, she was rated as most physically attractive, intelligent, and competent as a brunette. As a blonde, she was seen as needy.[364] This suggests that men approach blondes for short-term encounters either because they are being protective of vulnerable young women (so very unlikely!), or see blonds as less intelligent, less dominant, and easier to control (more likely). In a study of male university students, participants said that they preferred dating less intelligent women for short-term relationships, but wanted a more intelligent woman as a spouse.

In an experiment, a woman appeared to accidentally drop a glove while walking alone and appeared to be unaware of her loss. The woman had her hair either falling naturally on her back and shoulders, up in a bun, or in a ponytail. The hairstyle did not alter female passerby reactions, but men were more likely to gallantly retrieve the glove of the damsel with loose hair falling on her shoulders.[365]

Men may perceive women with tattoos, very tall high heels, loose hair, with a large busts, and with more masculine faces, as being more promiscuous. Women with blond hair may be perceived to be younger, less competent, and more vulnerable.

Makeup that creates the look of bedroom eyes with heavier eyelids appears to be a signal for sexual interest and availability, but it does not appear to increase attractiveness. Wide-open eyes convey childlike sincerity, trustworthiness, openness and perhaps vulnerability. In contrast, heavy, drooping eyelids, and makeup that cause the eyes to appear less wide open convey maturity and sexual readiness. Bedroom eyes also appears to be perceived as a willingness to poach mates, which creates a sense of distrusts and hostility from same-gender individuals and promotes mate-guarding.[366]

Testosterone levels quickly rise in men who have brief conversations with women, with the level of testosterone rising in accordance with the man's rating of the woman as a potential romantic partner. The man's testosterone level rise was also correlated with the woman's perception of how much the man was trying to impress her.[367] Cortisol levels also rise in this situation.[368] And it goes both ways. When women were shown a 20-minute video of an attractive young man courting a young woman, both testosterone and cortisol levels rose in the saliva of these women, but they did not rise in women watching a nature documentary or a film of an older, unattractive man courting a young woman.[369]

This release of hormones influences behavior - it increases bonding, risk-taking, and assertiveness. Thus, women should be aware how dress, makeup, and clothing can lure attention by increasing sexual attractiveness, and how this can influence not only men they interact with but also their own body's hormonal milieu.

Interestingly, falling in love lowers testosterone levels in men for about the first two years of the relationship[370] and levels usually fall again after a man becomes a father.[371] Having children lowers a man's testosterone levels, and lower testosterone levels decrease the likelihood of a man divorcing his wife.

Seeing Red

As with red lipstick, when women wear red clothing, it increases the sexual attractiveness of women with feminine faces. Men also rated women wearing red as warmer and more competent.[372] When men evaluated the attractiveness and sexual intent of women in photographs wearing blue, green or white tee-shirts, it did not affect the attractiveness rating of the women, but men rated the women wearing red tee-shirts as having sexual intent.[373] Even a woman carrying a red item can act as a red cue for men. Men sat closer to women wearing red that they had just met and asked more intimate questions.[374] Waitresses get more tips from men, but not from women, when wearing red shirts than when wearing the same shirt in blue, green, yellow, black, or white. Women wearing a red tee-shirt were more likely to be offered a lift by men than when wearing other colors.[375] Women placing photos on dating sites get more contact requests if the image showed them wearing red as compared to wearing other colors.[376] Waitresses wearing lipstick received more frequent tips and in higher amounts when wearing red lipstick, with progressively lower amounts with pink, brown, or no lipstick. Waitresses earned 2.5 times as much in tips from men and twice as much from women when wearing red lipstick as compared to no lipstick.[377]

In a series of experiments, men found women wearing the color red to be more attractive and sexually desirable relative to women wearing other colors. The color did not alter the men's assessments of the woman's intelligence, kindness or likability, and men seemed unaware of this red effect.[378] Somewhat surprisingly, the effect goes both ways. When women rated photographs of men wearing red or photographed in front of a red background, they considered the men to be more attractive and sexually desirable than with other colors. The use of red did not affect the women's perception of the men's likability, extraversion or agreeableness. The participants seemed unaware of the impact red coloring had on their perception.[379]

Men perceive women who are wearing red clothing to be more attractive and more sexually receptive than when women wear white. Women also perceive other women wearing red to be more sexually receptive, but not more attractive. Women are more likely to make derogatory comments about the sexual fidelity of a woman wearing red, and they are more likely to guard their partner against a woman wearing a red shirt relative to a green one.[380]

Women also were found to use the color red strategically. In a blinded study, women in their twenties were recruited to come in for an interview, and they sent a photo of the man scheduled to interview them. Some participants received a photo of an attractive young man while others received a photo of a not so attractive man. Upon arrival, the women were told that the man was not available, but as part of the interview process, they were photographed. A later assessment of the photos analyzed the color of clothing they wore. The women who believed that they would be meeting an attractive young man were 6.8 times more likely to be displaying red clothing than those that had expected to meet the less attractive man.[381]

Wearing red increases the perception of a woman's sexual availability. Although men may find women wearing red to be warmer and more competent, it also may increase their sexual interest, and when women wear red, it may garner animosity from other women.

Women can use red clothing, lipstick, and accessories strategically; however, red clothing should be subdued or avoided when a woman campaigns, seeks leadership consensus from other women, or interviews with a female employer. In an obvious double standard, men can get away with a red silk power tie, as women find it attractive and straight men miss the signal.

Note: Many female members of U.S. Congress wear red blazers in their official portraits. The red jacket is attention-grabbing and helps women stand out from their male counterparts wearing charcoal and navy blue. The bold red jacket helps these women gain media attention rather than be lost in the crowd among their male colleagues. The red jackets would likely not be helpful during professional job interviews or during a campaign, except in situations where there is a sea of other candidates one wants to be differentiated from.

The goal in culturing a professional persona is to appear competent, healthy, and educated. Appearing sexually alluring sends a different message. Sexually alluring styles are attractive but attract sexual attention. It does not raise the appraisal of competence or trust in either men or women. Men often interpret overt sexiness in a woman's appearance as availability, but not as competence (other than competently fertile) and women are often put off by other women who use sexy styles of dress and makeup. Women may perceive other women with a sexy appearance as artificial, competitive, mate-poaching, or male-baiting trollops.

The appraisal of sexual fitness is implicit and automatic. While the inherent internal response to these signals may be natural, we are responsible for our behavior. There is no place for sexual assault or sexual harassment in our society, and a person's appearing sexually attractive is never an excuse for sexual victimization or objectification.

I'm fairly certain that men were not built for platonic male-female relationships, and am unsure about women. I don't have much helpful advice here – like our implicit prejudices, this is another area of human behavior and foible we are far from mastering.

When men have fairly open opportunity, as in marriage, the average man seeks sex on about 12 occasions per month at the age of 21, and the frequency gradually declines to about five times per month by the age of 65. Men that are physically fit have a slower decline in sexual drive. Between the ages of 45 and 55, the average man seeks sexual relations about seven times a month or about every four days. Middle-aged women generally have a slower build-up of sexual drive and seek relationships less frequently.

Thus, it can be assumed that a healthy middle-aged man develops sufficient sexual appetite to initiate sexual advances at least every four days. Conventional wisdom of married men of this age who travel for work is that women start to catch their attention about the third day away from home. The longer the time a person is away from their regular sexual partner, the more likely that sex drive will overflow into other relationships.

To avoid unwanted sexual overtures in professional relations, one can try to avoid high-risk situations. One risk is spending time alone with co-workers that might be potential sexual partners when traveling away from home for more than a couple of days. Evenings, especially when alcohol is consumed is another time of increased risk of unwanted or unintended sexual advances. Avoid sexually alluring signals, such as wearing red, to lower risk of unwanted advances.

Understanding how appearance can influence how we react to each other allows us to tailor the use of dress and makeup to best serve how we wish to be perceived. People should be mindful that their appearance can broadcast implicit signals that are perceived as sexual readiness.

Elegance is also attractive. The word *elegant* has a couple of meanings; pleasingly graceful when speaking of demeanor and style, and pleasingly simple and effective when speaking of solutions to a problem. Elegance is practical, uncomplicated, and appropriate for professional situations.

Pearl: Glamorous styles in cosmetics, clothing, and jewelry should be avoided in most professional situations, and as a candidate.

Pebble: While women with a waist to hip ratio of 0.7 are most attractive to men, men with 12% body fat are most attractive to woman; this level of body fat is associated with a high immune competence. Testosterone levels in men were found to fall in association with increasing body fat levels.[382]

The weirder you're going to behave, the more normal you should look. It works in reverse, too. When I see a kid with three or four rings in his nose, I know there is absolutely nothing extraordinary about that person.

~P. J. O'Rourke

Pearl: The more you hope to be an instrument of change in the world, the more in tune you should be and more orthodox you should look.

Chapter 24: Voice

Men with lower-pitched voices are perceived to be physically stronger, more dominant and more attractive than men with higher pitched voices. It is somewhat different for women; women with higher-pitched voices are perceived to be more attractive, and those with lower-pitched voices are perceived to be more dominant.

For both genders, high-pitched, stressed voices are associated with negative emotions including stress, fear, and panic.[139] While female voices with a high fundamental pitch are considered to be more attractive, this is in large part because of its association with age; [383] both men's and women's voices become deeper into middle-age.

Voice is an important physical trait for a candidate. Hillary Clinton's voice during her speeches was often described as shrill, irritating, and annoying. Her vocal pitch is typical for her age, so that was not what people found objectionable. However, rather than controlling her breath from the abdomen, during speeches, she pushes air from the throat. This caused her voice to sound harsh and tight, and causes her to look as if she is straining and uncomfortable; her audience perceives and feels this discomfort. Recall from Chapter 7, the German study where viewers were able to discern subjects with an annoying voice just watching them read on video, with the sound off.[384]

Many people felt that Hilary Clinton's voice was annoying. When she wanted to make a point, she would speak louder. She used excessive force when speaking into the microphone during her speeches and this was amplified by the "mic proximity-effect" which can cause harsh penetrating sounds. When speaking in front of large crowds, her voice also lacked typical femininity. It lacked musicality (fluctuation in pitch) and softness; things expected in a woman's voice. Although Secretary Clinton annunciates very clearly, her speaking voice has no recognizable regionalism or folksiness as did Bill Clinton's. Her speech was not especially distinctive, a feature that voters like in candidates.[385] These traits make her voice less interesting and less pleasant to listen to.

Nevertheless, when she did use a Southern Black sociolect when speaking to a Southern Black audience, she was soundly criticized for pandering. It is not only women who are judged on their voice. Howard Dean let out an enthusiastic yelp at the end of a primary in 2004, and it contributed to the tanking of his campaign.

Analysis of US presidential debates between 1960 and 2000 found that the candidate with the lower voice was perceived to have performed better and went on to win a higher percentage of the popular vote. Both men and woman show a preference in voting for men with lower-pitched voices. In partisan politics, conservatives more strongly align with candidates with lower-pitched voices than do liberals. A similar finding has been observed in school board elections; men and women both preferred the female candidate with the lower-pitched voice. When women face women in an election, the one with the lower voice has a great advantage. When men face men in an election, having a lower voice gives a smaller, but still, several percentage point advantage.[386]

In contrast, however, when facing a female candidate for the House of Representatives, men with lower-than-average pitched-voices performed less well against a female candidate than did men with higher pitched voices.[387] This may result from the perception that the man with a higher pitched voice is less aggressive (towards the female candidate).

As people mature, the pitch of the voice falls until middle age; this deepening is a testosterone effect. After the age of sixty with a decline in testosterone, the pitch rises some. From the ages 40 to 60, the voice is at its lowest. This correlates with the ages at which candidates are most likely to win elective office.

In an experimental study, the voices of men and women were recorded while requesting voters to vote for them, along with a brief political, but non-partisan message. The voices were then digitally altered to control the pitch for playback. Subjects were then asked to listen to five voice pairs and select which voice in each pair was stronger, older, more competent, and which they would vote for. The questions and the voices were presented in random order. The lower voices were considered stronger, more competent, more mature, and selected as the preferred candidate they would vote for in over 60 percent of the pairs, giving the lower voice a greater than 20 percent advantage (60% vs. 40%). When the race was between women, the lower voice won over 70% of the voice parings.[388] [389]

For both men's and women's voices, lower-pitched voices are perceived to be more trustworthy than higher pitched ones. This is likely because the voice deepens with age, and older adults are deemed more trustworthy. However, the correlation with low timbre was stronger for competence than it was for age.[390] For men, but not for women, a lower voice was also perceived to be more dominant. In men, a lower voice is considered more attractive and preferred in most contexts. The preference for voice pitch in women is context dependent.[391] A higher pitched woman's voice is usually considered more attractive as it is associated with youth and fertility. Softer or higher pitched female voices are perceived as more caring, and more musical voices (with greater pitch variation) and higher pitched voices are perceived as friendlier, less threatening, and more cooperative.[392]

In a study evaluating speed dating, it was found that when flirting, the pitch of men's voices fall and the pitch range widens, meanwhile woman's pitches rise, and they speak more softly, as if more intimately. Friendly speech by men was higher pitched and had less pitch variation. In women, during friendly speech, there was more pitch variation, and the speech was louder. When people felt awkward, the speech was lower pitched, slowed, stilted and interrupted with uhs and ums.[393]

Pebble: In studies of the perception of male voices, a voice with the fundamental frequency of 96 Hz has been found to be the most attractive. This frequency is between F♮2 and G2 on a piano or one on the lowest string of a guitar, between the second and third fret. The average male voice has a mean fundamental frequency of 120 Hz, between A♭2 and B2 on the piano or just above the A string of a guitar.

Pearl: When we speak quickly, get excited, or stressed, the pitch of the voice tends to rise. By slowing down, the pitch will stay lower and sound more authoritative. Try to slow your speech by about ten percent to sound more competent and authoritative.

Find Your Radio Voice

Pearl: In the German study outlined in Chapter 7, people were able to discern which speakers had annoying voices from silent videos of people talking. The clue may have been posture. A head-forward posture will add strain to the voice and may give it a higher pitch and have it sound strained and unpleasant. The shoulders should be balanced and relaxed, not hunched forward. Also, when our posture is upright and balanced, and we are relaxed, we can more easily and are more likely to breathe from the diaphragm which gives more relaxed and smooth breath control and adds resonance. Correct posture is discussed in Chapter 21.

Avoid speaking from the throat. This can occur if one tries to speak with a lower than natural tone, speaks with a nasal tone, or is stressed. Nasal voices are also unpleasant and less resonant. Try this; take a breath so that the abdomen enlarges like a balloon, and only speak while the belly is going in so that the "balloon" is deflating. It is then time for another breath. Doing this will help you breathe from the diaphragm.

Your best voice is your relaxed, natural voice. A natural, relaxed voice, regardless of its fundamental pitch, will be resonant, expressive, and rich. A relaxed, resonant voice sounds deeper than a stressed voice. The expressiveness in a voice comes from being relaxed and using a natural range of pitches when speaking.

Pearl: To find your natural, relaxed voice, standing with correct posture and practice humming so that the lips buzz for a few minutes each morning. You should feel just a bit of vibration just below the cheekbones. Try practicing mmm-hmm, with the lips closed and count saying the number: Mmm-hmm 1, mmm-hmm 2, mmm-hmm 3, mmm-hmm, 4..., and focus on having the sound emanate from the face rather than the throat or nose. One can practice and warm-up the voice while getting ready for the day.

Prosody

We modulate our voice for different situations. When we speak with another person that is more dominant or of higher prestige, we are likely to raise the fundamental frequency of our speech in deference and submission. However, when we perceive ourselves to be dominant in a conversation, we are less likely to alter our pitch, and if we do, we may lower it slightly. When we enter a conversation where status and authority is unknown, we tend to lower our pitch, as if to not to give up any power points until the pecking order has been established.[394]

Prosody is the patterns of rhythm, inflection, and sounds in language that conveys emotional content and meaning beyond the words. A large amount of the semantic content in language is communicated through the intonation, pitch, and cadence, the musical elements in language. In 1871, Darwin noted in *The Descent of Man* that "Even monkeys express strong feelings in different tones – anger and impatience by low, – fear and pain by high notes."[395] The reason that music is perceived to express emotion is that it mimics the prosody of language.[396]

This morning, I walked past a man speaking with his wife on the beach and heard this smidgen of conversation: "It's just an idea; we don't have to go." But that does not convey what he said at all. What he actually voiced was that he highly wanted to and intended to do the activity being discussed and that he would be disappointed and annoyed with her if she put the kibosh on it. He said, "It's just an iDEa. We don't <u>HAVE</u> to go." If someone asks "Where did you get that?" it can be an accusation, ridicule, envy or just asking where they acquired the object. The changes in pitch, rhythm, and inflection change the meaning of language and change the dynamics of relationships people have with each other.

Anger, surprise, and sadness are easily recognized in vocal prosody, and happiness and fear are usually, but somewhat less reliably communicated. Disgust and sarcasm, however, are poorly recognized through prosody in language.[397]

Pearl: When we want something, we become supplicant, and the pitch of our voice rises. When we offer to give something, the pitch of the voice goes lower. Remember when speaking as a leader in directing activity, one is not asking for favors. Using the lower range of your voice shows confidence and authority. When asking for cooperation, it is a request, and the voice should reveal that.

Pearl: It is not just the fundamental pitch of the voice that communicates confidence and establishes authority. Just as, or perhaps more, important is the change of pitch during the sentence. If the pitch rises towards the end of the sentence, it signals either a question or a lack of dominance in the exchange. If the pitch rises and comes back down to where it started, it indicates that you are on equal footing with the other person. It the pitch falls to its lowest pitch at the end of the sentence, it indicates a command or authority. Pearl: Try recording a brief conversation with someone you are dominant to (your child), equal to (a friend) and to a superior (your boss, and listen to your vocal inflections. See how your voice changes, and practices speaking as an equal or authority for the appropriate situation.

A rising pitch and increasing speed towards the end of a sentence also shows excitement and enthusiasm, while a falling pitch and slowing at the end can denote that something is bad or final. If someone says "The hurricane caused a great disaster" with a rising tone and emphasis on the word great, we would likely conclude that they were happy about it. A rising pitch may indicate stress or fear.

Pearl: Use pauses to place emphasis, by separating phrases and concepts. Compare these two sentences: "Think of a great tree in a forest and how you would feel if I cut it down." Or instead, "Think of a great tree in a forest. (Pause) How would you feel if I cut it down?" The separation of connected ideas gives the listener time to create the image and adds drama to the point.

Pearl: When introducing yourself, say your first name with a rising inflection and after a tiny pause, your last name with a falling tonal inflection. Your first name is for friends and peers (rising, enthusiastic, and non-dominant), and your last name, more formal and authoritative.)

Pearl: If you don't like listening to your own recorded voice, then perhaps it's time to make it more pleasant for others to listen to.

Pearl: The voice is a musical instrument and inflection is an important part of communication. Use it to add melody. Practice using your instrument by singing. Prosody also makes language more understandable.

Pearl: Mouth breathing causes dry throat. Breathe in through the nose to moisturize it if you feel your throat starting to dry from talking.

Pearl: When responding to a question, use a similar verbal structure in your response, (such as repeating a central phrase without repeating the entire question). It shows that you are addressing the question rather than dodging it and that you are in tune with, and listening to the other party. It also makes for a smoother transition helping to connect the idea of the question with the answer.

Be cautious however not to blindly repeat metaphors that you do not agree with. "Tax-reform" is a metaphor where the word reform indicates the need to change iniquitous, immoral or abusive tax rules. The proposed changes in a tax plan, however, may make changes that create further inequity and economic disadvantage on some but not others. The metaphor that government should be run as a business supports the idea that profit is the central reason for government, and estate tax when called a "death tax" is something to be avoided at all cost.

Using a Microphone

Talking into a microphone can make novices sound terrible. Speaking too closely into a microphone can cause S's to sizzle and P's to pop and T's to explode, all of which are annoying. Speaking too loudly when the amplification is set high will cause squealing feedback. Any noise will be amplified. If you try to talk over a cheering crowd (in our dreams), or a over a jeering, booing, or otherwise noisy hoard, what you and they hear, and what will be recorded, may sound completely, and unflatteringly different.

One difficulty is that different microphones have different characteristics and the distance the mouth should keep from the microphone depends on the mic. With a lapel mic, one should not need to worry about loudness, breath or plosive sounds. But with any mic, the speaker still needs to project and speak clearly.

Pearl: When using a *handheld mic*, the appropriate speaking distance is usually close; one to two inches. Hold the mic below the lips and point it at your nose, so the air travels over the mic, but so the breath flows above it – and is not directed into it. Any change in the distance will change the volume. With handheld mics, make sure to keep the same distance from the microphone, especially if turning to answer questions as when turning to look at different parts of the audience. The microphone should come with you; otherwise, your voice will drop off. If this is too much to focus on, try just keeping the foam ball on the mic touching the chin.

Pearl: For most microphones, speak over the mic, rather than into it. This should decrease the wind effect from the breath and decrease hissing S's, popping plosives from P's, B', and T's, as well as breath sounds and smacking lip noises that are amplified the closer you are and more directly you speak into a mic.

Pearl: *Podium Microphones*: Point the microphone at your mouth, and speak into it from about eight inches. When adjusting the level of the mic, take hold of the neck or boom without touching the microphone to avoid causing feedback noise.

Pearl: If you are going to raise your voice for emphasis or shout, move away from the microphone. It will still capture the energy that is being displayed, with less distortion and without hurting ears.

Pearl: To test a microphone when an audience is gathered, do not blow on the microphone, thump it, or say testing 1-2-3. Just say hello, or gently tap the side of the mic below the mouthpiece. The sound tech will get it together, and you will not look unprepared as you do when you make the assumption that the mic needs testing.

Pearl: *Lavaliere microphones* are clipped to a lapel or collar, about eight inches below the chin. Speak as if you are talking to a small group. With these clip-on mics, you don't have to worry about the distance or direction of the microphone. These mics are usually wireless and have a battery pack that will clip onto a belt or slips into a pocket.

Pearl: If wearing a dress or other clothing without pocket or waistband, there may be no place to put the lavaliere microphone battery pack. Thus, such clothing may not work for interviews. Clothing that makes rustling sounds or necklaces that hit buttons or hit the mic will make unwanted noise.

Pearl: If you are speaking into a microphone for a one-on-one conversation, think of the microphone as a recording device, and speak as if you are talking to someone across the table or as if speaking to a small group in a conference room. If speaking to a crowd with a mic, you need to project even more, although the microphone will amplify your voice. Speak as if you are talking to a classroom or to the people in the first and second row in front of you.

Pearl: If you have the opportunity, practice with the microphone before using it publicly to get a sound check and test the best distance.

Pearl: if you have to clear your throat, try swallowing. If that does not work, move away from the mic to clear it.

Pearl: Smile while on radio – it will come across in your voice. Avoid sarcasm as it does not transmit well on radio.

Pearl: Find the off button so that you can turn it off when you're done speaking, and avoid being overheard making noises or saying things you had expected to be private.

P.S.: Avoid ever saying or writing anything you don't want public.

Vocal Fry

About two-thirds of young English speaking college women use vocal fry, also known as glottal fry, in their speech, especially at the end of sentences.[398] Vocal fry is phonation using the glottis to give a low pitched; it gives a creaking sound. American women commonly use a fry when attempting to sound more authoritative, intelligent, serious, and determined, as it lowers the fundamental pitch of their voice. The vocal fry is not considered pleasant or attractive sounding. However, the vocal fry is defended by some as giving young upwardly mobile women more credibility and gravitas. Others argue that it betrays an underlying lack of confidence. Thus, raising the question, of whether vocal fry is effective in empowering women.

In a study designed to elucidate the perception of vocal fry on listeners, participants were asked to evaluate voices with and without glottal fry for competence, attractiveness, intelligence and to choose which "candidate" from the pair they would be more likely to hire. The fry voice was lower pitched; however, it was rated, regardless of the listeners' ages or gender, as less competent, less trustworthy, less educated, less attractive, and the speaker was less likely to be chosen to be hired. This was true for both male and female speakers. Women's voices with a vocal fry were chosen as the more preferred voice in these categories only about 18 percent of the time. A vocal fry is apparently even slightly less desirable in men, as the fry voice was chosen only about 15 percent of the time. This data strongly argues that a fry is not helpful in augmenting the perception of competence or intelligence.[399]

Recall that facial typicality and health are considered attractive in both men and women. Men are perceived to be more attractive, competent, and trustworthy when they look typically male, and women when they look typically female. Additionally and more importantly, a healthy appearance is not only attractive but also seen as more trustworthy; disease is off-putting and potentially dangerous. A vocal fry sounds similar to a hoarse voice that may be caused by disease or screaming. Neither of these is endearing. A fry is similar to a growling sound made by animals, both large and small, including birds, in order to appear larger and more aggressive. Thus, the fry may be implicitly interpreted not as confident, but rather defensive and hostile.

If a fry is used, it should be used very sparingly, and only at the end of a sentence to emphasize a command.

Upspeak (Valley Girl)

Upspeak, a defining trait of the Valley Girl sociolect, is the use of a rising pitch in a declarative sentence. More typically, a rising terminal pitch is used in a sentence when making a query, but in upspeak, it signifies that the user has more to say. Nevertheless, persons outside of the sociolect group may interpret the speaker of declarative, upspeak statements as unsure of what they have said or as asking for permission.

Some upspeak is normal in the general American dialect, and it is especially used by women. However, in the typical use, it is used in a submissive tone or when requesting agreement. Men also sometimes use upspeak to signal the absence of hostile intent when speaking with women.[400]

Upspeak is common in some sociolects but not in others, so that it can be easily misinterpreted when speaking to those outside of one's group. A British survey was conducted, which included 700 business owners, managers, and executives to study their perception of upspeak among employees. Eighty-five percent of the business people considered upspeak to be a "clear indicator of a person's insecurity or emotional weakness." More than half felt it would hinder the person's prospects of promotions and pay raises in their organization, and that upspeak damages the speaker's professional credibility.[401]

In professional settings, upspeak should be limited to questions and to when intentionally signaling lack of dominance. Thus, it is not often helpful outside of when asking questions or requesting consensus.

String of Pearls

Pearl: Women have the most power when they are clear and direct, but lose power when perceived as aggressive, defensive, or angry.

Pearl: Avoid using volume as a sole device to create emphasis. It is important to vary volume to help people focus on the main points. If the volume and pitch of speech remain the same, people start to tune-out. We assume they have made their point, and there is no further emotional content. Speakers who talk in a monotone are monotonous, and listeners lose interest or get annoyed. When someone speaks in a monotone, the emotional message, which is the most important element in carrying interest, is missing, so there is no reason to continue listening. A musical voice is more pleasant and will hold attention better.

Pearl: You can't force anyone to change their mind, so force is ineffective. You may be able to persuade others once you understand them.

Remember that media is entertainment. Be entertaining, or at least interesting. If you are interviewed by a reporter or on air, it is because they want a story that is interesting; one that affects peoples affect. They want a story that creates an emotional response. That response may be humor, a sense of pride, imagination or indignation. The more entertaining you are, the more likely you will get more free air time.

Pearl: For every talk or appearance you give, choose your three main points you want to get across. Write them down on a 3x5 card and take it with you. Open your conversation with those three points. You should be able to say everything in 30 seconds. Use the rest of any airtime you have to expand on those points. If possible deliver those messages in a form that is quotable, makes an interesting sound bite, or a tease that motivates people to listen to the entire interview.

Media hosts and reporters may say things that are off-color, rude, offensive, derisive, or obscene. Be careful. This does not make it O.K. for you to do so.

If while being recorded you flub your sound bite, stop, take a breath and start from the beginning as if nothing had happened. The media wants that sound bite, and will likely edit out dead air and the rest.

Chapter 25: Mug Shots

As a candidate, your photos may be the most important source of information from which voters make their decision to support you or not. As a candidate for a non-supreme-leader elected position, your photos may be all that many voters know about you other than your name at the time of your first election. A photo will likely make and cement the first impression people make of you.

When selecting a photograph for developing an online persona, whether for professional, social, or romantic purposes, we select images that show us in a way that we hope we will be perceived. These images will often form the first impressions to those encountering the person's image for the first time. These images can affect our future by impacting our personal, social and professional relationships.

First impressions from photographs are important. Recall that when people were first shown an attractive photo of a person and later shown an unattractive photo of the same person, they rated the person as being more attractive than if they had not seen the first picture. If viewers saw the unattractive photo first but were shown the attractive photo of the person later, they rated the person as less attractive when seeing the attractive photo. [402] Be careful about what photos you make public.

In a study of just over 100 undergraduate students, each participant submitted 12 photos of their faces, downloaded from their Facebook account. The subjects were then asked to select from these 12 photos a profile-image for use on Facebook (social media), LinkedIn (professional) and the dating site Match.com. The assumption was that people would select the photo that presented them most favorably to friends for Facebook, most professionally for the business setting, LinkedIn, and use their most attractive photo for potential romantic partners for the dating site. The participants were then asked to rate their own photos according to attractiveness, trustworthiness, dominance, competence, and confidence, on a scale of one (low) to nine (high). Participants were then asked to rank these facial traits for another randomly-selected, same-gender participant that they had not previously known. Additionally, 20 internet-recruited "judges" also scored each set of 12 photos for these personality traits.

As would be expected, people chose images they rates as most attractive for social media and dating sites, and those rated as appearing most competent and trustworthy for the professional site. The surprising outcome of the study, as you might expect (why else would it be here?) was that people were not very adept at selecting images that showed them in the most favorable light for these traits. People actually were surprisingly lousy at selecting good pictures of themselves for the appropriate uses, while strangers were much more astute observers in rating faces. [403]

We are too familiar with our own faces, and thus, we consider our face to be normal; normal and familiar faces are perceived to be safer and more trusted. This causes us to perceive our face as being more trustworthy and attractive than others do. The lesson of this study is to recruit others, preferably people who are not close to you, to select photos of you for the context in which they are needed. People who are less biased by familiarity with you are more likely to select the photos in which you look most attractive, competent, trustworthy, dominant and confident.

Pearl: Have people, preferably people that do not know you choose photos of you after giving them the criteria you are looking for. They will choose better than you will.

News Flash

The dating site OkCupid uses software to match potential clients for dating; it matches people on attractiveness as well as age, location, and other attributes that help increase the likelihood of couples linking up. More attractive women prefer to date more attractive men, while less attractive men tend to have lower expectations for which women will be willing to date them.

The OkCupid software gathers data as people look at pictures of their clients. They can determine how attractive people are in the pictures that have been submitted by the amount of interest in that person. The website keeps score on how attractive and desirable people find the photos to be, and then uses an algorithm to match potential couples of similar attractiveness. This gives OkCupid a huge data set with millions of ratings of the attractiveness of people in over half a million photos. Most of these photos carry data encrypted as EXIF data that tell shutter speed, whether a flash was used, and other data from the camera.

A camera flash creates a single source, direct light that accentuates blemishes, scars, and wrinkles. After our mid-twenties, attractiveness decreases with age. OkCupid found that using a flash lowered the attractiveness of people in photographs by the equivalent of adding seven years of age.[404]

Pearl: Using a single source flash decreases attractiveness and increases perceived age by about seven years.

OkCupid also found that photos from camera phones gave the least attractive photos, and the digital SLR cameras with interchangeable lenses gave more attractive photos than did point and shoot cameras. It is not surprising that the more complex cameras, which are also likely used by more competent and experienced photographers, give better photographs. OkCupid also found that outdoor lighting, about an hour before sunset, gave the most flattering natural lighting. The effect of this lighting was likely to give people a healthy reddish glow, as well as being softer, more diffuse lighting that minimized shadows from wrinkles, scars and bumps.

Photos that focus on the subject and blur the background give a more intimate feel and have less distraction, giving more attractive portraits, especially for photos in which there is distracting stuff in the background. This is one reason that more complex cameras may give better portraits. Using a larger *f*-stop on the camera (using a larger lens aperture and requiring more glass) gives a shallower depth of focus, allowing the eyes of the person to be in focus and the background out of focus. An *f*-stop of 1.8 or lower (the lower the *f*-number, the larger the aperture) gave the best results. Most less-expensive cameras, however, do not have lenses this large. Thus a larger aperture can give a more attractive portrait. Try to use an f-stop of 2.2 or lower when having an open-air photo portrait done.

Aside: When OkCupid set up blind-dates on attributes that did not include attractiveness, the likelihood that a couple would continue to date between two people of similar attractiveness and two people of different attractiveness did not change. Once two well-matched people got through the first meeting and sat down and talked, looks

In a study of face perception, 45 male and female subjects were photographed using lenses of different focal lengths. A 50 mm lens, a standard length for general photography, an 85 mm lens, and a slightly longer, 105 mm, slightly telephoto, lens were used. All these lenses are used in portrait photography. Each subject was photographed with each lens. An *f*-stop of 8.0 was used for every photograph. The distance varied by lens used; the distance was set so that the head filled the same portion of the frame for each photo.

The photos were randomized and presented to reviewers who were asked to judge the triad of photos from most to least attractive, dominant, and masculine or feminine. The photos were also measured for their face width to height ratios.

In the photos, women were considered to be considerably less attractive and less feminine in the photos taken with the 50 mm lens, and slightly but not significantly more attractive and feminine when the 85 mm lens was used rather than with the 105 mm lens. Women were seen as considerably more dominant using the 105 mm lens than with the shorter lenses. Men were perceived to be more attractive, masculine and dominant in the photos taken with the 105 mm lens. In men, there were large differences in ratings of dominance and masculinity between the 85 mm and 105 mm lenses, but the difference in attractiveness was small. Finally, the face width to height ratio was significantly smaller with the 50 mm lens, which explains the decreased perception of masculinity and dominance using the short 50 mm lens.[405]

This effect from lens length may be attributed to the distance from which the photo was taken rather than the lens used, as this study changed the distance from the subject for each lens.

In a separate study, 45 subjects were given $100 to play a computer investing game. In the game, they were shown images of 18 pairs of men's faces. Each man had two simultaneous photos taken, one from 18 inches and the other from 53 inches, creating 36 different images. The participants were asked to decide on randomly paired photos of different men, which was more trustworthy and then to decide how much to invest with that man in a round of the game. At the end, from one randomly selected pair, if the man was the more trustworthy, they would go home with $300. This game has been demonstrated to motivate participants to choose more trustworthy faces accurately. The participants invested about four times as much cash when shown images taken from 53 inches as they did from photos taken from 18 inches. The participants then rated the faces for age and weight, and on a scale of one to seven on trustworthiness, attractiveness, and competence. There was no difference in perceived age, but the more distant photos made the men appear a bit heavier. The increased distance widens the face and does cause the person to look heavier. The photos taken from 53 inches were rated as more trustworthy and competent. The photos from a greater distance were also judged to be more average (typical), and thus more attractive. The authors suggest that the near photos are interpreted as invading the personal space of the viewer, and thus breaching trust.[406]

Pearl: Avoid having your picture taken with a short lens and from short distances. If you want to project dominance, a 105 mm lens will help, with only a minor decline in the perception of femininity and attractiveness. Men who would prefer to appear less dominant and masculine might have a photo done using an 85 mm lens without a loss in attractiveness. Do not publish selfies unless you have five foot long arms.

When photographed with the head tilted down, it makes men appear more aggressive, as it makes the brows appear lower and increases the perceived face width to height ratio. In at least young women in a mating choice context, when the face is tilted down, it gives a more attractive, feminine and submissive appearance.[407]

Leaders are often photographed from slightly below, perhaps to make them appear taller, more dignified, and perhaps, larger than life so that we look up to them. Photos taken from a lower viewpoint, however, increase the perception of body weight, while those taken from above decrease the estimation of body weight.[408] A downwards view is perceived to be younger, and upwards view appears to be older.

Three-quarter view and full-frontal view photos are rated similarly on personality traits (aggressiveness, competence, dominance, likeability, and trustworthiness) with very brief viewing (50/1000 of a second), but attractiveness and facial maturity take slightly more time to discriminate for the three-quarters perspective.[409] However, our faces are not laterally symmetrical. One side of our face shows different characteristics than the other side. This means that if we are photographed in a three-quarters view, halfway between a profile and a frontal view, only those features of that side of the face will be seen. Thus, by selecting the side of the face visible to the camera, we can highlight certain characteristics.

In a study judging the perception of the "big-five personality traits" plus health, views of the right side of the face of women were *more accurate* in judging agreeableness, emotional stability, and health. The view of the left side of the face allowed for a more accurate view of extraversion. Neither conscientiousness nor intellect was significantly differentiated. While the right side of the face gives more accurate discrimination of personality, the left side gives, on average, higher values for health, attractiveness, emotional stability, openness, and conscientiousness. Thus, the right face provides more accurate and often more negative information on these traits.[410] The left side of the face is less revealing and tends to obscure lower values of these traits, raising the assessment of those with lower scores.

At least among women, faces that have high health, attractiveness, emotional stability, and openness can use right, three-quarter view photos that emphasize these positive characteristics. Women with more average facial characteristics might choose a left, three-quarters view as giving a more positive presentation.

This advantage of the left view may explain the left cheek bias for selfies. Women, but not men, are considerably more likely to take selfies of the left side of their faces.[411] In fact, throughout the history of photography and in portrait painting, there has been a bias towards portraying the left side of the face. When painters do self-portraits using a mirror, they are more likely to do a right face view – showing the anatomical left side of their face. Similarly mirror selfies also more often show the anatomical left side of the face.[412]

In spite of this, in a study of 5829 photos of faculty members from official university websites, both men and women scientist in the fields of mathematics, engineering and chemistry showed a bias towards showing the right side of the face, while women in the social sciences, literature, psychology, and the performing arts had the typical bias towards posting photos of the left side of the face.[413] The reason for this is that, apparently, the right side of the face shows intellect more strongly, whereas the left side is more attractive.

The left side of the face is more revealing of emotions for both men and women, other than spontaneous anger which is easier to see on the right side of the face. The left side of a smiling face appears happier, more emotive and more trustworthy. In most studies, the right side of the face, however, is judged to be more attractive in women.[414]

In a study done to understand the effect of viewpoint on the heuristic perception of faces, 3D scans of the faces of seven men and seven women were made. The use of a 3D scan allowed several different images to be made where there was no variation of facial expression between images of the individual. The computer images created various perspectives; 30° below, 30° right, 15° right, frontal view, 15° left, 30° left, and 30° above. Each viewpoint was then rated on a seven-point scale by 172 participants for attractiveness, helpfulness, sympathy, dominance, distinctiveness, and intelligence. The participants also estimated body mass of the individuals for each perspective. It should be noted that only the frontal view "looked" at the viewer in these images, as the gaze did not change between perspectives.

The most attractive perspective was the 15° left hemiface view, followed by either 30° hemiface views and then the 15° right hemiface view. The least attractive perspectives for women and men were 30° above followed by the frontal and below views. Right 30° hemiface views gave the highest ratings for being helpful, sympathetic and intelligent. The finding that the right side of the face appears more intelligent explains the reason that university academics in the field of science would select right sided images, as this trait is highly valued while attractiveness, more evident on the left side, is more favored by women in the humanities.

The view from 30° from above stood out as being strongly perceived to be less helpful than other perspective views. This is not surprising as a downwards head tilt and gaze are a sign of submission[415] and physical smallness. The average estimated weight for men and women in their frontal views was 162 and 159 pounds respectively. It was a few pounds less for the 15° and 30° side viewpoints. Both men and women were estimated to be considerably smaller in the 30° from above images, with estimated average body masses of 150 and 144 pounds respectively. Men and women were judged to be considerably larger when viewed from 30° below, with estimated body masses of 176 and 167 pounds respectively. This difference in mass should not be assumed to be associated primarily with a perception of obesity, but rather of stature and size, as well as weight.

Pearl: a photo from below can make one appear to be larger.

In this study, the viewpoint of the face did not affect the perception of dominance. The authors suggest this occurred because these computer images did not show the neck; neck muscle mass may be an important clue to the perception of dominance.[416] A head-forward posture stretches the neck and gives a less dominant appearance. This is further discussed in the chapter on posture.

Pearl: If you are in a profession or political contest that values intelligence, a 30° right hemiface photo can give a more intelligent and helpful appearance for your professional and LinkedIn pictures.

Pearl: If you are in a profession or political contest that values attractiveness, or need a photo for other purposes that accentuates attractiveness, try a 15° left hemiface photo.

Pearl: The right side of the face gives a more accurate perception of agreeableness, emotional stability, while the left side gives a more flattering view.

Pearl: If you would like to appear more massive, have a picture taken from below.

Pearl: If you would like to appear strong and dominant, make sure your posture is perfect in the photo. No matter the angle from which the photo is taken, if you want to look competent and level-headed, be level-headed when the picture is taken.

Pearl: Women look most attractive with an 85 mm lens and men look more dominant with a 105 mm lens that gives a slightly wider appearing face.

Pearl: A better quality camera, with a larger lens and larger aperture, allowing for a smaller f-stop and with a shallower depth of field can put the background out of focus making for a less cluttered image in which the subject stands out. A better-qualified finger on the shutter button can also give a more flattering and dynamic portrait.

Pearl: For elected office, the goal is to appear as a competent adult. It's O.K. to hide blemishes, but avoid "Photoshopping" that removes character and maturity and gives baby-butt smooth skin.

TV and Video

TV and video have their own idiosyncrasies. Your dress should be as for other professional settings, neat, wrinkle-free, and well-fit, comfortable, but not tight.

Video cameras do not see the world the same way we do, not even the way still cameras do. An important difference is that video cameras have limited lines of information and this can cause a moiré phenomenon when recording small patterns. You have likely seen this, where fabric seems to move on TV. It is quite distracting. Another problem is that video cameras do automatic white balancing. This can wash out white clothing so that details are lost, can glow, or worse, cause the camera to darken other colors as it seeks to balance brightness. A third problem is bleeding. Red tends to bleed on video cameras. Some of the cautions listed in this section have become less important with the use of high-definition television, but may still be a problem for local news stations or for viewers using older TVs.

Fabric with patterns should be avoided, especially narrow stripes, herringbone, checks, and other textured patterns that cause moiré. Solid colors work well.

Both black and white clothing should be avoided. Blue, charcoal, and tan jackets look better than black jackets on TV. Rather than a white shirt or blouse, a light pastel color will show more detail and look better on TV. A white shirt under a jacket is O.K.

Red can easily over saturate and bleed into adjacent areas on a video camera. A red power tie may make a man look flushed. Bright yellow, hot pink and bright orange should also be avoided. Bright red lipstick should be toned down as well, as it will appear brighter on TV. Blues, berry, and blue-green work well on camera. Lush colors are fine for women; men should stick to more staid colors. Blues are one of the best colors for TV cameras, and more likely to have you look your best.

If wearing a tie, wear one without a pattern, and one that is not shiny.

Green can be a problem if the studio uses green screen – you might disappear into the background.

Pearl: Check out the set before you go to an interview or TV event. At least look on TV to see what the set looks like and how the host dresses to gauge what will be appropriate for you to wear. Always bring a change of clothing for a TV event, in case what you wear clashes with the set.

Pearl: Show less cleavage than you usually feel comfortable with – it will look lower and deeper on TV. Pleats, such as a pleated skirt, make women's hips look bigger on TV. Avoid see-through blouses, short skirts, plunging necklines, or very tall high heels. Looking beautiful is an asset, but sexy and flirtatious appearance decrease a woman's perceived competence and gravitas. Glamorous and sexy makeup should be avoided as a candidate or for a professional look. While you should look your best, unless you are promoting a fashion line, your clothing, accessories, and makeup should be so boring that they don't merit discussion. The focus should be first on your message, second on your message, and third and last, on you.

Anything that can distract, will distract people from you and your message. Avoid shiny and sparkly clothing, accessories or makeup. Shiny fabrics can create glare. The studio light will make things more sparkling and shiny. A slightly matte lipstick will look better than a wet or glossy one. Any bling will be distracting. Do not wear more than one ring per hand. Avoid dangling earrings as they can be distracting. Do not wear bracelets that may make noise that will be picked up and amplified by the microphones. As a candidate, do not wear extravagant jewelry; it sends a message of flaunting privilege. Make sure that your clothes are not wrinkled.

Pearl: Stick to the dress code outlined in previous chapters. Unless the goal is to look eccentric or like a diva, avoid flashy and large jewelry, long or brightly colored fingernails, false eyelashes, sparkly eyeshadow, and candy-colored lipstick. Avoid big hair and extreme styles. Anything that catches the attention will do it more on TV than in person.

Wear clothing that is comfortable so that you look comfortable and relaxed. Bring a bag for your wallet, phone, keys, and other items that you can leave with a trusted person while on the set. You don't need the bulge in your pocket or the distraction of your phone.

If wearing pants, wear socks that are high enough that your calf will not show if you cross your legs. No one wants to see that. Make sure your undergarments cannot be seen when you sit. You don't want your underwear to be what people remember from your TV appearance.

Contact lenses are better than glasses for TV, as glasses can reflect, glare, and make it hard for the audience to see your eyes. If you prefer your look with glasses, get glasses with front and back anti-reflective coatings.

Pebble: Most men never wear makeup, but almost everyone on TV does. Under the bright lights, the nose, forehead, bald and thinning areas of the scalp will look oily and shiny and may look plastic. The makeup will help hide the sweating from the heat of the lights. Use a powder makeup that closely matches your skin color. Men, keep it subtle. I have seen interviews in which men use lipstick to give a better color, but when it is too much − it is all I see. If using lipstick, use one that is matt and on the brownish end of the spectrum.

Under stage lights, things can get hot. Wear a lighter weight suit than you might otherwise for the time of year. Bring a handkerchief. Men should wear a cotton undershirt to help absorb sweat. Antiperspirant is a good idea on these occasions.

If you are delivering a prepared message, practice. Do at least one recorded run on your smartphone to see how you come off.

Be yourself. Assume that the producer invited you to use you to boost their ratings. Don't get conned into supporting a position or issue because it makes for a good story. Use the opportunity to tell your story in the way you want it told.

Even though your mission may be better public policy, politics, and patriotism, when you are invited on the air, it becomes entertainment. If you are entertaining and interesting, dynamic and fun, you will likely be invited back. If you are monotonous, you will not catch the interest of the station or the voters, and will likely not be invited back.

Practice at home, video record, watch, rinse, and repeat. To see how you look, listen to the video with the sound off. Next, watch with the sound on and with your eyes closed.

The camera will make your voice ten pounds wimpier. When on camera, be enthusiastic and speak to the audience. Even though the interviewer is close to you and you are wearing a microphone, project as if you are speaking to a small conference room full of people. Make sure your voice has plenty of inflection and variation in volume, as the microphone will tend to balance it out and make it sound more monotonous. Show that you have a passion for the issues you support. Be thoughtful, and take your time to express yourself clearly. Don't be timid. Have fun!

Zoom and Computer Conferencing

While it is a rare experience to go on TV or cable shows, it is almost impossible to avoid video calls and conferences. Most of these will be done from your home or office, and not in a well lit studio with acoustic isolation. While low quality video and sound are so common-place on these calls, you can still look and sound professional. Most TV interviews are no longer done in a studio, but more often with the interviewee at home.

Dress the part you wish to portray, and prep as if you were going to be interviewed on TV other than you do not need to worry as much about getting hot and sweaty in your at home as you would in a studio. A suit jacket is usually not needed, as you are portraying yourself at home. Nevertheless, it is appropriate to portray yourself as you would in a professional setting. For example, dress as you might be dressed, seated in the office of the job you wish to hold or if you were being interviewed at home by a camera crew.

Lighting: Find the best lighting in your home for video calls. Using your smartphone camera in selfie mode, explore different areas of the home, looking for the best lighting for your face. Look for a spot with bright, disperse lighting that evenly illuminates your face. Avoid backlighting, or having windows to your back. Avoid overhead lighting that will cast shadows on your face. Generally, during day-light hours, the best spots will be facing a window. Hopefully you can find a spot with good lighting to set your computer that is uncluttered and quiet. If you need to add light or to do video calls at night, place light(s) near face level behind the camera to illuminate your face. Using LED lights with a color temperature of 3000° K to 4000 °K gives good skin color tone while 2700 °K incandescent bulbs make people look orange on camera. Light rings with multiple LEDs placed behind or around the camera can give even lighting that make the person appear attractive and minimizes wrinkles and shadows on the face, helping to make you look healthy and attractive.

Webcam criteria: At the time of this writing (2022), the video camera and microphone on most laptops is of insufficient quality to portray us with sufficient clarity. Most webcams currently sold, even those with good ratings, do not have sufficient resolution to give a non-fuzzy image.

Purchase a minimum 1024 pixel wide webcam rated at least HD. A higher pixel rating, for example 2048 pixel or 4K, will allow zooming in. A minimum resolution for reasonable quality image after zooming in is 800 X 600.

I suggest a camera that can do 60 frames per second (FPS), but 30 FPS is sufficient. A webcam that has the capacity to do 60 FPS should have the electronics to do 30 frames per second with ease and not have a jerky image.

Most web cams are wide angle; they give a 100 to 120 degree view. This is a problem as either you will be small in the image, or need to be very close to the camera, which can distort the face, as explained above. The wide angle will also show much more of the room, making it harder to find an attractive background that you can control. If you zoom in, most cameras just use fewer pixels, so then you lower the resolution. I suggest looking for a web cam that either has an optical zoom (expensive), very high resolution (less expensive) or one with a 60 to 80 degree view.

Webcams with dual microphones can generally do automatic noise reduction, and often give decent sound without sounding hollow or amplifying echoes in the room. Alternatively the use of a large diaphragm USB microphone just out of sight of the camera can give excellent sound quality.

Webcam placement: Whether using a separate or built in video camera, it should be positioned so that the camera is just above eye level so that you are looking slightly up into it. This gives the most attractive lighting on your face and avoids shadows. It also makes you look engaged. For a laptop webcam, this generally requires putting the computer on a pedestal or stack of books.

Webcam Use: When videoconferencing, especially if it might be recorded or broadcast, put the window or windows you are actually watching at the top of the screen, just below the webcam, even if it only takes up the top inch or two of the screen. You can place your own image at the top center if you would like to monitor how you appear, or put the view-box of the person that you are paying most to attention to in the top center or just to the side. This allows the other viewer to see your eyes looking as if you are speaking with them, rather than watching you looking down throughout the meeting. You do not need to fix your gaze and stare directly into the camera, but most of the time it should appear that you are paying attention the people who are speaking or who you are listening to, with your eyes up, rather than looking down as one does when watching the middle of the screen. It is best to look directly into the camera, but it gets tiring, especially if using bright lights, and you want to look relaxed, not worn out.

Pearl: Video software usually has a mirror image feature that allows the user to flip the image. This makes it easier to adjust one's posture and control how we appear on camera, as we are used to seeing ourselves in a mirror. Any type or print in the image, such as that on a poster or book cover, however, will be reversed.

Practice: Take time to set up and make sure the camera and lighting are correct before each call. It may take some time learning how to adjust the camera using the conferencing or other software, and get situated so that you look good and feel comfortable. Once you figure it out, write down the adjustment steps so that you can easily set up before calls. Cover the camera lens when you don't want to be seen.

Final TV Check List

Before going on camera:

Make sure your tongue is clean and pink and not coated with your last meal. You should be well groomed and make sure your hair and makeup are in place without lipstick on your teeth.

Always assume the camera and microphones are live, even after your appearance is done, as long as you are in the studio or a reporter is around. The same is true for your webcam.

Lean in. Lean towards the camera ten degrees even if not looking into it. It will make you appear more engaged and interesting and make you look more confident, taller and leaner. Leaning back in a chair can make the person appear aloof and disconnected as if they are avoiding engagement. It also causes them to appear shorter and heavier.

Sitting straight up will make a person appear stiff and uncomfortable. Sitting very still makes one look stiff, so it is good to move the head and body, and appear relaxed. Be cautious that the chair will likely swivel and may lean back. Avoid swinging or rocking.

If you are being interviewed or part of a discussion, avoid looking into the camera when on TV. You will likely be more comfortable and look more natural talking with others in the room. Generally, only look into the camera if there is no one else on camera to speak to.

If you talk with your hands, try to keep the gestures smaller while on TV or video. When seated and the camera is zoomed in on you, you don't need your arms flapping about, cut off from view. When talking with your hands, keep them above the belly button and below the chin, and not wider than the shoulders; thus, keep them mostly in front of the chest, and below the ears. Don't obscure your face by having your hands in front of it. You can rest your hands in your lap when not speaking. Avoid touching your neck or face while on camera, as it will make you look nervous. If standing and giving a talk, wider motions of the arms and hands are needed, in front of a classroom, on stage, and on camera. A speaker that stands with their hands clasped, in their pockets, hanging at their sides, or clutching the podium for dear life is uninspiring at best. Use your hands to emphasize your points. Look around the room, making eye contact with different members of the audience. This eye contact makes the speaker appear to connect with the audience, even for those watching at home. If the eye contact makes you nervous, pretend that they are all friends or just focus on their eyebrows.

In the gubernatorial election video study from Chapter 3, and the German video study in Chapter 8, stage presence had a large impact on the perception of the individuals being watched. Appearing comfortable, graceful, and confident, and having good eye contact was pleasing while looking stiff was not.

Pearl: Own the stage! Don't be a shrinking violet. Act as if you are in your living room with invited guests. Use the space with a full, open posture and movement. Even if standing in one spot, do not stand still – you can shift your weight from one foot to the other. Use your hands in large gestures to create a larger presence.

Have a drink of water before going on, so that you don't get a dry mouth. Avoid licking your lips, darting your eyes or making funny faces. Men may try using a thin coat of lip balm, such as ChapStick® to help prevent the sensation of dry lips, but should practice with it to make sure they do not lick their lips even more with it.

Smile. If you are attacked, smile and be Zen. Freaking out will make for great TV, but will likely not be so good for you.

Don't get creative on camera. Be ready. Stick to your prepared material, and avoid thinking on your feet. If you are searching for an answer, remember to look for it on the floor; this will make you will look thoughtful. If you instead look up to the heavens for inspiration, rolling up your eyes will make it look like you are inventing folderol on the fly.[417]

Chapter 26: How We Choose

In elections, partisan voters, those who vote consistently for members of the party they affiliated with are unlikely to flip their vote to the other party based on the facial characteristics of most candidates. Well-informed voters also are less swayed by a candidate's physical appearance.

Suppose that 26 percent of the electorate in a district are committed Republicans that always turn out to vote in partisan elections and that 24 percent are committed Democrats. And suppose that 10 percent of the voters are swing voters that usually vote and 40 percent are non-committed voters that occasionally vote.

Committed Democrat	Left-leaning		Right-leaning	Committed Republican

Figure 26-1: A representation of the main political spectrum in the U.S.

In this scenario, the most common one, it is almost always the swing voters who decide partisan elections. Thus, it ends up being the least-partisan, least well-informed, and often the least-committed voters that decide most competitive partisan elections. These are the voters most likely to be influenced by a candidate's physical characteristics. Thus, we are stuck with elections that are decided by heuristic choices of the least informed and least connected voters.

In primary elections, especially early on, when little about the candidates is known, and when candidates of the same party are likely to have similar platforms, physical characteristics of the candidates also have a large impact on the vote.

It can be assumed that when two job candidates for the same position in the private sector or other professional positions are ranked similarly on experience and qualifications, differences in their appearance often become deciding criteria.

Actually, the most qualified applicant is often not selected for a position. The role of the human resource officer is to find qualified applicants. As long as a person is selected to be in the "qualified pool of applicants," then other criteria can be used in hiring. Deciding criteria may be such things as conformity to corporate culture. In truth, the decision is often made from gut-level, first impressions.. Our career paths are often decided, and limited, by implicit evaluations that have no objective bearing on our abilities.

Additionally, there are several reasons not to hire the most qualified applicant. The most qualified person may be deemed overqualified. The organization may feel that the highest qualified candidate may demand a higher salary, or see the position as a temporary stepping stone to a different job. A highly qualified candidate may be seen as a threat to the job of the person they are being hired by.

When several people are scheduled to be interviewed for a position, the last person to be interviewed for a job has the highest chance of being selected.[418]

The last-interviewee biases towards choosing the final candidate for a job position appears to result from the subjective nature of the hiring process and difficulty in comparing and remembering relative heuristic evaluations. Since a numeric score is not usually assigned when judging people on a heuristic, emotion-based judgment, we cannot easily compare more than two or three candidates easily, and we tend to remember final information better than other similar events.

Imagine that you are a judge for a contest where there are ten entries for red wine, blueberry muffins, or blackberry-apple pie, and your job is to choose the prize-winning item. You get one taste of each item and cannot go back. So you taste entry A and B and determine that you like A better than B. Then you try C and compare it to your memory of A, and on and on until the final item J.

Assume for a moment that entries A, C, E, F, and J, each had a combination of different desirable and less desirable qualities, but all were good and had similar summary ratings. In this scenario, in a sequential selection, the most recently tasted of these pies always has a 50% chance of being selected. It would be A or C, and then (A/C) or E, and next (A/C/E) or F in a sequential choice pattern, with the latest comparator getting a 50% chance of selection. Even if we can compare three items at a time the last item considered (if equal to the others) has a one-third chance of being selected compared to a 20% chance if the four others were of equal appraisal.

By the time we get to F, G, and H, how well do we really remember the

unique flavor of apple pie A or those qualities that had us preferring it over pie C, even if one of them was superior? Since memory, especially of subjective appraisal, fades, the last item evaluated, the last thing we taste or experience, and the most recent person we met gets stronger ratings and is better remembered (in a positive or negative light).
This effect of bias in a sequential appraisal of job candidates becomes more pronounced when the interviews are subjective, and when the interviews are brief. It is even harder when those appraisals are spread over several days or even weeks.

Pearl: If you have the choice, try to be the final person interviewed for a job or other position.

Partisans

When there is a partisan choice, most partisan voters choose the candidate of their own party. Swing voters with less party affinity may make choices that are more like dating choices. They choose the candidate with the highest implicit attractiveness and stick with them unless there is enough reason to discount them.

If voters can be convinced that their choice of candidate cannot be trusted, they will often not vote rather than vote for an alternate candidate. This is especially true for less partisan voters; while more committed voters may hold their nose and vote for a un-likable candidate. The purpose of negative advertising is not to get people to switch votes, but rather to get voters to skip voting. The successful candidate is the one that can get less committed voters that lean towards their camp to show up and vote, and lower the appetite for voting in those that lean in the other direction.

People do not like to think of themselves as inconsistent and will stick with a choice, especially if they have made a public commitment to that choice until it is painfully evident the choice was wrong. People will go ahead and get married to a partner they have strong apprehensions about after having made public commitments and often stay in unhappy relationships that are dysfunctional too long. The strength of commitment to a political candidate can be greatly enhanced if the person makes a public act supporting this endorsement, such as making a donation, no matter how small to a political campaign, placing a bumper sticker on their car, or a yard sign on their lawn[419]

It typically takes two years for people to fall out of love and a similar amount of time to let go of their commitment to a person or idea. In the days leading up to the 2016 election, 38 percent of the likely voters stated that they strongly supported Trump. One year after the election, Trump had the lowest approval rating of any president for which polling data is available, thus since World War II. Nevertheless, he continued to have a 37.7 percent job approval rating after one and two years in office.[420] In a poll taken after Trump defended Nazi and white supremacist terrorists, two-thirds of those identifying as members of his political party stated that they approved of his handling of the situation.

During campaigns, supporters generally either disbelieve or dismiss negative news about their candidate. In December 2017, even after the Republican Senate majority leader Mitch McConnell said the sexual misconduct allegations concerning a 14-year-old girl and several other underage girls were credible, and Alabama Republican Senator Richard Shelby publicly stated he could not vote for Republican Roy Moore, 52% of White, college-educated women and 68% of all White voters in Alabama chose him on polling day. Ninety percent of his supporters reported that they did not believe the allegations of sexual misconduct; ten percent of them accepted that the allegations were probably true, and voted for him anyway.[421]

Simultaneously, supporters will believe even the most outrageous negative fabrication about the opposition. Consider the internet allegations that Hillary Clinton was running a child sex trafficking ring out of a Virginia pizza parlor, as an example.

We make choices emotionally and implicitly using the right half of our brains, and then we justify that choice with the left brain, the area of reason. The left half of the brain acts like a lawyer defending a client with a rationalized argument, rather than actually making a rational choice. In a competitive district, the best face can usually win, unless the incumbent is unusually popular. Most of the time, the incumbent is the incumbent because they had a better face to begin with.

A political candidate has little chance of changing the mind of those who do not favor them. Trump has an over 50% approval rating in 15 states, and in 13 of these 15 states, Obama's job performance approval was less than 35% in at his lowest point of job approval in 2014.[422] [423] The same cohort that despised Obama, falsely believe that Trump won the 2020 election against Biden. If people change their minds, they do it slowly.

In 2016, 26 percent of U.S. voters identified as Republican, 33 percent identified as Democrat and 34 percent identified as independent. Forty-eight percent of the entire electorate self-identified as leaning Democrat and 44 percent leaned Republican.

Depending on the district, less than a quarter of the registered voters will show up for a midterm primary election; these elections are highly important, especially for winning a seat in the U. S. House of Representatives. Since most seats are not competitive, the winner of the primary for the party that controls the district almost always wins.

In 2010, only about 19 percent of voters (eight percent Democrats and eleven percent Republicans) voted in congressional primaries. These midterm primaries decide who will win most House seats, as most Congressional seats are in safe districts, and the winner of the primary for the safe party usually goes on to win.

Most of the voters that show up for primary elections are not swing voters, but party-line voters. In a party primary without an incumbent, where candidates are usually not differentiated by policy, the best face, the face that looks like a leader, can often win just on their face. Since only about ten percent of a party's voters turn out for these elections, a candidate for the party that has a safe district can win by getting a tiny bit larger voter turnout.

In a midterm election, those in which the President is not elected, about 40 percent of the registered voters turn out to vote in the general midterm election. Although each congressman may have limited power, the party in power has a lock on power and control over future elections through gerrymandering. These elections determine the course of policy that the country takes.

It is an unrealistic goal to try changing the minds of those with opposing political views in the short timeframe of an election; candidates shouldn't even try. People will change their minds and agree with a candidate after they decide to support them, not before. In a contested election, the Republicans will almost always vote for a

Republican candidate and the Democrats for a Democratic one. If a candidate is one of these, they should not need to worry about their base unless they really screw up. People will discount news of horrible things about a candidate they back rather than condemn them, and they will believe ridiculous lies about the opponent, rather than switch loyalty. People want to feel internally consistent; they are reluctant to switch sides and only when the reality is forced on them later, they will feel betrayed, rather than take responsibility for their poor implicit choices.

It is the swing voters a candidate needs to sway to show up to vote or dissuade from voting for the other candidate. You can sway folks into your camp with your face. You can discourage swing voters from showing up to vote with negative ads against your opponent. But it is a rare rare event to get a party loyalist to vote for the other camp.

Random Pearl

According to a 2007 Gallup poll, four percent of Americans would not vote for a Catholic, five percent said that they would not vote for a Black person, and 11% said they would not vote for a woman as president of the United States. The actual rates of voter biases are likely much higher than what these respondents admitted to.

Fifty-three percent of Americans in this survey said that they would not vote for a presidential candidate that was an atheist. Only 48 percent of moderates and 29 percent of conservatives say they would vote for an atheist presidential candidate.[424]

People don't trust atheists. Atheists were found to be the least desirable of several criteria as a potential daughter or son-in-law, and people say they would be less likely to hire an atheist for a position of trust or responsibility.[425] When asked who would be most likely to engage in immoral acts, atheists topped the list ranking alongside rapists. Even atheists have low opinions of the morality of atheists.[426]

Pearl: If you are an atheist, or even agnostic, you may be best off keeping that aspect of your life to yourself.

Chapter 27: Where Power Lies

Perspective

Absolute power corrupts absolutely. Cliché; but sadly true. With power, people assume further privilege and are more likely to cheat and lie. They actually become better liars as power loosens moral inhibitions and strengthens the sense of privilege. People with power become more self-serving and less generous. They find it easy to justify unethical and unfair behavior that benefits them. Interestingly, a paucity of power may promote a Robin Hood effect, where those who lack power are more likely to engage in unethical behavior to benefit others.[427]

In a democracy, we negotiate over policy and negotiate with other countries. In business, we negotiate with other businesses and clients. Thus a balance of giving and taking is required in negotiation and cooperation.

When one side has absolute power, however, they can take what they want, but doing so destroys relationships. Both empathy and perspective-taking are essential tools for understanding the other side. Empathy helps understand what others are feeling and perspective-taking provides the cognitive understanding of the other side and what they need. Although understanding the feelings of the other side is helpful, it is the cognitive understanding of the needs of the other side that allows negotiations to benefit both sides, including the dominant one. Thus, it does not create a loss for the dominant party to understand the weaker side, but rather allows for better solutions that benefit each side.[428]

Perspective-taking is simply looking at the situation from the other party's vantage point. It expands our viewpoint and allows us to think about what the other side desires and needs, and why they need it. When those needs are not in conflict, it allows the more powerful side to give the others what they need to have to cooperate with you. Destroying the other side may seem the straightforward way to get what you want, but it rarely works out well. You are more likely to end with a Pyrrhic victory. Perspective-taking can allow both sides to win.

Successful leaders are perspective-takers that listen to the needs and ideas of those they serve, those they lead with and those they negotiate with. By being flexible and offering choices, a leader can get more done and score more victories. Sadly for America, our politicians seem locked into extreme, uncompromising, polarized viewpoints, where little progress is made. Perhaps that's the plan.

When resources are scarce, people become competitive. And they can become terribly, viciously competitive. Wars are fought over perceived limited resources. People are willing to pay more for an item, such as diamonds that are considered rare, even though they may have no great intrinsic value. Diamonds are not more beautiful than are cubic zirconium, but the supply of diamonds is controlled to maintain high prices and perception of scarcity and value. People trample each other in Walmart stores on Black Fridays in a rush to limited deals; people that would not hurt another person in other situations or for the equal value. Many students will sabotage their classmates if the number of A's available in a class is limited and will have animosity against a student that "ruins the curve" by making too high a score. Siblings will fight, bite, scream and scratch each in attempts to gain limited attention from their parents. Humans are very willing to be inhumane when wanting a limited resource, such as wealth, privilege or power. It brings out the worse in us.

In contrast, if the number A's depends on just on a performance standard, students will often cooperate in meeting that standard. When coupons are available for a great deal, people will share them on the internet for strangers to use.

A predominant contemporary viewpoint is one of scarcity. In this perspective, wealth is a zero-sum game, and opportunity is a limited resource that needs to be fought for in order to maintain and accumulate status, wealth, and privilege for themselves and their heirs. By denying access to others, they increase their share of the pie. The pie is only so big, and they need to fight to maintain their share of it.

While the number of seats for new students in Princeton's undergraduate class is limited to about 1700, there is not an intrinsic limit to the number of high-quality college degrees that can be earned. There may be a limit to mineral resources, such as and gold, coal, oil, and petroleum gas. Wars are fought over such resources. But there is no intrinsic limit to the supply of energy. There is plenty of solar energy to be harvested and there can be sufficient fusion power when brought to practical use in a few years. We can meet our energy needs if we are willing as a society to invest in it. While there is a limit on how many waterfront vacation mansions can be built, there is not a limit on decent housing, as long as people work together to make it happen.

We would have had multiple if not continuous famines in the United States if we had not improved crop yields through improved farming equipment, practices, and crops. Much of the research came from the United States Department of Agriculture and agricultural universities in the United States.

Most of the resources humans required for healthy, happy, prosperous, and productive lives depend on resources that can be multiplied like the miracle of the five loaves and two fish. There is not an intrinsic limit on education, health, energy, or housing. We are not at overcapacity as to the number of humans on the planet, but we are far past sustainability as man overexploits the planet's resources in a competitive struggle to corner wealth while ignoring the obvious consequences.

Don't assume that the resources needed for equitable, prosperous, productive, happy and rewarding lives are limited by finite limitations in resources. It is instead intelligence, imagination, and grit, which are in short supply.

There are also a limited number of leadership positions, and people fight for these too. Democracy could be a way to distribute power and leadership, but that is a dangerous notion. Democracy has always been a dangerous notion.

No one hates democracy more than a politician.

"If you look back at 10 negotiations, and you find that you're satisfied with your outcome every single time, you're probably not setting your goals high enough. If you look back across an arc of negotiations, and you find that you've ruptured relationships nine out of 10 times, you're probably being too competitive."

Maurice Schweitzer, Professor at Wharton School of Business

Chapter 28: Executive Presence

Portraying an executive presence is an important part of gaining a leadership position. At some time, the candidate will need to prove their competence, but they will not get the chance to do so if they cannot attain the position.

There are many components to presenting an executive presence.

❖ It is important to look the part and develop a polished executive appearance.

❖ Fast talk, like that of a salesman, may make one appear to be more knowledgeable, but slowing down makes a person appear to be considering their words carefully, and this makes the speaker sound more authoritative. Slow your speech down by 10 percent. Use the extra time to choose your words carefully.

❖ Listen actively. Use exploratory questions to find out what is going on and where the trouble and difficulties lie. Find out what is working and what is not before making decisions. You will look smarter when asking great questions than coming up with solutions that have been tried and failed.

❖ Have three questions ready for every meeting. Examples:

  ✓ What are their problems? What do they need?
  ✓ What solutions do they think would work? How would it help? How do they get by now in the current situation?

❖ If you think that you are the smartest person in the room, then you are probably not. Cato the Elder said, "Wise men learn more from fools than fools from the wise." Listen and learn.

❖ Every meeting should have clear goals set ahead of time and finish with something of value. Meetings should create value; not be a waste of time. If the meeting accomplishes nothing, it is a waste.

❖ As a candidate and leader always ask for a commitment from those you talk to, no matter how small.

❖ Communicate clearly. Use stories to bring the emotional connection home to the listener and make your position more compelling.

❖ Have a positive and engaged body language.

❖ Be on time. Not only is it polite; you will feel more at ease.

❖ Avoid giveaways that you feel nervous:[429]

   ❧ Avoiding eye contact
   ❧ Pressured or rushed speech
   ❧ Putting things in the mouth that don't belong there, such as paperclips your fingers or fingernails
   ❧ Playing with your hair or repeatedly checking it
   ❧ Cracking your knuckles
   ❧ Fidgety fingers
   ❧ Touching your face, neck, or ears
   ❧ Biting your lip or fingernails
   ❧ Nervous laughter
   ❧ Foot bouncing, leg shaking
   ❧ Swiveling or rocking in a chair

If you realize that you are doing a nervous tic during an interview, just stop doing it and don't worry about it. Remind yourself it is O.K. to be nervous; it is just excitement, and you are the best person for the position.

Charisma

The word charisma was derived from Greek (khárisma) in the first century AD. It referred to a divinely imparted gift that empowers a believer to share God's work with others to inspire them to carry out God's plans for his people. Charisma is a compelling charm or attractiveness that influences and inspires devotion and actions from others. Although by definition it is a divine gift, this ability to motivate and excite others can be learned.

The keys to charisma include empathy, eye contact, and listening to others – really listening and being attentive. The second set of skills includes enthusiasm and moral conviction. Charismatic leaders set high expectations for themselves and their followers. If you don't have a fervent belief in your mission, it is unlikely that you will convince others of it. Thirdly, it requires self-efficacy; the confidence in one's own ability to achieve the intended results. Charisma requires not only confidence that the mission is essential for the greater good and that it is achievable, but also that the leader is capable of heading the movement to achieve the goal; so that they can inspire and motivate others to join in. Belief sells.

Self-confidence is essential for the ability to sell. Self-confidence that arises from malignant arrogance and narcissism works; it can be used to sell cages to crows. Alternatively, the confidence of conviction can provide self-efficacy that sells solutions that benefit the community. Both types of confidence are an asset in sales, one is self-serving and sleazy, and other can serve society.

A charismatic leader can solve great problems, but authenticity is essential. This moral authority is given to those leaders who share the dangers and hardships of the struggle one is rallying for, not for those who entice others to take the risk, while they watch from the palace. Eye contact, attentiveness, and listening create a sense of interaction with the audience that bolsters a sense of connection and authenticity.

Finally, charisma takes speaking skills. Charismatic leaders frequently use metaphors, stories, and anecdotes to make the message easier to understand and remember, and to create an emotional response. They use inclusive terms (we and us) to share the feelings as a group. They use rhetorical devices include contrasts, lists (best a list of three) and use rhetorical questions to create anticipation and draw in the audience.[430]

Chapter 29: Getting It Done

Nice guys don't finish last. It's the nice girls that do.

Social power is seen as a limited resource for which there is competition. Thus, when one tries to change things and have influence, it often creates conflict, even when one does not view their actions as power-seeking. Speaking up, and worse, voicing an alternative viewpoint, suggesting a new paradigm or idea, or asking for privileges reserved for the more powerful can get a person of lower power status into trouble.

Social scientist and Columbia Business School professor Adam Galinsky explains that each of us has a "range of acceptable behavior" in regard to our place in the power pecking order in our social setting.

Too Weak	Acceptable Behavior Range			Too Strong
Punishment	Pass	Reward	Pass	Punishment

Figure 29-1: A representation of ranges of acceptable power.

As long as one stays in their expected Range of Acceptable Behavior (RAB), and don't cause waves, people can stay out of trouble. But if someone with a lower power status voices an opposing viewpoint, seeks higher status, or assumes a position of influence, they are likely to be knocked down. If someone does not stand up for themselves sufficiently for their status and "rank" or take on the expected responsibilities, they too are punished or knocked further down the ladder. This hierarchical status creates expectations of behavior that can constrain or enhance one's opportunities for advancement based on the status quo.

Women, minorities, those who come from disadvantaged or less affluent homes, and those who are physically smaller or less robust have less access to social power and a lower level of influence.

We can see this power play in the classroom, schoolyard, and boardroom. It is in the plot of nearly every movie set in a middle or high school. And all too often, people settle into and limit their lifetime power status RAB based on the perceived status they had in high school.

We may be top dog in our own home but far from it in our place of work. We can act within our acceptable range of power, but we get punished if we push the limits, we may be discounted as having a voice, demeaned, ostracized, treated dismissively, or booted from the organization.

But do any of these things act to limit the ability to contribute to an organization? The answer is yes if the organization is based on physical strength and aggression – so it's true for football and hand to hand combat. But being smaller, less physically strong or minority does not limit intelligence, creativity, drive, passion, or the ability to lead most other teams or organizations. Yet, our instinctual behavior continues to lead us to dismiss those who do not look the part

Women have less power in most organizations. Women who seek a position of leadership above their Level of Influence are considered, uppity, usurpers, illegitimate, untrustworthy, opportunistic, manipulative, and avaricious for power. When men are ambitious it is considered admirable; when women are ambitious, it is considered deviant. It is within the range of acceptable behavior for men with no previous experience in public administration to run for high office, but when the former senator and Secretary of State Hillary Clinton woman did, she was vilified, as power hungry, self-serving, and dangerous.

It is not just women, but also ethnic minorities that are automatically assigned a lower rank on the power totem pole.

In the old days, a woman that learned the use herbs to cure disease might be considered a witch. Even in a modern usage, the word "witch" has a connotation of an ugly, self-serving, evil woman, while the male counterpart, a wizard, connotates a man of learning and talent with extraordinary skills.

In a brief study done at the NYU Stern School of business in 2013, students were asked to score the trustworthiness of two hypothetical executives. The description of the two executives was exactly the same, except for their first name. The executive named Catherine scored significantly lower than the hypothetical executive named Martin when it came to trustworthiness. And it was not only male students that scored the executive with a woman's name lower.[431]

Galinsky says that those who want to have a stronger voice can do so with much less likelihood of ruffling feathers and being seen as a usurper, by working as a social advocate for others. In this way, the person is not seen as trying to take power for themselves and thus is seen as less of a threat. When people advocate for others, they expand their range of acceptable behavior, at least in their own minds, and this allows them to become more assertive.

Pearl: Women and minorities generally have less perceived power and may be considered illegitimate usurpers if they seek leadership positions. However, when someone is seen as an advocate for an underprivileged minority, it can be perceived as a legitimate reason for seeking power.

Galinsky also advises that asking for advice from someone in power will build a bond of trust. Asking for advice is inherently a submissive act; it makes the person doing the asking appear less of a threat.

Along this same line, is the Benjamin Franklin effect: a person that has done a favor for someone is more likely to view the person favorably and to help them in the future.

Franklin wrote: "He that has once done you a kindness will be more ready to do you another, than he whom you yourself have obliged."

Thus, asking for even a small favor, and having it granted, will raise the person's liking of the person who requests it. We end up admiring and liking those we have helped. Just getting the advice of a supervisor will have them like you more.

This psychological phenomenon is explained by the cognitive dissonance theory. People justify their actions a posteriori. If someone helps another person, they end up liking the person; why else would they have done the favor? If one person has harmed another, they will soon vilify or otherwise disparage the person they harmed to justify their actions. We like to think that we act rationally. Our brains like our beliefs about ourselves to match what we have done. Soldiers and prison guards come to hate those they have harmed and dehumanize them as it allows them to justify their actions. It is easy to rationalize having killed "vermin." It is much more difficult to come to terms with killing a family in their own home who happened to live in a country whose leader was at war with the leader of the soldier's country.[432]

One of the first self-help books, How to Win Friends and Influence People, was published in 1937 by Dale Carnegie. Carnegie thought of asking a favor as a subtle form of flattery, acknowledging the person's legitimate power and competency, and showing respect and admiration. This should be especially true when the resource being requested is advice, rather than a request for other resources.

Pearl: A key to the Franklin effect is to ask, at least for the first favor, one favor small enough that the person would likely feel that they would appear petty if they deny the request. Next, remind them of the favor they have granted a week or so later, by thanking them and again showing respect. When possible, avoid reciprocating the favor, at least until a friendship with the person has jelled. If favors are returned too soon, they can be considered quid pro quo; a fair trade, and they would not promote the Franklin effect.

The Franklin effect can be used to gain acceptance into the circle of power, where you have more voice in solving problems and serving the greater good. It can help turn a teacher or supervisor into a mentor and ally.

A candidate benefits from asking for small commitments at every meeting. The request may be asking voters to put a bumper sticker on their car, a small contribution, a commitment to vote. A commitment of time, even two minutes to answer a few questions, a public endorsement such as placing a yard sign, or money, even if only a dollar, is enough. Anyone that has made even a small commitment to a candidate will be likely to vote for them. Just asking them to show up to vote, for whoever they like, even if it's not you, will have them liking and favoring you if they complete the favor.

It is important to gauge what is asked for. Ask for something small enough to be sure they will grant the request. People will agree to minor requests in order not to seem miserly or rude. If one asks for too much, if they feel overly pressured to comply, or if they refuse, they may like you less.

Since we are on the topic, I would like to request a small favor. Please write a 5-star review of this book on Google Play or Amazon. It will help share this information with others; my hope is that this information can help democratize our democracy.

Women and minorities will not gain equity in power until they see themselves and other women and minorities as legitimate leaders and support leadership roles for each other.

Women often limit themselves and other women from positions of power. Only a small percentage of Caucasian women say they are interested in leadership roles in their profession.[433] This lack of aspiration and lower sights on achievement does not begin in college. At the time of university graduation, women's aspirations for leadership are on par or above that of their male classmates. At graduation, women's perspective of their own abilities and future is based on their classroom performance, which often outstrips that of their male counterparts. It is later that women become discouraged and lose interest as they see doors of opportunity narrowing to them.

Women more frequently lack role models and mentors, either male or female, in their professional lives, have fewer inroads to building personal contacts with leaders, and are discouraged from seeking leadership. Women should proactively seek out a mentor and use the Franklin effect to develop advocates for their success and for developing friendships with those in higher positions. These alliances are the keys to the corner offices, boardrooms, and advancement. Although not as easily available, women may benefit more by seeking out a male mentor within their organization than a female one.[434]

One of the pitfalls to mentoring relationships is that it is natural to form feeling for those we care about. It is not uncommon for sexual feelings to develop between a mentor and the trainee. Some men may avoid mentoring young women just to sidestep this risk. Avoiding unwanted sexual overtures in mentoring relationships can be a challenge, especially for single persons. Avoiding high-risk situations, such as travel, alcohol, and non-work hour alone time, as discussed in Chapter 23, may help. It may also be helpful to make sure the mentor is aware of that the mentee is in a close, long-term, monogamous relationship, even if the relationship is much less than that.

Our personal power and range of acceptable behaviors in an organization are constrained by how we are seen by the other people within that power structure. There are externally imposed restraints and perceptions as well as those we present.

We create our societal role with our self-confidence, or lack of it, and from numerous other social cues. In high school, status, which is a corollary to power, is based on affluence, self-confidence, attractiveness, dominance, competence in sports or other skills, and likeability. Those with prior status advantage have an easier route, while those at the bottom of the status ladder have a difficult time moving up. Since early physical maturity is something that gives status in middle school, if you are a late bloomer, you may still feel inadequate. If your family could not afford the trendy clothing that was in style and a new car back then, you may still feel un-cool. Most adult's social status self-opinion was set and remains close to what it was during adolescence.

When we apply for a job in a different company, join an organization, move to a new city, we are the ones taking our power estimate and our RAB with us. The people in these organizations do not have private investigators researching your high school social status score to assign you to the same level, nor have insight into the economic status of your family.

Nevertheless, people easily pick up on the clues we give them. We are the ones that create many of our own limitations. We often set our own limitations or RAB expectations both by our behavior, but as well by the image we project to the world. People really don't look that deeply.

We limit ourselves based on the narrative we tell ourselves about who we are in relation to those around us. Others judge us on the clues that we supply them, including a judgment based on our physical presence. Thus, there are internal and external restraints to access to power.

This book has focused on the things we can change to increase our power and influence and thus be able to effect positive changes in our world. To raise your RAB and increase your influence, you need to raise your own perception of your power and to project competence and leadership in the eyes of others. And since we rely on social feedback to assess our social status, the internal and external perceptions reinforce each other.

When you feel powerful, confident, and unfearful, you can expand your own range. When others see you as powerful, they grant you a wider range of acceptable behavior.

Creating a more competent and attractive external persona takes some discipline, but is fairly straightforward, as described throughout this book. Three to four months of a healthy diet, sufficient sleep and exercise, and caring for your skin, will have most people looking, feeling and thinking much better. Correcting posture with exercise and the correct aids will also take a few months of self-discipline. Dressing appropriately, makeup, and grooming are the easy parts.

The other half is believing in yourself. It is not so easy to overcome your own self-image of powerlessness. After all, the world has been reinforcing your self-image like a mirror most of your life. That is why it is often easiest to move forward if one changes their outward image first. It is easier to change your self-image when you see it in a mirror.

Remind yourself of a time when you felt powerful and in control before you walk into a room where your power will be tested. Putting yourself in the power mindset changes your perspective. It will change the tone and prosody of your voice, body language, and your posture. This will be implicitly perceived by those you meet with. Others are more likely to see you as competent and leader and give you respect.

☙

Congratulations! You have completed the book. The author greatly appreciates your allowing him to share these ideas with you.

❧

References

1 When and Why Did Human Brains Decrease in Size? A New Change-Point Analysis and Insights From Brain Evolution in Ants. DeSilva JM, Traniello JFA, Claxton AG,Fannin DL. Front. Ecol. Evol., 22 October 2021. https://www.frontiersin.org/article/10.3389/fevo.2021.742639

2 Coevolution of the neocortical size, group size and language in humans. Dunbar RIM. Behavioral and Brain Sciences 1993 (16)681-735.

3 Segregation in Social Networks Based on Acquaintanceship and Trust. DiPrete TA, Gelman A, McCormick T, Teitler J, and Zheng T. Am. J. of Sociology. Jan 2014. 116(4)1234-83

4 Social network size in humans. Hill RA, Dunbar RIM. Human Nature 2003 14(1)53-72.

5 Perceived intelligence is associated with measured intelligence in men but not women. Kleisner K, Chvátalová V, Flegr J. PLoS One. 2014 Mar 20;9(3):e81237. PMID:24651120

6 Trust and Credit: The Role of Appearance in Peer-to-peer Lending. Duarte J, Siegel S, Young L. The Review of Financial Studies. Aug. 2012. 23(8):2455-84.

7 Racial bias in neural empathic responses to pain. Contreras-Huerta LS, Baker KS, Reynolds KJ, Batalha L, Cunnington R. PLoS One. 2013 Dec 23;8(12):e84001. PMID:24376780

8 Manipulations of cognitive strategies and intergroup relationships reduce the racial bias in empathic neural responses. Sheng F, Han S. Neuroimage. 2012 Jul 16;61(4):786-97. PMID:22542636

9 Cognitive Reflection and Decision Making. Frederick, S. Journal of Economic Perspectives. Fall 2005. 19(4):25-42.

10 Thin-Slice Forecasts of Gubernatorial Elections. Benjamin DJ, Shapiro JM. Rev Econ Stat. 2009 Aug 1;91(33):523-536. PMID:20431718

11 Predicting political elections from rapid and unreflective face judgments. Ballew CC 2nd, Todorov A. Proc Natl Acad Sci U S A. 2007 Nov 13;104(46):17948-53. PMID:17959769

12 Predicting Elections: Child's Play! Antonakis J, Dalgas O. Science. 27 Feb 2009. 323(5918):1183

13 The influence of political candidates' facial appearance on older and younger adults' voting choices and actual electoral success. Franklin RG Jr., Zebrowitz LA, & Craig T. Cogent Psychology Vol. 3, Iss. 1,2016

14 Polling the Face: Prediction and Consensus Across Cultures. Rule NO, Ambady A. Journal of Personality and Social Psychology, 2010, Vol. 98, No. 1, 1–15

15 Cultural effects on the association between election outcomes and face-based trait inferences. Lin C, Adolphs R, Alvarez RM. PLoS One. 2017 Jul 10;12(7):e0180837. PMID:28700647

16 Competence ratings in US predict presidential election outcomes in Bulgaria. Sussman AB, Petkova K, Todorov A. J Exp Social Psychology. july 2013, 49(4):771-775.

17 Leaders' smiles reflect cultural differences in ideal affect. Tsai JL, Ang JY, Blevins E, et al. Emotion. 2016 Mar;16(2):183-95. PMID:26751631

18 The looks of a winner: Beauty, gender, and Electoral Success. Berggren N, Jordahl H, Poutvaarr P. CESIFO WORKING PAPER NO. 2002, CATEGORY 2: PUBLIC CHOICE MAY 2007. Presented at CESifo Area Conference on Public Sector Economics

19 Facial attractiveness: evolutionary affects hypothetical voting decisions differently in wartime and peacetime scenarios. Little AC, Roberts SC, Jones BC, Debruine LM. Q J Exp Psychol (Hove). 2012;65(10):2018-32. PMID:22650610

20 The perception of attractiveness and trustworthiness in male faces affects hypothetical voting decisions differently in wartime and peacetime scenarios. Little AC, Roberts SC, Jones BC, Debruine LM. Q J Exp Psychol (Hove). PMID:22650610

21 Caveman Executive Leadership: Evolved Leadership Preferences and Biological Sex. Murry GR, Murray SM. Evolutionary Psychology in the Business Sciences, pp.135-163. Springer 2011

22 http://www.people-press.org/2016/09/13/2-party-affiliation-among-voters-1992-2016/ Accessed August 2017

23 Is There Gender Bias Among Voters? Evidence from the Chilean Congressional Elections. Pino F. April 2017. Department of Economics, University of Chile

24 Ironic effects of explicit gender prejudice on women's test performance. Mendoza-Denton R, Shaw-Taylor L, Chen S, Chang E. Journal of Experimental Social Psychology. 2009 45(2009):275–278

25 Thought of a Woman President Rattles Male Voters in New Jersey. Cassino D. http://publicmind.fdu.edu/2016/160323/final.pdf Accessed August 2017.

26 Women Want Five Things. Hewlett SA, Marshall M. Center for Talent Inovation, Dec. 2014

27 Gender is costing Hillary Clinton big among men. Dan Cassino. http://blogs.lse.ac.uk/usappblog/2016/03/24/gender-is-costing-hillary-clinton-big-among-men/ Accessed August 2017.

28 The political gender gap: gender bias in facial inferences that predict voting behavior. Chiao JY, Bowman NE, Gill H. PLoS One. 2008;3(10):e3666. PMID:18974841

29 The political gender gap: gender bias in facial inferences that predict voting behavior. Chiao JY, Bowman NE, Gill H. PLoS One. 2008;3(10):e3666. PMID:18974841

30 Caveman Executive Leadership: Evolved Leadership Preferences and Biological Sex. Murry GR, Murray SM. Evolutionary Psychology in the Business Sciences, pp.135-163. Springer 2011

31 Pioneer Advantage: Marketing Logic or Marketing Legend? Golder PN, Tellis GJ. 1993. Journal of Marketing Research, 30(2):158–170.

32 Economic and Identity. Akerlof GA, Kranton R. The Quarterly Journal of Economics. 2000. 115(3):715-753

33 http://gizmodo.com/exclusive-heres-the-full-10-page-anti-diversity-screed-1797564320 Accessed August 2017

34 National Center for Education Statistics https://nces.ed.gov/ Accessed August 2017.

35 https://www.aaeteachers.org/index.php/blog/757-the-teacher-gender-gap

36 http://aasa.org/SchoolAdministratorArticle.aspx?id=14492

37 Intent to harm or injure? Gender and the expression of anger. Campbell A, Muncer S. Aggress Behav. 2008 May-Jun;34(3):282-93.PMID:17849395

38 Gender differences in social representations of aggression: the phenomenological experience of differences in inhibitory control? Driscoll H, Zinkivskay A, Evans K, Campbell A.Br J Psychol. 2006 May;97(Pt 2):139-53. PMID:16613646

39 https://www.washingtonpost.com/news/on-leadership/wp/ 2017/06/07/ the-number-of-women-ceos-in-the-fortune-500-is-at-an-all-time-high-of-32/ Accessed August 2017.

40 http://www.catalyst.org/knowledge/women-sp-500-companies Accessed August 2017.

41 Women Want Five Things. Hewlett SA, Marshall M. Center for Talent Inovation, Dec. 2014

42 Everyday Moments of Truth: Frontline Managers Are Key to Women's Career Aspirations. Coffman J and Nuenfeldt B. Bain & Company Insights. June 17, 2014.

43 How chronic self-views influence (and potentially mislead) estimates of performance. Ehrlinger J, Dunning D. J Pers Soc Psychol. 2003 Jan;84(1):5-17.PMID:12518967

44 Is There Gender Bias Among Voters? Evidence from the Chilean Congressional Elections. Pino F. April 2017. Department of Economics, University of Chile

45 Face and fortune: Inferences of personality from Managing Partners' faces predict their law firms' financial success. Rule NO.Ambady N. The Leadership Quarterly August 201122(4): 690-696

46 Judgments of Power From College Yearbook Photos and Later Career Success. Rule NO.Ambady N. Social Psychological and Personality Science. 2011. 2(2) 154-158

47 Facial Dominance of West Point Cadets as a Predictor of Later Military Rank. Muller U, Mazur A. Social Forces. March 1996. 3(1):823-850.

48 The Facial Appearance of CEOs: Faces Signal Selection but Not Performance. Stoker JI, Garretsen H, Spreeuwers LJ. PLoS One. 2016 Jul 27;11(7):e0159950. PMID:27462986

49 Predicting Firm Success From the Facial Appearance of Chief Executive Officers of Non-Profit Organizations. Re DE, Rule NO. Perception. 2016 Oct;45(10):1137-50. PMID:27329518

50 Perceived trustworthiness is associated with position in a corporate hierarchy. Linke L, Saribay SA, Kleisner K. Personality and Individual Differences. 99 (2016) 22–27

51 She's Got the Look: Inferences from Female Chief Executive Officers' Faces Predict their Success. Rule NO, Ambady N. Sex Roles, Nov. 2009, 61(9–10):644–652

52 The height leadership advantage in men and women: Testing evolutionary psychology predictions about the perceptions of tall leaders. Baker NB, Rompa, I, Inge H, et al. Jan.10, 2013. Group Processes & Intergroup Relations. Volume: 16 issue: 1, page(s): 17-27.

53 http://ac360.blogs.cnn.com/2013/03/12/how-are-powerful-women-perceived/ Accessed Sept. 2017

54 Perceived aggressiveness predicts fighting performance in mixed-martial-arts fighters. Trebicky V, Havlícek J, Roberts SC, Little AC, Kleisner K. Psychol Sci. 2013 Sep;24(9):1664-72. PMID:23818656

55 Geometric morphometrics of male facial shape in relation to physical strength and perceived attractiveness, dominance, and masculinity. Windhager S, Schaefer K, Fink B. Am J Hum Biol. 2011 Nov-Dec;23(6):805-14. PMID:21957062

56 The morphometrics of "masculinity" in human faces. Mitteroecker P, Windhager S, Müller GB, Schaefer K. PLoS One. 2015 Feb 11;10(2):e0118374. PMID:25671667

57 Male facial appearance signals physical strength to women. Fink B, Neave N, Seydel H. Am J Hum Biol. 2007 Jan-Feb;19(1):82-7. PMID:17160983

58 Ibid Ref 54. PMID:23818656

59 Further evidence for links between facial width-to-height ratio and fighting success: Commentary on Zilioli et al. (2014). Třebický V, Fialová J, Kleisner K, Roberts SC, Little AC, Havlíček J. Aggress Behav. 2015 Jul-Aug;41(4):331-4. PMID:25236530

60 Ibid Ref 54. PMID:23818656 Image used with permission

61 In your face: facial metrics predict aggressive behaviour in the laboratory and in varsity and professional hockey players. Carré JM, McCormick CM. Proc Biol Sci. 2008 Nov 22;275(1651):2651-6. PMID:18713717

62 Valid facial cues to cooperation and trust: male facial width and trustworthiness. Stirrat M, Perrett DI. Psychol Sci. 2010 Mar;21(3):349-54. PMID:20424067

63 Fearless dominance mediates the relationship between the facial width-to-height ratio and willingness to cheat. Geniolea SN, Keyesa AE, Carréc JM, McCormick CM. Personality and Individual Differences. Jan. 2104 57(1):59-64.

64 Facial width-to-height ratio predicts self-reported dominance and aggression in males and females, but a measure of masculinity does not. Lefevre CE, Etchells PJ, Howell EC, Clark AP, Penton-Voak IS. Biol Lett. 2014 Oct;10(10):20140729. PMID:25339656

65 Facial structure is indicative of explicit support for prejudicial beliefs. Hehman E, Leitner JB, Deegan MP, Gaertner SL. Psychol Sci. 2013 Mar 1;24(3):289-96. PMID:23389425

[66] Evidence from Meta-Analyses of the Facial Width-to-Height Ratio as an Evolved Cue of Threat. Geniole SN, Denson TF, Dixson BJ, Carré JM, McCormick CM. PLoS One. 2015 Jul 16;10(7):e0132726. PMID:26181579

[67] The effects of facial adiposity on attractiveness and perceived leadership ability. Re DE, Perrett DI. Q J Exp Psychol (Hove). 2014;67(4):676-86. PMID:23971489

[68] Apparent height and body mass index influence perceived leadership ability in three-dimensional faces. Re DE, Dzhelyova M, Holzleitner IJ, Tigue CC, Feinberg DR, Perrett DI. Perception. 2012;41(12):1477-85. PMID:23586287

[69] Prenatal testosterone exposure is related to sexually dimorphic facial morphology in adulthood. Whitehouse AJ, Gilani SZ, Shafait F, et al. Proc Biol Sci. 2015 Oct 7;282(1816):20151351. PMID:26400740

[70] Testosterone-mediated sex differences in the face shape during adolescence: subjective impressions and objective features. Marečková K, Weinbrand Z, Chakravarty MM, et al. Horm Behav. 2011 Nov;60(5):681-90. PMID:21983236

[71] Facial Width-To-Height Ratio (fWHR) Is Not Associated with Adolescent Testosterone Levels. Hodges-Simeon CR, Hanson Sobraske KN, Samore T, Gurven M, Gaulin SJ. PLoS One. 2016 Apr 14;11(4):e0153083. PMID:27078636

[72] Hypermasculinised facial morphology in boys and girls with Autism Spectrum Disorder and its association with symptomatology. Tan DW, Gilani SZ, Maybery MT, Mian A, Hunt A, Walters M, Whitehouse AJO. Sci Rep. 2017 Aug 24;7(1):9348. PMID:28839245

[73] The association between perinatal testosterone concentration and early vocabulary development: a prospective cohort study. Hollier LP, Mattes E, Maybery MT, et al. Biol Psychol. 2013 Feb;92(2):212-5. PMID:23153707

[74] Sex-specific associations between umbilical cord blood testosterone levels and language delay in early childhood. Whitehouse AJ, Mattes E, Maybery MT, Sawyer MG, Jacoby P, Keelan JA, Hickey M. J Child Psychol Psychiatry. 2012 Jul;53(7):726-34. PMID:22276678

[75] Facial width-to-height ratio in a large sample of Commonwealth Games athletes. Kramer RS. Evol Psychol. 2015 Feb 25;13(1):197-209.PMID:25714799

[76] Face Shape and Behavior: Implications of Similarities in Infants and Adults. Zebrowitz LA, Franklin RG Jr, Boshyan J. Pers Individ Dif. 2015 Nov 1;86:312-317. PMID:26217067

[77] Ibid Ref 71. PMID:27078636

[78] Photo by Stiendy, Wikimeida Commons 4.0

[79] Facial appearance affects voting decisions. Little AC, Burrriss RP, Jones BC, Roberts SC. Evolution and Human Behavior. Jan. 2007. 28(1):18-27

[80] Васин Юрий, Wikimedia Creative Commons 4.0

[81] How components of facial width to height ratio differently contribute to the perception of social traits. Costa M, Lio G, Gomez A, Sirigu A. PLoS One. 2017 Feb 24;12(2):e0172739. PMID:28235081

[82] The perception of attractiveness and trustworthiness in male faces affects hypothetical voting decisions differently in wartime and peacetime scenarios. Little AC, Roberts SC, Jones BC, Debruine LM. Q J Exp Psychol (Hove). PMID:22650610

83 Facial cues to perceived height influence leadership choices in simulated war and peace contexts. Re DE, DeBruine LM, Jones BC, Perrett DI. Evol Psychol. 2013 Jan 31;11(1):89-103. PMID:23372088

84 The perception of attractiveness and trustworthiness in male faces affects hypothetical voting decisions differently in wartime and peacetime scenarios. Little AC, Roberts SC, Jones BC, Debruine LM. Q J Exp Psychol (Hove). 2012;65(10):2018-32. PMID:22650610

85 Democrats and republicans can be differentiated from their faces. Rule NO, Ambady N. PLoS One. 2010 Jan 18;5(1):e8733. PMID:20090906

86 Winning Faces Vary by Ideology: How Nonverbal Source Cues Influence Election and Communication Success in Politics. Laustsen L, Petersen MB. Political Communication Aug 2015. 33(2):188-211

87 Facial appearance affects voting decisions. Little AC, Burriss, RP, Jones BC. Roberts SC. Evol Hum Behav. 2007;28:18–27

88 High seroprevalence of Toxoplasma gondii infection in inmates: A case control study in Durango City, Mexico. Alvarado-Esquivel C, Hernández-Tinoco J, Sánchez-Anguiano LF, et al. Eur J Microbiol Immunol (Bp). 2014 Mar;4(1):76-82. PMID:24678408

89 https://www.cdc.gov/parasites/toxoplasmosis/epi.html Center for Disease Control and Prevention Accessed August 2017

90 Looking like a leader-facial shape predicts perceived height and leadership ability. Re DE, Hunter DW, Coetzee V, Tiddeman BP, Xiao D, DeBruine LM, Jones BC, Perrett DI. PLoS One. 2013 Dec 4;8(12):e80957. PMID:24324651

91 Tall claims? Sense and nonsense about the importance of height of US presidents. Stulp, G., Buunk, AP, Verhulst S, Pollet, T. The Leadership Quarterly (2012)

92 Ibid Ref. 91 PMID:24324651

93 Influence of Perceived Height, Masculinity, and Age on Each Other and on Perceptions of Dominance in Male Faces. Batres C, Re DE, Perrett DI. Perception. 2015;44(11):1293-309. PMID:26562897

94 https://www.nytimes.com/2017/10/10/us/politics/trump-corker-feud-tweet-liddle-bob.html Accessed Oct. 2017

95 https://www.inc.com/john-warrillow/the-surprising-role-height-plays-in-your-potential-as-a-leader.html Accessed August 2017.

96 Caveman Politics: Evolutionary Leadership Preferences and Physical Stature. Murray G, Schmitz DJ. Social Science Quarterly Oct. 2011. 92(1215-1235). DOI 10.1111/j.1540-6237.2011.00815.x

97 The relationship between physical work and the height premium: finnish evidence. Böckerman P, Johansson E, Kiiskinen U, Heliövaara M. Econ Hum Biol. 2010 Dec;8(3):414-20. PMID:20934925

98 The Effect of Adolescent Experience on Labor Market Outcomes: The Case of Height. Perisco N, Posltewaite A, Silverman D.Journal of Political Economy, 2004, 112(5)1099-1053.

99 Height and leadership. Lindquist E. IFN Working Paper No. 835, 2010 Research Institute of Industrial Economics. May 2010 Stockholm, Sweden www.ifn.se

[100] Stature and Status: Height, Ability, and Labor Market Outcomes. Case A, Paxson C. Journal of Political Economy, University of Chicago Press,2008 116(3)499-532. NBER working paper 12466

[101] Stature and Status: Height, Ability, and Labor Market Outcomes. Case A, Paxson C. Journal of Political Economy, University of Chicago Press,2008 116(3)499-532. NBER working paper 12466

[102] Tall claims? Sense and nonsense about the importance of height of US presidents. Stulp, G., Buunk, AP, Verhulst S, Pollet, T. The Leadership Quarterly (2012)

[103] Presidential IQ, Openness, Intellectual Brilliance, and Leadership: Estimates and Correlations for 42 U.S. Chief Executives. Simonton KD.. Political Psychology. 27 (4): 511–526. (Aug. 2006)

[104] Anthropometric Reference Data for Children and Adults: United States, 2011–2014 US Dept. of Health and Human Services; et al. (August 2016).

[105] The curse of the superstar CEO. Khurana R. Harvard Business Review, Sept. 2002. https://hbr.org/2002/09/the-curse-of-the-superstar-ceo

[106] http://www.flickr.com/photos/99527366@N00/13927310340/ (Photo by Andrew H. Walker/Getty Images for Yahoo News).

[107] Myths and Truths About Successful CEOs. Williams R. Psychology Today. Sept. 2017.

[108] Mate choice and human stature: homogamy as a unified framework for understanding mating preferences. Courtiol A, Raymond M, Godelle B, Ferdy JB. Evolution. 2010 Aug;64(8):2189-203. PMID:20199563

[109] Height and leadership. Lindquist E. IFN Working Paper No. 835, 2010 Research Institute of Industrial Economics. May 2010 Stockholm, Sweden www.ifn.se

[110] Table 205.Cumulative Percent Distribution of Population by Height and Sex: 2007 to 2008. NHANES Data

[111] The height leadership advantage in men and women: Testing evolutionary psychology predictions about the perceptions of tall leaders. Baker NB, Rompa, I, Inge H, et al. Jan.10, 2013. Group Processes & Intergroup Relations. Volume: 16 issue: 1, page(s): 17-27.

[112] Evolutionary preferences for physical formidability in leaders. Murray GR. Politics Life Sci. 2014 Spring;33(1):33-53. PMID:25514522

[113] https://www.nhlbi.nih.gov/health/educational/lose_wt/risk.htm Accessed Sept. 2017

[114] Ailing voters advance attractive congressional candidates. Zebrowitz LA, Franklin RG Jr, Palumbo R. Evol Psychol. 2015 Jan 6;13(1):16-28. PMID:25562113

[115] Ibid Ref. 91 PMID:24324651

[116] Ibid Ref. 5. PMID:24651120

[117] Perceived intelligence is associated with measured intelligence in men but not women. Kleisner K, Chvátalová V, Flegr J. PLoS One. 2014 Mar 20;9(3):e81237. PMID:24651120

[118] Adaptation to facial trustworthiness is different in female and male observers. Wincenciak J, Dzhelyova M, Perrett DI, Barraclough NE. Vision Res. 2013 Jul 19;87:30-4. PMID:23727267

[119] Verbal and non-verbal intelligence changes in the teenage brain. Ramsden S, Richardson FM, Josse G, Thomas MS, Ellis C, Shakeshaft C, Seghier ML, Price CJ. Nature. 2011 Oct 19;479(7371):113-6. PMID:22012265

[120] The influence of reading ability on subsequent changes in verbal IQ in the teenage years. Ramsden S, Richardson FM, Josse G, Shakeshaft C, Seghier ML, Price CJ. Dev Cogn Neurosci. 2013 Oct;6:30-9. PMID:23872197

[121] Eyelid-openness and mouth curvature influence perceived intelligence beyond attractiveness. Talamas SN, Mavor KI, Axelsson J, Sundelin T, Perrett DI. J Exp Psychol Gen. 2016 May;145(5):603-620. PMID:26913618

[122] Cues of fatigue: effects of sleep deprivation on facial appearance. Sundelin T, Lekander M, Kecklund G, Van Someren EJ, Olsson A, Axelsson J. Sleep. 2013 Sep 1;36(9):1355-60. PMID:23997369

[123] Somatic growth of lean children: the potential role of sleep. Jiang YR, Spruyt K, Chen WJ, Shen XM, Jiang F. World J Pediatr. 2014 Aug;10(3):245-50. doPMID:25124976

[124] Reduced risk for overweight and obesity in 5- and 6-y-old children by duration of sleep--a cross-sectional study. von Kries R, Toschke AM, Wurmser H, Sauerwald T, Koletzko B. Int J Obes Relat Metab Disord. 2002 May;26(5):710-6. PMID:12032757

[125] Sleep duration and growth outcomes across the first two years of life in the GUSTO study. Zhou Y, Aris IM, Tan SS, Cai S, Tint MT, Krishnaswamy G, Meaney MJ, Godfrey KM, Kwek K, Gluckman PD, Chong YS, Yap F, Lek N, Gooley JJ, Lee YS. Sleep Med. 2015 Oct;16(10):1281-6. PMID:26429758

[126] Bedtime in Preschool-Aged Children and Risk for Adolescent Obesity. Anderson SE, Andridge R, Whitaker RC. J Pediatr. 2016 Sep;176:17-22. 27426836

[127] Blinded by Beauty: Attractiveness Bias and Accurate Perceptions of Academic Performance. Talamas SN, Mavor KI, Perrett DI. PLoS One. 2016 Feb 17;11(2):e0148284. PMID:26885976

[128] Sensitivity to "Bad Genes" and the Anomalous Face Overgeneralization Effect: Cue Validity, Cue Utilization, and Accuracy in Judging Intelligence and Health. Zebrowitz LA, Rhodes G.Journal of Nonverbal Behavior. Sept. 2004, 28(3):167–185

[129] Internal facial features are signals of personality and health. Kramer RS, Ward R. Q J Exp Psychol (Hove). 2010 Nov;63(11):2273-87. PMID:20486018

[130] Inferring character from faces: a developmental study. Cogsdill EJ, Todorov AT, Spelke ES, Banaji MR. Psychol Sci. 2014 May 1;25(5):1132-9. PMID:24570261

[131] The influence of political candidates' facial appearance on older and younger adults' voting choices and actual electoral success. Franklin RG, Zebrowitz LA. Cognet Psychology. March 2016. 3(1)1-13

[132] The face-time continuum: lifespan changes in facial width-to-height ratio impact aging-associated perceptions. Hehman E, Leitner JB, Freeman JB. Pers Soc Psychol Bull. 2014 Dec;40(12):1624-36. PMID:25278108

[133] Observable attributes as manifestations and cues of Personality and intelligence. Borkenau P, Liebler A. Journal of Personality. March 1995. 63(1):1-25 10.1111/j.1467-6494.1995.tb00799.x

[134] Cultural effects on the association between election outcomes and face-based trait inferences. Lin C, Adolphs R, Alvarez RM. PLoS One. 2017 Jul 10;12(7):e0180837. PMID:28700647

[135] Observable attributes as manifestations and cues of Personality and intelligence. Borkenau P, Liebler A. Journal of Personality. March 1995. 63(1):1-25 10.1111/j.1467-6494.1995.tb00799.x

[136] Perceptual and Social Attributes Underlining Age-Related Preferences for Faces. Kiiski HS, Cullen B, Clavin SL, Newell FN. Front Hum Neurosci. 2016 Aug 31;10:437. PMID:27630553

[137] Adiposity, compared with masculinity, serves as a more valid cue to immunocompetence in human mate choice. Rantala MJ, Coetzee V, Moore FR, Skrinda I, Kecko S, Krama T, Kivleniece I, Krams I. Proc Biol Sci. 2013 Jan 22;280(1751):20122495. doi: 10.1098/rspb.2012.2495. PMID: 23193134

[138] Effects of Facial Maturity on Voting Preference. Nixon B, Pollom S 2006 *psych.hanover.edu/research/Thesis06/NixonandPollom.pdf*

[139] Perceptions of Competence, Strength, and Age Influence Voters to Select Leaders with Lower-Pitched Voices. Klofstad CA, Anderson RC, Nowicki S. PLoS One. 2015 Aug 7;10(8):e0133779. PMID:26252894

[140] Attractiveness of blonde women in evolutionary perspective: studies with two Polish samples. Sorokowski P. Percept Mot Skills. 2008 Jun;106(3):737-44. PMID:18712194

[141] The influence of skin tone, hair length, and hair colour on ratings of women's physical attractiveness, health and fertility. Swami V, Furnham A, Joshi K. Scand J Psychol. 2008 Oct;49(5):429-37. PMID:18452501

[142] A sex difference in facial contrast and its exaggeration by cosmetics. Russell R. Perception. 2009;38(8):1211-9. PMID:19817153

[143] British men's hair color preferences: an assessment of courtship solicitation and stimulus ratings. Swami V, Barrett S. Scand J Psychol. 2011 Dec;52(6):595-600. PMID:21883260

[144] Ibid Ref 141. PMID:18712194

[145] Image by Tomasz W. Kozlowski, Wikimedia commons.

[146] Synophrys: Epidemiological Study. Kumar P. Int J Trichology. 2017 Jul-Sep;9(3):105-107. PMID:28932060

[147] Face Value: Facial Appearance and Assessments of Politicians. Carpinella CM, Johnson KL. Aug. 2016. Oxford Research Encyclopedias. DOI: 10.1093/acrefore/9780190228637.013.62

[148] Forming impressions of facial attractiveness is mandatory. Ritchie KL, Palermo R, Rhodes G. Sci Rep. 2017 Mar 28;7(1):469. PMID:28352107

[149] Electrophysiological correlates of processing facial attractiveness and its influence on cooperative behavior. Chen J, Zhong J, Zhang Y, Li P, Zhang A, Tan Q, Li H. Neurosci Lett. 2012 May 31;517(2):65-70. PMID:22410307

150 Hello handsome! Male's facial attractiveness gives rise to female's fairness bias in Ultimatum Game scenarios-An ERP study. Ma Q, Qian D, Hu L, Wang L. PLoS One. 2017 Jul 5;12(7):e0180459. PMID:28678888

151 Identifying cognitive preferences for attractive female faces: an event-related potential experiment using a study-test paradigm. Zhang Y, Kong F, Chen H, Jackson T, Han L, Meng J, Yang Z, Gao J, Najam ul Hasan A. J Neurosci Res. 2011 Nov;89(11):1887-93. PMID:21805493

152 Insular and hippocampal contributions to remembering people with an impression of bad personality. Tsukiura T, Shigemune Y, Nouchi R, Kambara T, Kawashima R. Soc Cogn Affect Neurosci. 2013 Jun;8(5):515-22. PMID:22349799

153 Remembering beauty: roles of orbitofrontal and hippocampal regions in successful memory encoding of attractive faces. Tsukiura T, Cabeza R. Neuroimage. 2011 Jan 1;54(1):653-60. PMID:20659568

154 Faces with Light Makeup Are Better Recognized than Faces with Heavy Makeup. Tagai K, Ohtaka H, Nittono H. Front Psychol. 2016 Mar 1;7:226. PMID:26973553

155 Forming impressions of facial attractiveness is mandatory. Ritchie KL, Palermo R, Rhodes G. Sci Rep. 2017 Mar 28;7(1):469. PMID:28352107

156 Genetic diversity revealed in human faces. Lie HC, Rhodes G, Simmons LW. Evolution. 2008 Oct;62(10):2473-86. PMID:18691260

157 Facial appearance reveals immunity in African men. Phalane KG, Tribe C, Steel HC, Cholo MC, Coetzee V. Sci Rep. 2017 Aug 7;7(1):7443. PMID:28785075

158 Exploring the relationship between attractiveness and a good sense of humour. In: Psychology of Interpersonal Perception and Relationships. Cowan, M. L. and Little, A. C., 2014. Nova Science Publishers Inc, pp. 71-94. (Psychology of Emotions, Motivations and Actions) http://opus.bath.ac.uk/54253/

159 Attractiveness, Competence or Likeability? Appearance Effects in the 2013 German Election. Jackle S, Metz T. European Consortium for Political Research. Presented at the ECPR General Conference in Montreal, August 26th – 29th 2015

160 http://www.uni-regensburg.de/Fakultaeten/phil_Fak_II/Psychologie/_Psy_II /beautycheck/english/sozialewahrnehmung/sozialewahrnehmung.htm. Accessed Oct. 2017

161 Expressions of positive emotion in women's college yearbook pictures and their relationship to personality and life outcomes across adulthood. Harker L, Keltner D. J Pers Soc Psychol. 2001 Jan;80(1):112-24. PMID:11195884

162 Smile intensity in photographs predicts longevity. Abel EL, Kruger ML. Psychol Sci. 2010 Apr;21(4):542-4. doi: 10.1177/0956797610363775. PMID:20424098

163 A winning smile? Smile intensity, physical dominance, and fighter performance. Kraus MW, Chen TW. Emotion. 2013 Apr;13(2):270-9. PMID:23356564

164 Smiles as signals of lower status in football players and fashion models: evidence that smiles are associated with lower dominance and lower prestige. Ketelaar T, Koenig BL, Gambacorta D, Dolgov I, Hor D, Zarzosa J, Luna-Nevarez C, Klungle M, Wells L. Evol Psychol. 2012 Jul 10;10(3):371-97. PMID:22947668

165 The contingent smile: a meta-analysis of sex differences in smiling. LaFrance M, Hecht MA, Paluck EL. Psychol Bull. 2003 Mar;129(2):305-34. PMID:12696842

166 Smiling faces rated more feminine than serious faces in Japan. Kawamura S, Kageyama K. Percept Mot Skills. 2006 Aug;103(1):210-4. PMID:17037662

167 Smiling when distressed: when a smile is a frown turned upside down. Ansfield ME. Pers Soc Psychol Bull. 2007 Jun;33(6):763-75. PMID:17483396

168 Be Careful Where You Smile: Culture Shapes Judgments of Intelligence and Honesty of Smiling Individuals. Krys K, Melanie Vauclair C, Capaldi CA, et al. J Nonverbal Behav. 2016;40:101-116. PMID:27194817

169 It is better to smile to women: gender modifies perception of honesty of smiling individuals across cultures. Krys K, Hansen K, Xing C, Espinosa AD, Szarota P, Morales MF. Int J Psychol. 2015 Mar;50(2):150-4. PMID:25066890

170 Reading a smiling face: messages conveyed by various forms of smiling. Otta E, Folladore Abrosio F, Hoshino RL. Percept Mot Skills. 1996 Jun;82(3 Pt 2):1111-21. PMID:8823879

171 The effect of smiling and of head tilting on person perception. Otta E, Lira BB, Delevati NM, Cesar OP, Pires CS. J Psychol. 1994 May;128(3):323-31. PMID:8046666

172 Smiling makes you look older. Ganel T. Psychon Bull Rev. 2015 Dec;22(6):1671-7. PMID:25855200

173 You may look unhappy unless you smile: the distinctiveness of a smiling face against faces without an explicit smile. Park HB, Han JE, Hyun JS. Acta Psychol (Amst). 2015 May;157:185-94. PMID:25819385

174 Smiling emphasizes perceived distinctiveness of faces. Kawamura S, Komori M. Percept Mot Skills. 2008 Aug;107(1):119-20. PMID:18986039

175 Trustworthy-looking face meets brown eyes. Kleisner K, Priplatova L, Frost P, Flegr J. PLoS One. 2013;8(1):e53285. PMID:23326406

176 What is typical is good: the influence of face typicality on perceived trustworthiness. Sofer C, Dotsch R, Wigboldus DH, Todorov A. Psychol Sci. 2015 Jan;26(1):39-47. PMID:25512052

177 Facial Skin Smoothness as an Indicator of Perceived Trustworthiness and Related Traits. Tsankova E, Kappas A. Perception. 2016 Apr;45(4):400-8. PMID:26621963

178 Intensity of smiling and attractiveness as facial signals of trustworthiness in women. Schmidt K, Levenstein R, Ambadar Z. Percept Mot Skills. 2012 Jun;114(3):964-78. PMID:22913033

179 Adaptation to facial trustworthiness is different in female and male observers. Wincenciak J, Dzhelyova M, Perrett DI, Barraclough NE. Vision Res. 2013 Jul 19;87:30-4. PMID:23727267

180 The effect of eyelid constriction on perceptions of mating strategy: Beware of the squinty-eyed guy! Kruger DJ, Piglowski JS. Personality and Individual Differences Apr. 2012. 52)5):576-580.

181 Do characteristics of faces that convey trustworthiness and dominance underlie perceptions of criminality? Flowe HD. PLoS One. 2012;7(6):e37253. PMID:22675479

[182] Bright, bad, babyfaced boys: appearance stereotypes do not always yield self-fulfilling prophecy effects. Zebrowitz LA, Andreoletti C, Collins MA, Lee SY, Blumenthal J. J Pers Soc Psychol. 1998 Nov;75(5):1300-20. PMID:9866189

[183] The functional basis of face evaluation. Oosterhof NN, Todorov A.Proc Natl Acad Sci U S A. 2008 Aug 12;105(32):11087-92. PMID:18685089

[184] Evaluating faces on trustworthiness: an extension of systems for recognition of emotions signaling approach/avoidance behaviors. Todorov A. Ann N Y Acad Sci. 2008 Mar;1124:208-24. PMID:18400932

[185] http://www.uni-regensburg.de/Fakultaeten/phil_Fak_II/Psychologie/Psy_II/beautycheck/english/prototypen/prototypen.htm Accessed Oct. 2017

[186] Beauty sleep: experimental study on the perceived health and attractiveness of sleep deprived people. Axelsson J, Sundelin T, Ingre M, Van Someren EJ, Olsson A, Lekander M. BMJ. 2010 Dec 14;341:c6614. PMID:21156746

[187] Negative effects of restricted sleep on facial appearance and social appeal. Sundelin T, Lekander M, Sorjonen K, Axelsson J. R Soc Open Sci. 2017 May 17;4(5):160918. PMID:28572989

[188] The following sections are taken from Unraveling Cancer, Chapter 30. Charles Lewis, 2016.Carrabelle. ISBN-13: 978-1535593724

[189] Sleep deprivation: Impact on cognitive performance. Alhola P, Polo-Kantola P. Neuropsychiatr Dis Treat. 2007;3(5):553-67. PMID:19300585

[190] Fatigue, alcohol and performance impairment. Dawson D, Reid K. Nature. 1997 Jul 17;388(6639):235. PMID:9230429

[191] Does abnormal sleep impair memory consolidation in schizophrenia? Manoach DS, Stickgold R. Front Hum Neurosci. 2009 Sep 1;3:21. PMID:19750201

[192] Micropillar arrays as a high-throughput screening platform for therapeutics in multiple sclerosis. Mei F, Fancy SP, Shen YA, et al. Nat Med. 2014 Aug;20(8):954-60. PMID:24997607

[193] Systematic interindividual differences in neurobehavioral impairment from sleep loss: evidence of trait-like differential vulnerability. Van Dongen HP, Baynard MD, Maislin G, Dinges DF. Sleep. 2004 May 1;27(3):423-33. PMID: 15164894

[194] The cumulative cost of additional wakefulness: dose-response effects on neurobehavioral functions and sleep physiology from chronic sleep restriction and total sleep deprivation. Van Dongen HP, Maislin G, et al. Sleep. 2003 Mar 15;26(2):117-26. PMID: 12683469

[195] Sleep drives metabolite clearance from the adult brain. Xie L, Kang H, Xu Q, et al. Science. 2013 Oct 18;342(6156):373-7. PMID:24136970

[196] Meta-analysis of short sleep duration and obesity in children and adults. Cappuccio FP, Taggart FM, Kandala NB, Currie A, Peile E, Stranges S, Miller MA. Sleep. 2008 May;31(5):619-26. PMID:18517032

[197] Enteroimmunology. Chapter 42. Charles Lewis Psy Press. 2015

[198] Ibid Ref 198. Lewis

199 Cues of fatigue: effects of sleep deprivation on facial appearance. Sundelin T, Lekander M, Kecklund G, Van Someren EJ, Olsson A, Axelsson J. Sleep. 2013 Sep 1;36(9):1355-60. PMID:23997369

200 These pearls are taken from Unraveling Cancer, Chapter 30. Charles Lewis, 2016.Carrabelle. ISBN-13: 978-1535593724

201 Daily exercise facilitates phase delays of circadian melatonin rhythm in very dim light. Barger LK, Wright KP Jr, Hughes RJ, Czeisler CA. Am J Physiol Regul Integr Comp Physiol. 2004 Jun;286(6):R1077-84. PMID:15031136

202 Physical exercise accelerates reentrainment of human sleep-wake cycle but not of plasma melatonin rhythm to 8-h phase-advanced sleep schedule. Yamanaka Y, Hashimoto S, Tanahashi Y, Nishide SY, Honma S, Honma K. Am J Physiol Regul Integr Comp Physiol. 2010 Mar;298(3):R681-91. PMID:20042689

203 Ibid Ref. 201. Lewis

204 Evening use of light-emitting eReaders negatively affects sleep, circadian timing, and next-morning alertness. Chang AM, Aeschbach D, Duffy JF, Czeisler CA. Proc Natl Acad Sci U S A. 2015 Jan 27;112(4):1232-7. PMID:25535358

205 Acute ethanol modulates glutamatergic and serotonergic phase shifts of the mouse circadian clock in vitro. Prosser RA, Mangrum CA, Glass JD. Neuroscience. 2008 Mar 27;152(3):837-48. PMID: 18313277

206 Habitual moderate alcohol consumption desynchronizes circadian physiologic rhythms and affects reaction-time performance. Reinberg A, Touitou Y, Lewy H, Mechkouri M. Chronobiol Int. 2010 Oct.;27(9-10):1930-1942. PMID: 20969532

207 Skin colour changes during experimentally-induced sickness. Henderson AJ, Lasselin J, Lekander M, Olsson MJ, Powis SJ, Axelsson J, Perrett DI. Brain Behav Immun. 2017 Feb;60:312-318. PMID:27847284

208 Integrating shape cues of adiposity and color information when judging facial health and attractiveness. Fisher CI, Hahn AC, DeBruine LM, Jones BC. Perception. 2014;43(6):499-508. PMID:25154284

209 Perception of health from facial cues. Henderson AJ, Holzleitner IJ, Talamas SN, Perrett DI. Philos Trans R Soc Lond B Biol Sci. 2016 May 5;371(1693). pii: 20150380. PMID:27069057

210 Ibid Ref 138. PMID: 23193134

211 Facial appearance reveals immunity in African men. Phalane KG, Tribe C, Steel HC, Cholo MC, Coetzee V. Sci Rep. 2017 Aug 7;7(1):7443. PMID:28785075

212 Fruit over sunbed: carotenoid skin colouration is found more attractive than melanin colouration. Lefevre CE, Perrett DI. Q J Exp Psychol (Hove). 2015;68(2):284-93. PMID:25014019

213 Facial coloration tracks changes in women's estradiol. Jones BC, Hahn AC, Fisher CI, Wincenciak J, Kandrik M, Roberts SC, Little AC, DeBruine LM. Psychoneuroendocrinology. 2015 Jun;56:29-34. PMID:25796069

214 Oxygenated-blood colour change thresholds for perceived facial redness, health, and attractiveness. Re DE, Whitehead RD, Xiao D, Perrett DI. PLoS One. 2011 Mar 23;6(3):e17859. PMID:21448270

215 Redness enhances perceived aggression, dominance and attractiveness in men's faces. Stephen ID, Oldham FH, Perrett DI, Barton RA. Evol Psychol. 2012 Aug 17;10(3):562-72. PMID:22947678

216 Visible skin colouration predicts perception of male facial age, health and attractiveness. Fink B, Bunse L, Matts PJ, D'Emiliano D. Int J Cosmet Sci. 2012 Aug;34(4):307-10. PMID:22515406

217 Colour homogeneity and visual perception of age, health and attractiveness of male facial skin. Fink B, Matts PJ, D'Emiliano D, Bunse L, Weege B, Röder S. J Eur Acad Dermatol Venereol. 2012 Dec;26(12):1486-92PMID:22044626

218 Anti-inflammatory efficacy of topical preparations with 10% hamamelis distillate in a UV erythema test. Hughes-Formella BJ, Filbry A, Gassmueller J, Rippke F. Skin Pharmacol Appl Skin Physiol. 2002 Mar-Apr;15(2):125-32. PMID:11867970

219 You are what you eat: within-subject increases in fruit and vegetable consumption confer beneficial skin-color changes. Whitehead RD, Re D, Xiao D, Ozakinci G, Perrett DI. PLoS One. 2012;7(3):e32988. PMID:22412966

220 Daily Consumption of a Fruit and Vegetable Smoothie Alters Facial Skin Color. Tan KW, Graf BA, Mitra SR, Stephen ID. PLoS One. 2015 Jul 17;10(7):e0133445. PMID:26186449

221 Assessment of dietary lutein, zeaxanthin and lycopene intakes and sources in the Spanish survey of dietary intake (2009-2010). Estévez-Santiago R, Beltrán-de-Miguel B, Olmedilla-Alonso B. Int J Food Sci Nutr. 2016;67(3):305-13PMID:26903293

222 Molecular mechanisms of green tea polyphenols with protective effects against skin photoaging. Roh E, Kim JE, Kwon JY, Park JS, Bode AM, Dong Z, Lee KW. Crit Rev Food Sci Nutr. 2017 May 24;57(8):1631-1637. PMID:26114360

223 African perceptions of female attractiveness. Coetzee V, Faerber SJ, Greeff JM, Lefevre CE, Re DE, Perrett DI. PLoS One. 2012;7(10):e48116. PMID:23144734

224 Cross-cultural agreement in facial attractiveness preferences: the role of ethnicity and gender. Coetzee V, Greeff JM, Stephen ID, Perrett DI. PLoS One. 2014 Jul 2;9(7):e99629. PMID:24988325

225 Facial appearance reveals immunity in African men. Phalane KG, Tribe C, Steel HC, Cholo MC, Coetzee V. Sci Rep. 2017 Aug 7;7(1):7443. PMID:28785075

226 β-Carotene and other carotenoids in protection from sunlight. Stahl W, Sies H. Am J Clin Nutr. 2012 Nov;96(5):1179S-84S. PMID:23053552

227 Carotenoids and flavonoids contribute to nutritional protection against skin damage from sunlight. Stahl W, Sies H. Mol Biotechnol. 2007 Sep;37(1):26-30. PMID:17914160

228 Molecular evidence that oral supplementation with lycopene or lutein protects human skin against ultraviolet radiation: results from a double-blinded, placebo-controlled, crossover study. Grether-Beck S, Marini A, Jaenicke T, Stahl W, Krutmann J. Br J Dermatol. 2017 May;176(5):1231-1240. PMID:27662341

229 Tomatoes protect against development of UV-induced keratinocyte carcinoma via metabolomic alterations. Cooperstone JL, Tober KL, Riedl KM, Teegarden MD, Cichon MJ, Francis DM, Schwartz SJ, Oberyszyn TM. Sci Rep. 2017 Jul 11;7(1):5106. PMID:28698610

230 [Influence of cooking procedure on the bioavailability of lycopene in tomatoes]. Perdomo F, Cabrera Fránquiz F, Cabrera J, Serra-Majem L. Nutr Hosp. 2012 Sep-Oct;27(5):1542-6. PMID:23478703

231 Increases in plasma lycopene concentration after consumption of tomatoes cooked with olive oil. Fielding JM, Rowley KG, Cooper P, O' Dea K. Asia Pac J Clin Nutr. 2005;14(2):131-6. PMID:15927929

232 Coloration in different areas of facial skin is a cue to health: The role of cheek redness and periorbital luminance in health perception. Jones AL, Porcheron A, Sweda JR, Morizot F, Russell R. Body Image. 2016 Jun;17:57-66. PMID:26967010

233 Facial contrast is a cue for perceiving health from the face. Russell R, Porcheron A, Sweda JR, Jones AL, Mauger E, Morizot F. J Exp Psychol Hum Percept Perform. 2016 Sep;42(9):1354-62. PMID:27100405

234 Aspects of facial contrast decrease with age and are cues for age perception. Porcheron A, Mauger E, Russell R. PLoS One. 2013;8(3):e57985. PMID:23483959

235 Facial Contrast Is a Cross-Cultural Cue for Perceiving Age. Porcheron A, Mauger E, Soppelsa F, Liu Y, Ge L, Pascalis O, Russell R, Morizot F. Front Psychol. 2017 Jul 25;8:1208. PMID:28790941

236 Aspects of facial contrast decrease with age and are cues for age perception. Porcheron A, Mauger E, Russell R. PLoS One. 2013;8(3):e57985. PMID:23483959

237 Reliance on head versus eyes in the gaze following of great apes and human infants: the cooperative eye hypothesis. Tomasello M, Hare B, Lehmann H, Call J. J Hum Evol. 2007 Mar;52(3):314-20. PMID:17140637

238 Metrics of the normal anterior sclera: imaging with optical coherence tomography. Ebneter A, Häner NU, Zinkernagel MS. Graefes Arch Clin Exp Ophthalmol. 2015 Sep;253(9):1575-80. PMID:26067393

239 Bulbar conjunctival thickness measurements with optical coherence tomography in healthy chinese subjects. Zhang X, Li Q, Xiang M, Zou H, Liu B, Zhou H, Han Z, Fu Z, Zhang Z, Wang H. Invest Ophthalmol Vis Sci. 2013 Jul 12;54(7):4705-9. PMID:23744999

240 Age-related changes and diseases of the ocular surface and cornea. Gipson IK. Invest Ophthalmol Vis Sci. 2013 Dec 13;54(14):ORSF48-53. PMID:24335068

241 Aqueous Tear Deficiency Increases Conjunctival Interferon-γ (IFN-γ) Expression and Goblet Cell Loss. Pflugfelder SC, De Paiva CS, Moore QL, Volpe EA, Li DQ, Gumus K, Zaheer ML, Corrales RM. Invest Ophthalmol Vis Sci. 2015 Nov;56(12):7545-50. PMID:26618646

242 Effects of Oxidative Stress on the Conjunctiva in Cu, Zn-Superoxide Dismutase-1 (Sod1)-Knockout Mice. Kojima T, Dogru M, Ibrahim OM, Wakamatsu TH, Ito M, Igarashi A, Inaba T, Shimizu T, Shirasawa T, Shimazaki J, Tsubota K. Invest Ophthalmol Vis Sci. 2015 Dec;56(13):8382-91. 26747769

243 Sclera color changes with age and is a cue for perceiving age, health, and beauty. Russell R, Sweda JR, Porcheron A, Mauger E. Psychol Aging. 2014 Sep;29(3):626-35. PMID:25244481

244 Red, yellow, and super-white sclera : uniquely human cues for healthiness, attractiveness, and age. Provine RR, Cabrera MO, Nave-Blodgett J. Hum Nat. 2013 Jun;24(2):126-36. PMID:23660975

[245] Binocular symmetry/asymmetry of scleral redness as a cue for sadness, healthiness, and attractiveness in humans. Provine RR, Cabrera MO, Nave-Blodgett J. Evol Psychol. 2013 Aug 16;11(4):873-84. PMID:23955871

[246] Comparative study of treatment of the dry eye syndrome due to disturbances of the tear film lipid layer with lipid-containing tear substitutes. Dausch D, Lee S, Dausch S, Kim JC, Schwert G, Michelson W. Klin Monbl Augenheilkd. 2006 Dec;223(12):974-83. PMID:17199193

[247] Goblet Cells Contribute to Ocular Surface Immune Tolerance-Implications for Dry Eye Disease. Barbosa FL, Xiao Y, Bian F, Coursey TG, Ko BY, Clevers H, de Paiva CS, Pflugfelder SC. Int J Mol Sci. 2017 May 5;18(5). pii: E978. PMID:28475124

[248] Revisiting the vicious circle of dry eye disease: a focus on the pathophysiology of meibomian gland dysfunction. Baudouin C, Messmer EM, Aragona P, et al. Br J Ophthalmol. 2016 Mar;100(3):300-6. PMID:26781133

[249] Ubiquity and diversity of human-associated Demodex mites. Thoemmes MS, Fergus DJ, Urban J, Trautwein M, Dunn RR. PLoS One. 2014 Aug 27;9(8):e106265. PMID:25162399

[250] Prevalence of Demodex spp. in eyelash follicles in different populations. Wesolowska M, Knysz B, Reich A, Blazejewska D, Czarnecki M, Gladysz A, Pozowski A, Misiuk-Hojlo M. Arch Med Sci. 2014 May 12;10(2):319-24. PMID:24904668

[251] Potential role of Demodex mites and bacteria in the induction of rosacea. Jarmuda S, O'Reilly N, Zaba R, Jakubowicz O, Szkaradkiewicz A, Kavanagh K. J Med Microbiol. 2012 Nov;61(Pt 11):1504-10. PMID:22933353

[252] Exposure of a corneal epithelial cell line (hTCEpi) to Demodex-associated Bacillus proteins results in an inflammatory response. McMahon FW, Gallagher C, O'Reilly N, Clynes M, O'Sullivan F, Kavanagh K. Invest Ophthalmol Vis Sci. 2014 Oct 2;55(10):7019-28. PMID:25277231

[253] Demodex-associated Bacillus proteins induce an aberrant wound healing response in a corneal epithelial cell line: possible implications for corneal ulcer formation in ocular rosacea. O'Reilly N, Gallagher C, Reddy Katikireddy K, Clynes M, O'Sullivan F, Kavanagh K. Invest Ophthalmol Vis Sci. 2012 May 31;53(6):3250-9. PMID:22531699

[254] Clinical and immunological responses in ocular demodecosis. Kim JH, Chun YS, Kim JC. J Korean Med Sci. 2011 Sep;26(9):1231-7. doi: 10.3346/jkms.2011.26.9.1231. PMID:21935281

[255] Edible Plants and Their Influence on the Gut Microbiome and Acne. Clark AK, Haas KN, Sivamani RK. Int J Mol Sci. 2017 May 17;18(5). pii: E1070. PMID:28513546

[256] Correlation between serum reactivity to Demodex-associated Bacillus oleronius proteins, and altered sebum levels and Demodex populations in erythematotelangiectatic rosacea patients. Jarmuda S, McMahon F, Zaba R, O'Reilly N, Jakubowicz O, Holland A, Szkaradkiewicz A, Kavanagh K. J Med Microbiol. 2014 Feb;63(Pt 2):258-62. PMID:24248990

[257] Ocular Demodicosis as a Potential Cause of Ocular Surface Inflammation. Luo X, Li J, Chen C, Tseng S, Liang L. Cornea. 2017 Sep 7. PMID:28902017

258 A meta-analysis of association between acne vulgaris and Demodex infestation. Zhao YE, Hu L, Wu LP, Ma JX. J Zhejiang Univ Sci B. 2012 Mar;13(3):192-202. dPMID:22374611

259 Interventions for rosacea. van Zuuren EJ, Fedorowicz Z, Carter B, van der Linden MM, Charland L. Cochrane Database Syst Rev. 2015 Apr 28;(4):CD003262. PMID:25919144

260 In vivo confocal microscopy evaluation of ocular and cutaneous alterations in patients with rosacea. Liang H, Randon M, Michee S, Tahiri R, Labbe A, Baudouin C. Br J Ophthalmol. 2016 May 24. pii: bjophthalmol-2015-308110. PMID:27222243

261 http://eyedoc2020.blogspot.com/2016/05/how-to-use-tea-tree-oil-for-eyelid.html Accessed Sept 2017.

262 Ocular surface discomfort and Demodex: effect of tea tree oil eyelid scrub in Demodex blepharitis. Koo H, Kim TH, Kim KW, Wee SW, Chun YS, Kim JC. J Korean Med Sci. 2012 Dec;27(12):1574-9. PMID:23255861

263 In vitro and in vivo killing of ocular Demodex by tea tree oil. Gao YY, Di Pascuale MA, Li W, Baradaran-Rafii A, Elizondo A, Kuo CL, Raju VK, Tseng SC. Br J Ophthalmol. 2005 Nov;89(11):1468-73. PMID:16234455

264 Contact lens wear is associated with decrease of meibomian glands. Arita R, Itoh K, Inoue K, Kuchiba A, Yamaguchi T, Amano S. Ophthalmology. 2009 Mar;116(3):379-84. PMID:19167077

265 Association of contact lens-related allergic conjunctivitis with changes in the morphology of meibomian glands. Arita R, Itoh K, Maeda S, Maeda K, Tomidokoro A, Amano S. Jpn J Ophthalmol. 2012 Jan;56(1):14-9. PMID:22109632

266 Increased numbers of Demodex in contact lens wearers. Jalbert I, Rejab S. Optom Vis Sci. 2015 Jun;92(6):671-8. PMID:25882593

267 Prevalence of Demodex spp. in eyelash follicles in different populations. Wesolowska M, Knysz B, Reich A, Blazejewska D, Czarnecki M, Gladysz A, Pozowski A, Misiuk-Hojlo M. Arch Med Sci. 2014 May 12;10(2):319-24. PMID:24904668

268 Comparative study of treatment of the dry eye syndrome due to disturbances of the tear film lipid layer with lipid-containing tear substitutes. Dausch D, Lee S, Dausch S, Kim JC, Schwert G, Michelson W. Klin Monbl Augenheilkd. 2006 Dec;223(12):974-83. PMID:17199193

269 Preservatives in eyedrops: the good, the bad and the ugly. Baudouin C, Labbé A, Liang H, Pauly A, Brignole-Baudouin F. Prog Retin Eye Res. 2010 Jul;29(4):312-34. PMID:20302969

270 Pterygium as an early indicator of ultraviolet insolation: a hypothesis. Coroneo MT. Br J Ophthalmol. 1993 Nov;77(11):734-9. PMID: 8280691

271 The Role of UV Damage in Ocular Disease. Karpecki R. Review of Optometry. Oct. 2012.

272 January 2015 Wills Eye Resident Case Series - Diagnosis & Discussion. Finklea B. Review of Opthalmology, April 15, 2015.

273 A randomized, double-blind, placebo-controlled study of oral antioxidant supplement therapy in patients with dry eye syndrome. Huang JY, Yeh PT, Hou

YC. Clin Ophthalmol. 2016 May 9;10:813-20. doi: 10.2147/OPTH.S106455. PMID:27274185

274 Short-Term Omega 3 Fatty Acids Treatment for Dry Eye in Young and Middle-Aged Visual Display Terminal Users. Bhargava R, Kumar P, Arora Y. Eye Contact Lens. 2016 Jul;42(4):231-6. PMID:26322917

275 Oral omega-3 fatty acids treatment in computer vision syndrome related dry eye. Bhargava R, Kumar P, Phogat H, Kaur A, Kumar M. Cont Lens Anterior Eye. 2015 Jun;38(3):206-10. PMID:25697893

276 Oral omega-3 fatty acid treatment for dry eye in contact lens wearers. Bhargava R, Kumar P. Cornea. 2015 Apr;34(4):413-20. PMID:25719253

277 Short-term consumption of oral omega-3 and dry eye syndrome. Kangari H, Eftekhari MH, Sardari S, Hashemi H, Salamzadeh J, Ghassemi-Broumand M, Khabazkhoob M. Ophthalmology. 2013 Nov;120(11):2191-6. PMID:23642375

278 Unraveling Cancer. Chapter 13. Lewis CA Psy Press, 2016

279 Enteroimmunology, Chapter 37. Lewis CA. Psy Press, 2015

280 Exercise-induced stress behavior, gut-microbiota-brain axis and diet: a systematic review for athletes. Clark A, Mach N. J Int Soc Sports Nutr. 2016 Nov 24;13:43. eCollection 2016. PMID:27924137

281 Edible Plants and Their Influence on the Gut Microbiome and Acne. Clark AK, Haas KN, Sivamani RK. Int J Mol Sci. 2017 May 17;18(5). pii: E1070. PMID:28513546

282 Choline: an essential nutrient for public health. Zeisel SH, da Costa KA. Nutr Rev. 2009 Nov;67(11):615-23. PMID:19906248

283 Impact of Eye Cosmetics on the Eye, Adnexa, and Ocular Surface. Ng A, Evans K, North RV, Jones L, Purslow C. Eye Contact Lens. 2016 Jul;42(4):211-20. PMID:26398576

284 Enhanced eyelashes: prescription and over-the-counter options. Jones D. Aesthetic Plast Surg. 2011 Feb;35(1):116-21. PMID:20730536

285 Ibid Ref 283. PMID:26398576

286 Mascara induced milphosis, an etiological evaluation. Kadri R, Achar A, Tantry TP, Parameshwar D, Kudva A, Hegde S. Int J Trichology. 2013 Jul;5(3):144-7. PMID:24574694

287 Eyelash loss. Jordan DR. Semin Plast Surg. 2007 Feb;21(1):32-6. PMID:20567654

288 Ibid Ref 283. PMID:26398576

289 Optical properties of hair: effect of treatments on luster as quantified by image analysis. McMullen R, Jachowicz J. J Cosmet Sci. 2003 Jul-Aug;54(4):335-51. PMID:14528387

290 Sex Differences in the Perceived Dominance and Prestige of Women With and Without Cosmetics. Mileva VR, Jones AL, Russell R, Little AC. Perception. 2016 Oct;45(10):1166-83. PMID:27288188

291 Miscalibrations in judgements of attractiveness with cosmetics. Jones AL, Kramer RS, Ward R. Q J Exp Psychol (Hove). 2014 Oct;67(10):2060-8. PMID:24670156

292 Facial Cosmetics and Attractiveness: Comparing the Effect Sizes of Professionally-Applied Cosmetics and Identity. Jones AL, Kramer RS. PLoS One. 2016 Oct 11;11(10):e0164218. PMID:27727311

293 Faces with Light Makeup Are Better Recognized than Faces with Heavy Makeup. Tagai K, Ohtaka H, Nittono H. Front Psychol. 2016 Mar 1;7:226. PMID:26973553

294 The light-makeup advantage in facial processing: Evidence from event-related potentials. Tagai K, Shimakura H, Isobe H, Nittono H. PLoS One. 2017 Feb 24;12(2):e0172489. PMID:28234959

295 Remembering beauty: roles of orbitofrontal and hippocampal regions in successful memory encoding of attractive faces. Tsukiura T, Cabeza R. Neuroimage. 2011 Jan 1;54(1):653-60. PMID:20659568

296 A sex difference in facial contrast and its exaggeration by cosmetics. Russell R. Perception. 2009;38(8):1211-9. PMID:19817153

297 Cosmetics alter biologically-based factors of beauty: evidence from facial contrast. Jones AL, Russell R, Ward R. Evol Psychol. 2015 Feb 28;13(1):210-29. PMID:25725411

298 Facial contrast is a cue for perceiving health from the face. Russell R, Porcheron A, Sweda JR, Jones AL, Mauger E, Morizot F. J Exp Psychol Hum Percept Perform. 2016 Sep;42(9):1354-62. PMID:27100405

299 Measurement of eye size illusion caused by eyeliner, mascara, and eye shadow. Matsushita S, Morikawa K, Yamanami H. J Cosmet Sci. 2015 May-Jun;66(3):161-74. PMID:26454904

300 A real-life illusion of assimilation in the human face: eye size illusion caused by eyebrows and eye shadow. Morikawa K, Matsushita S, Tomita A, Yamanami H. Front Hum Neurosci. 2015 Mar 20;9:139. PMID:25852522

301 Cosmetics alter biologically-based factors of beauty: evidence from facial contrast. Jones AL, Russell R, Ward R. Evol Psychol. 2015 Feb 28;13(1):210-29. PMID:25725411

302 Sex Differences in the Perceived Dominance and Prestige of Women With and Without Cosmetics. Mileva VR, Jones AL, Russell R, Little AC. Perception. 2016 Oct;45(10):1166-83. PMID:27288188

303 Cosmetics as a feature of the extended human phenotype: modulation of the perception of biologically important facial signals. Etcoff NL, Stock S, Haley LE, Vickery SA, House DM. PLoS One. 2011;6(10):e25656. PMID:21991328

304 Facial Skin Smoothness as an Indicator of Perceived Trustworthiness and Related Traits. Tsankova E, Kappas A. Perception. 2016 Apr;45(4):400-8. PMID:26621963

305 Influence of facial skin attributes on the perceived age of Caucasian women. Nkengne A, Bertin C, Stamatas GN, Giron A, Rossi A, Issachar N, Fertil B. J Eur Acad Dermatol Venereol. 2008 Aug;22(8):982-91. PMID:18540981

306 Hand attractiveness—its determinants and associations with facial attractiveness. Kościński K. Behavioral Ecology. Nov. 2011. 23(2):334-342

307 Analysis of facial soft tissue changes with aging and their effects on facial morphology: A forensic perspective. Kaur M,Garg RK, SInla S.Egyptian Journal of Forensic Sciences, June 2015. 5(2):45056

308 Lip colour affects perceived sex typicality and attractiveness of human faces. Stephen ID, McKeegan AM. Perception. 2010;39(8):1104-10.PMID:20942361

309 Does Red Lipstick Really Attract Men? An Evaluation in a Bar. Guéguen N. International Journal of Psychological Studies. June 2012. 4(2)206-209

310 Rating by vlogger Angie Hotandflashy.

311 College Prep Guidebook. Charles Lewis 2015 Psy Press, Carrabelle FL. ISBN-13: 978-1505261578

312 Halitosis. Scully C. BMJ Clin Evid. 2014 Sep 18;2014. pii: 1305. PMID:25234037

313 Effects of zinc and fluoride on the remineralisation of artificial carious lesions under simulated plaque fluid conditions. Lynch RJ, Churchley D, Butler A, Kearns S, Thomas GV, Badrock TC, Cooper L, Higham SM. Caries Res. 2011;45(3):313-22. PMID:21720159

314 Anticalculus effect of two zinc citrate/essential oil-containing dentifrices. Santos SL, Conforti N, Mankodi S, Kohut BE, Yu D, Wu MM, Parikh R. Am J Dent. 2000 Sep;13(Spec No):11C-13C. PMID:11763907

315 Should Candidates Smile to Win Elections? An Application of Automated Face Recognition Technology. Horiuchi Y, Loatsu T, Nakaya F. Political Psychology. Mar 2011.

316 Unattractive, promiscuous and heavy drinkers: perceptions of women with tattoos. Swami V, Furnham A. Body Image. 2007 Dec;4(4):343-52. PMID:18089280

317 Effects of a tattoo on men's behavior and attitudes towards women: An experimental field study. Guéguen N. Arch Sex Behav. 2013 Nov;42(8):1517-24. PMID:23657810

318 Effect of tattoos on perceptions of credibility and attractiveness. Seiter JS, Hatch S. Psychol Rep. 2005 Jun;96(3 Pt 2):1113-20. PMID:16173380

319 http://www.npr.org/sections/health-shots/2017/09/18/551212312/teen-wants-a-tattoo-pediatricians-say-heres-how-to-do-it-safely Accessed Sept. 2017

320 Para-phenylenediamine allergy: current perspectives on diagnosis and management. Mukkanna KS, Stone NM, Ingram JR. J Asthma Allergy. 2017 Jan 18;10:9-15. PMID:28176912

321 http://ncojournal.dodlive.mil/2014/09/17/army-releases-latest-policies-on-female-hairstyles-tattoos/

322 Hairstyle as an adaptive means of displaying phenotypic quality. Mesko N, Bereczkei T. Hum Nat. 2004 Sep;15(3):251-70. PMID:26190549

323 https://www.theatlantic.com/magazine/archive/1999/06/the-mirror-of-dorian-gray/377630/ Accessed Spt.2017

324 http://udel.edu/~mcdonald/mythhairwhorl.html Accessed Sept. 2017

325 Association between scalp hair-whorl direction and hemispheric language dominance. Weber B, Hoppe C, Faber J, Axmacher N, Fliessbach K, Mormann F, Weis S, Ruhlmann J, Elger CE, Fernández G. Neuroimage. 2006 Apr 1;30(2):539-43. PMID:16289721

326 Handedness, eyedness, and hand--eye crossed dominance in patients with schizophrenia: sex-related lateralisation abnormalities. Dane S, Yildirim S, Ozan E, Aydin N, Oral E, Ustaoglu N, Kirpinar I. Laterality. 2009 Jan;14(1):55-65. PMID:19130640

327 Handedness, eyedness, and crossed hand-eye dominance in male and female patients with migraine with and without aura: a pilot study. Aygül R, Dane S, Ulvi H. Percept Mot Skills. 2005 Jun;100(3 Pt 2):1137-42. PMID:16158700

328 Shorn Scalps and Perceptions of Male Dominance. Mannes AE. Social Psychological and Personality Science. 2012 4(2):198-205.

329 A lover or a fighter? Opposing sexual selection pressures on men's vocal pitch and facial hair. Saxton TK, Mackey LL, McCarty K, Neave N. Behav Ecol. 2016 Mar-Apr;27(2):512-519. PMID:27004013

330 http://www.oprah.com/omagazine/7-things-nobody-ever-tells-you-about-aging_1. Accessed Sept. 2017

331 https://www.linkedin.com/pulse/when-interviewing-job-lose-ring-bruce-hurwitz Accessed August 2017

332 Wearing A Class Ring From Your Law School Is An Expensive Way To Advertise That You Are A Loser Who Has No Friends. Ellie Mystal. AboveTheLaw.com February 2013

333 Looking younger: cosmetics and clothing to look more vibrant. Palma DD. Clin Dermatol. 2008 Nov-Dec;26(6):648-51. PMID:18940547

334 Macaques exhibit a naturally-occurring depression similar to humans. Xu F, Wu Q, Xie L, Gong W, Zhang J, Zheng P, Zhou Q, Ji Y, Wang T, Li X, Fang L, Li Q, Yang D, Li J, Melgiri ND, Shively C, Xie P. Sci Rep. 2015 Mar 18;5:9220. PMID:25783476

335 Ibid Ref 335. Image used with permission. PMID:25783476

336 Head and neck anthropometry, vertebral geometry and neck strength in height-matched men and women. Vasavada AN, Danaraj J, Siegmund GP. J Biomech. 2008;41(1):114-21. Epub 2007 Aug 13. PMID:17706225

337 Why is muscularity sexy? Tests of the fitness indicator hypothesis. Frederick DA, Haselton MG. Pers Soc Psychol Bull. 2007 Aug;33(8):1167-83. PMID:17578932

338 Taking the Perfect Selfie: Investigating the Impact of Perspective on the Perception of Higher Cognitive Variables. Schneider TM, Carbon CC. Front Psychol. 2017 Jun 9;8:971. PMID:28649219

339 The 2016 HIGh Heels: Health effects And psychosexual BenefITS (HIGH HABITS) study: systematic review of reviews and additional primary studies. Barnish M, Morgan HM, Barnish J. BMC Public Health. 2017 Aug 1;18(1):37. PMID:28760147

340 High Heels Increase Women's Attractiveness. Guéguen N. Arch Sex Behav. 2015 Nov;44(8):2227-35. PMID:25408499

341 Epidemiology of High-Heel Shoe Injuries in U.S. Women: 2002 to 2012. Moore JX, Lambert B, Jenkins GP, McGwin G Jr. J Foot Ankle Surg. 2015 Jul-Aug;54(4):615-9. PMID:25977152

342 A 6-Week dynamic core stability plank exercise program traditional supine core stability strengthening program on diastasis recti abdominis. Walton LM, Costa A, LaVanture D, et al. Physical Therapy and Rehabilitation. 2016. 3(3)1-9

343 Inter-rectus distance in postpartum women can be reduced by isometric contraction of the abdominal muscles: a preliminary case-control study. Pascoal AG, Dionisio S, Cordeiro F, Mota P. Physiotherapy. 2014 Dec;100(4):344-8. PMID:24559692

344 Behavior of the Linea Alba During a Curl-up Task in Diastasis Rectus Abdominis: An Observational Study. Lee D, Hodges PW. J Orthop Sports Phys Ther. 2016 Jul;46(7):580-9. PMID:27363572

345 The effect of bridge exercise method on the strength of rectus abdominis muscle and the muscle activity of paraspinal muscles while doing treadmill walking with high heels. Kang T, Lee J, Seo J, Han D. J Phys Ther Sci. 2017 Apr;29(4):707-712. PMID:28533614

346 This and similar exercise drawings are from http://db.everkinetic.com

347 Hand attractiveness—its determinants and associations with facial attractiveness. Kościński K. Behavioral Ecology. Nov. 2011. 23(2):334-342

348 Body shape preferences: associations with rater body shape and sociosexuality. Price ME, Pound N, Dunn J, Hopkins S, Kang J. PLoS One. 2013;8(1):e52532. PMID:23300976

349 Judging a man by the width of his face: the role of facial ratios and dominance in mate choice at speed-dating events. Valentine KA, Li NP, Penke L, Perrett DI. Psychol Sci. 2014 Mar;25(3):806-11.PMID:24458269

350 Partnership status and the temporal context of relationships influence human female preferences for sexual dimorphism in male face shape. Little AC, Jones BC, Penton-Voak IS, Burt DM, Perrett DI. Proc Biol Sci. 2002 Jun 7;269(1496):1095-100. PMID:12061950

351 Testosterone and Men's Marriages. Booth A, Dabbs JM. Social Forces. Dec. 1993. 72(2):463-477

352 Human preferences for facial masculinity change with relationship type and environmental harshness. Little C, Cohen DL, Jones BC, Belsky J. Behavioral Ecology and Sociobiology April 2007, 61(6): 967–973

353 Body shape preferences: associations with rater body shape and sociosexuality. Price ME, Pound N, Dunn J, Hopkins S, Kang J. PLoS One. 2013;8(1):e52532. PMID:23300976

354 Eye-tracking of men's preferences for waist-to-hip ratio and breast size of women. Dixson BJ, Grimshaw GM, Linklater WL, Dixson AF. Arch Sex Behav. 2011 Feb;40(1):43-50. PMID:19688590

355 Judging female figures: a new methodological approach to male attractiveness judgments of female waist-to-hip ratio. Schützwohl A. Biol Psychol. 2006 Feb;71(2):223-9. PMID:16019126

356 Bust size and hitchhiking: a field study. Guéguen N. Percept Mot Skills. 2007 Dec;105(3 Pt 2):1294-8. PMID:18380130

357 Women's bust size and men's courtship solicitation. Gueguen N. Body Image. 2007 Dec;4(4):386-90. PMID:18089285

358 The effect of facial makeup on the frequency of drivers stopping for hitchhikers. Guéguen N, Lamy L. Psychol Rep. 2013 Aug;113(1):1109-13. PMID:24340803

359 Does Red Lipstick Really Attract Men? An Evaluation in a Bar. Guéguen N. International Journal of Psychological Studies. June 2012. 4(2)206-209

360 Ibid Ref. 338 PMID:28760147

361 Effects of a tattoo on men's behavior and attitudes towards women: An experimental field study. Guéguen N. Arch Sex Behav. 2013 Nov;42(8):1517-24. PMID:23657810

362 Q-cgi: new techniques to assess variation in perception applied to facial attractiveness. Burt DM, Kentridge RW, Good JM, Perrett DI, Tiddeman BP, Boothroyd LG. Proc Biol Sci. 2007 Nov 22;274(1627):2779-84. PMID:17848367

363 Hitchhiking women's hair color. Guéguen N, Lamy L. Percept Mot Skills. 2009 Dec;109(3):941-8. PMID:20178293

364 British men's hair color preferences: an assessment of courtship solicitation and stimulus ratings. Swami V, Barrett S. Scand J Psychol. 2011 Dec;52(6):595-600. PMID:21883260

365 Women's hairstyle and men's behavior: A field experiment. Guéguen N. Scand J Psychol. 2015 Dec;56(6):637-40. PMID:26565731

366 The effect of eyelid constriction on perceptions of mating strategy: Beware of the squinty-eyed guy! Kruger DJ, Piglowski JS.Personality and Individual Differences Apr. 2012. 52)5):576-580.

367 Rapid endocrine responses of young men to social interactions with young women. Roney JR, Lukaszewski AW, Simmons ZL. Horm Behav. 2007 Sep;52(3):326-33. PMID:17585911

368 Contact with attractive women affects the release of cortisol in men. van der Meij L, Buunk AP, Salvador A. Horm Behav. 2010 Aug;58(3):501-5. PMID:20427019

369 Attractive men induce testosterone and cortisol release in women. López HH, Hay AC, Conklin PH. Horm Behav. 2009 Jun;56(1):84-92. PMID:19303881

370 Hormonal changes when falling in love. Marazziti D, Canale D. Psychoneuroendocrinology. 2004 Aug;29(7):931-6. PMID:15177709

371 Changes in testosterone, cortisol, and estradiol levels in men becoming fathers. Berg SJ, Wynne-Edwards KE. Mayo Clin Proc. 2001 Jun;76(6):582-92. PMID:11393496

372 Red is romantic, but only for feminine females: sexual dimorphism moderates red effect on sexual attraction. Wen F, Zuo B, Wu Y, Sun S, Liu K. Evol Psychol. 2014 Aug 8;12(4):719-35. PMID:25300050

373 Color and women attractiveness: when red clothed women are perceived to have more intense sexual intent. Guéguen N. J Soc Psychol. 2012 May-Jun;152(3):261-5. PMID:22558822

374 Clothing Color and Tipping: Gentlemen Patrons Give More Tips to Waitresses With Red Clothes," Guéguen N, Jacob C. *Journal of Hospitality and Tourism Research*, 2014. 38(2):275-280.

375 Strategic Sexual Signals: Women's Display versus Avoidance of the Color Red Depends on the Attractiveness of an Anticipated Interaction Partner. Niesta Kayser D, Agthe M, Maner JK. PLoS One. 2016 Mar 9;11(3):e0148501. PMID:26960135

376 Color and Cyber-Attractiveness: Red Enhances Men's Attraction to Women's Internet Personal Ads. Guéguen N, Jacob C, Color Research and Application, 2013. 38(4):309-312.

377 Lipstick and Tipping Behavior: When Red Lipstick Enhance Waitresses Tips. Guéguen N, Jacob C International Journal of Hospitality Management, 2012. 31(4):1333-1335.

378 Romantic red: red enhances men's attraction to women. Elliot AJ, Niesta D. J Pers Soc Psychol. 2008 Nov;95(5):1150-64. PMID:18954199

379 Red, rank, and romance in women viewing men. Elliot AJ, Kayser DN, Greitemeyer T, Lichtenfeld S, Gramzow RH, Maier MA, Liu H. J Exp Psychol Gen. 2010 Aug;139(3):399-417. PMID:20677892

380 Red and romantic rivalry: viewing another woman in red increases perceptions of sexual receptivity, derogation, and intentions to mate-guard. Pazda AD, Prokop P, Elliot AJ. Pers Soc Psychol Bull. 2014 Oct;40(10):1260-9. PMID:25015338

381 Strategic Sexual Signals: Women's Display versus Avoidance of the Color Red Depends on the Attractiveness of an Anticipated Interaction Partner. Niesta Kayser D, Agthe M, Maner JK. PLoS One. 2016 Mar 9;11(3):e0148501. PMID:26960135

382 Adiposity, compared to masculinity, serves as a more valid cue to immunocompetence in human mate choice (Corrected). Rantala MJ, Coetzee V, Moore FR, et al. Proc Biol Sci. 2017 Apr 12;284(1852). pii: 20170103. PMID:28404778

383 Facial visualizations of women's voices suggest a cross-modality preference for femininity. Röder S, Fink B, Feinberg DR, Neave N. Evol Psychol. 2013 Mar 1;11(1):227-37.PMID:23531807

384 Observable attributes as manifestations and cues of Personality and intelligence. Borkenau P, Liebler A. Journal of Personality. March 1995. 63(1):1-25 10.1111/j.1467-6494.1995.tb00799.x

385 The Science Behind Hating Hillary's Voice. Lomborsis D, Khazan O. The Atlantic. https://www.theatlantic.com/video/index/493814/the-science-behind-hating-hillarys-voice. Accessed August 2017

386 Preference for leaders with masculine voices holds in the case of feminine leadership roles. Anderson RC, Klofstad CA. PLoS One. 2012;7(12):e51216. PMID:23251457

387 Candidate Voice Pitch Influences Election Outcomes. Klofstad CA. Political Psychology www.as.miami.edu/personal/cklofstad/25_polpsych_pitch.pdf

388 Perceptions of Competence, Strength, and Age Influence Voters to Select Leaders with Lower-Pitched Voices. Klofstad CA, Anderson RC, Nowicki S. PLoS One. 2015 Aug 7;10(8):e0133779. PMID:26252894

389 Sounds like a winner: voice pitch influences perception of leadership capacity in both men and women. Klofstad CA, Anderson RC, Peters S. Proc Biol Sci. 2012 Jul 7;279(1738):2698-704. PMID:22418254

390 Ibid Ref. 387. PMID:26252894

391 Low Vocal Pitch Preference Drives First Impressions Irrespective of Context in Male Voices but Not in Female Voices. Tsantani MS, Belin P, Paterson HM, McAleer P. Perception. 2016 Aug;45(8):946-963. PMID:27081101

392 Vocal fundamental and formant frequencies affect perceptions of speaker cooperativeness. Knowles KK, Little AC. Q J Exp Psychol (Hove). 2016;69(9):1657-75. PMID:26360784

393 Extracting social meaning: identifying interactional style in spoken conversation. Jurafsky D, Ranganath R, McFarland D. Proceedings of Human Language Technologies: The 2009 Annual Conference of the North American Chapter of the Association for Computational Linguistics. 638-646

394 Perceived differences in social status between speaker and listener affect the speaker's vocal characteristics. Leongómez JD, Mileva VR, Little AC, Roberts SC. PLoS One. 2017 Jun 14;12(6):e0179407. PMID:28614413

395 Charles Darwin (1871). "The Descent of Man"

396 Communication of emotions in vocal expression and music performance: different channels, same code? Juslin PN, Laukka P. Psychol Bull. 2003 Sep;129(5):770-814. PMID:12956543

397 Handbook of Emotions. Lewis M, Haviland-Jones, JM, Feldman Barrett L., eds. 3rd edit. 2008. Guilford Press. New York

398 Habitual use of vocal fry in young adult female speakers. Wolk L, Abdelli-Beruh NB, Slavin D. J Voice. 2012 May;26(3):e111-6. PMID:21917418

399 Vocal fry may undermine the success of young women in the labor market. Anderson RC, Klofstad CA, Mayew WJ, Venkatachalam M. PLoS One. 2014 May 28;9(5):e97506. PMID:24870387

400 What Does How You Talk Have to Do With How You Get Ahead? Winter C. April 24. 2014. Bloomberg Business. Accessed August 2017 https://web.archive.org/web/20150216083104/http://www.bloomberg.com/bw/articles/2014-04-24/upspeaks-use-by-smart-men-and-women-and-what-it-means

401 http://www.dailymail.co.uk/sciencetech/article-2538554/Want-promotion-Dont-speak-like-AUSSIE-Rising-pitch-end-sentences-make-sound-insecure.html Accessed August 2017.

402 Forming impressions of facial attractiveness is mandatory. Ritchie KL, Palermo R, Rhodes G. Sci Rep. 2017 Mar 28;7(1):469. PMID:28352107

403 Choosing face: The curse of self in profile image selection. White D, Sutherland CAM, Burton AL. 2017. Cognitive Research: Principles and Implications 2017 2:23

404 https://theblog.okcupid.com/dont-be-ugly-by-accident-b378f261dea4 Accessed Aug.2017.

405 Focal Length Affects Depicted Shape and Perception of Facial Images. Třebický V, Fialová J, Kleisner K, Havlíček J. PLoS One. 2016 Feb 19;11(2):e0149313. PMID:26894832

[406] Perspective distortion from interpersonal distance is an implicit visual cue for social judgments of faces. Bryan R, Perona P, Adolphs R. PLoS One. 2012;7(9):e45301. PMID:23028918

[407] https://theblog.okcupid.com/dont-be-ugly-by-accident-b378f261dea4 Accessed Aug.2017.

[408] Judging body weight from faces: the height-weight illusion. Schneider TM, Hecht H, Carbon CC. Perception. 2012;41(1):121-4. PMID:22611670

[409] Personality in perspective: judgmental consistency across orientations of the face. Rule NO, Ambady N, Adams RB Jr. Perception. 2009;38(11):1688-99. PMID:20120266

[410] Different signals of personality and health from the two sides of the face. Kramer RS, Ward R. Perception. 2011;40(5):549-62. PMID:21882719

[411] Consistently Showing Your Best Side? Intra-individual Consistency in #Selfie Pose Orientation. Lindell AK. Front Psychol. 2017 Feb 21;8:246. PMID:28270790

[412] Selfie-Takers Prefer Left Cheeks: Converging Evidence from the (Extended) selfiecity Database. Manovich L, Ferrari V, Bruno N. Front Psychol. 2017 Sep 4;8:1460. PMID:28928683

[413] How academics face the world: a study of 5829 homepage pictures. Churches O, Callahan R, Michalski D, Brewer N, Turner E, Keage HA, Thomas NA, Nicholls ME. PLoS One. 2012;7(7):e38940. PMID:22815695

[414] Ibid Ref. 336.PMID:17578932

[415] Knowing Who's Boss: fMRI and ERP Investigations of Social Dominance Perception. Chiao JY, Adams RB, Tse PU, Lowenthal L, Richeson JA, Ambady N. Group Process Intergroup Relat. 2008 Apr 1;11(2):201-214. PMID:19893753

[416] Ibid Ref. 336 PMID:17578932

[417] 1001 Ways to Wow the Media and Speaking Audiences, Chpt. 5: Dressing for Television. TJ Walker. www.mediatrainingworldwide.com

[418] Friend and Foe: When to Cooperate, When to Compete, and How to Succeed at Both Adam Galinsky and Maurice Schweitzer. Galinski 2015 ISBN: 9780307720214

[419] Influence; The Psychology of Persuasion. Cialdini RB. 2007 HarperCollins, New York

[420] https://projects.fivethirtyeight.com/trump-approval-ratings/?ex_cid=rrpromo Accessed Jan. 2018

[421] https://www.washingtonpost.com/graphics/2017/politics/alabama-exit-polls/?utm_term=.c44c0809e79f

[422] http://www.businessinsider.com/trump-approval-rating-every-state-gallup-2017-7 Accessed Aug. 2017

[423] http://news.gallup.com/poll/181463/majorities-five-states-approved-obama-2014.aspx. Accessed Oct.2017

[424] http://news.gallup.com/poll/26611/some-americans-reluctant-vote-mormon-72yearold-presidential-candidates.aspx Accessed Sept 2017.

425 Atheists As "Other": Moral Boundaries and Cultural Membership in American Society. Edgell P, Gerties J, Hartmand D. American Sociological Review. April 2006 71(2)211-234.

426 Everything is permitted? People intuitively judge immorality as representative of atheists. Gervais WM. PLoS One. 2014 Apr 9;9(4):e92302. PMID:24717972

427 Power and morality. Lammers J, Galinsky AD, Dubois D, Rucker D. Current Opinion in Psychology. Dec. 2015, 6: 15-19

428 When to use your head and when to use your heart: the differential value of perspective-taking versus empathy in competitive interactions. Gilin D, Maddux WW, Carpenter J, Galinsky AD. Pers Soc Psychol Bull. 2013 Jan;39(1):3-16. PMID:23150199

429 http://www.developgoodhabits.com/nervous-habits/ Accessed Sept. 2017

430 Can Charisma Be Taught? Tests of Two Interventions. Antonakis J, Fenley M, Liechta S. Acad. of Management Learning and Education. 2011 10(3):374-396.

431 http://ac360.blogs.cnn.com/2013/03/12/how-are-powerful-women-perceived/

432 You are Now Less Dumb; The Franklin Effect. David McRaney. Avery. 978-1592408795

433 Women Want Five Things. Hewlett SA, Marshall M. Center for Talent Inovation, Dec. 2014

434 Everyday Moments of Truth: Frontline Managers Are Key to Women's Career Aspirations. Coffman J and Nuenfeldt B. Bain & Company Insights. June 17, 2014.

Search/Index/Links: To search this book, either used the ebook edition on Amazon or GooglePlay. The "Look Inside" feature on Amazon. Also allows some searching. References are hyperlinked in the ebook edition.

Errors: If the reader comes across typos, errors or other problems with the content of this book, please contact Pys Press at PsyPress✳email.com. Please include the edition number from the copyright page, and page on which the problem was found.

If the reader finds the book helpful, the author is always appreciative of 5-star reviews on Amazon or GooglePlay!